Richard Byrne was educated at the London School of
Economics and Bec...   ...l
the probation servic...

RICHARD BYRNE

Safecracking

Grafton
An Imprint of HarperCollins*Publishers*

For Leah, Patrick and Bunty
and for Stephen Ball and David Jones.

Grafton
An Imprint of HarperCollins*Publishers*
77–85 Fulham Palace Road,
Hammersmith, London W6 8JB

A Grafton Original 1991
9 8 7 6 5 4 3 2 1

A catalogue record for this book
is available from the British Library

ISBN 0 586 20672 8

Printed in Great Britain by
HarperCollinsManufacturing Glasgow

Set in Times

Contents

Introduction   7
Prelude: The Great Cornhill Robbery   11

PART ONE: THE BOX   19

1 Stronger and Stronger Boxes   21
2 The Arms Race   36
3 Wood and Iron, Steel and Plastic   49
4 Fillings   57
5 Raising the Alarm   62
   Locked In   71
6 Vaults   77
   Brothers in Crime   92

PART TWO: THE LOCK   97

7 Tumblers and Keys   99
   The Picking of the Bramah Lock   109
8 Dial-a-Crime   116
9 The Invisible Locks   133
   Escapology   139

PART THREE: THE CRACK   145

10 Kings of Their Craft   147
11 Learning the Trade   154
12 The Burgling Life   159
    A Burglar's Tale   173
13 Muscle Power, Motor Power   184

14 Explosives   203
15 New Flames   223
     Nice, 1976   238

PART FOUR: THE PAYOFF   245

16 Government Burglars   247
17 Catching the Safecracker   264
18 The End of the Game   273

     Appendix: Raffles and Rififi – Safecracking in
        Films   281
     A Note on Sources   289
     Index   293

Introduction

This book began from just a few conversations, in the early 1970s, with a man called Jack who had given up safecracking. He was just approaching his fiftieth birthday, and I met him first in the greenhouse at Parkhurst prison, and then again while he was on parole from that ten-year prison sentence, trying to work out what to make of his next few years.

Jack had a fund of tales, many of them hilarious, about the safeblowing life – about packing a vast amount of butter around a gelignite charge, enough to deluge one of the gang completely when he scorned to take cover; about a young tearaway who pestered Jack to let him set off the charge himself, and was shell-shocked when he did so, because Jack had doubled the charge just to teach him his place in the gang.

He was a slim, mild-mannered, thoughtful and courtly man, who had moved in very respectable circles during the short gaps between sentences – among his girlfriends had been a niece of an important politician – and was held in high regard by other serious criminals.

But in 1974 he was redundant. As troublesome as the new decimal currency, and the inflation and property boom which made a nonsense of all his calculations, was the fact that Jack's trade was no longer needed. When he had gone to prison, he had been one of the last successful safemen; by the time he came out there was no money in the game, and the safecrackers' place at the top of the criminal tree had been taken by the robbers who stole money by force not stealth, who used violence by day not craftsmanship by night.

I was intrigued not only by Jack's story, but by the history of a contest between two very determined bodies of workers: the locksmiths and safemakers had for six generations invented and developed stronger and more cunning ways to defend wealth, and the safecrackers had matched them, move for move, device for device. Locks and boxes were produced which would resist each challenge: lockpicking, hammers and levers, drills, gunpowder, nitroglycerine, and gas torches were tried in turn, and defeated by new mechanisms and new metals.

The final sudden collapse of safecracking seemed to have so many industrial, even national parallels. We have become used to hearing about trades no longer needed, countries whose crops and products can no longer find a market; here was an example from the underworld. There had to be a story there too.

For years I made notes when I could, kept newspaper clippings, and asked questions of anyone who might have something to say, while working on other projects, until a telephone call came from Rhona Mitchell, the archivist of the Chubb safemaking and security company.

The vast Chubb records hold not only the history of the company, but an extraordinary wealth of material, stretching back to the 1830s, on crimes and criminals, rival products, patents and product tests, manufacturing and labour relations, which makes it one of the most valuable records of an industry and its market I have ever seen. I was enormously lucky to be permitted to read through files, and to draw on the memories of the many people to whom Rhona Mitchell was in turn kind enough to introduce me, often lock collectors and locksmiths who had asked for her help with quests of their own.

My understanding with Chubb, indeed with all the

people with whom I have spoken who make a living from security, was that I would neither ask about, nor seek access to any material on any products or ideas of the last twenty-five years, or which might prove useful to a thief of the 1990s. Any reference to more recent designs is based on published information freely available.

There are also limits on what can sensibly be written about criminal methods. Most older criminal memoirs offer nothing to a modern thief, but they were written before explosives became the weapon of terrorists rather than a tool for thieves. When drawing on them, and on personal interviews, cuts have had to be made.

Anyone with a daydream about becoming a cracksman should be clear about why skilled and experienced men stopped attacking safes – there isn't enough money in them today to make the effort worthwhile.

This is why the story of safecracking came to an end in the 1960s, why the story can now be told, and why Jack gave up. I haven't seen him for a long time but I know that after being caught for a couple of unimpressive jobs, which involved no safe work, he has been convicted of no crime for many years. I hope that he is happy in his retirement.

During my research I was greatly helped by a number of other individuals from among criminals, security craftsmen and others. Special thanks go to Arthur Briant for being so very generous with his time and notes; to George Glenton for letting me consult cuttings from his many years of reporting crime; to Sid Smythe, Don Murfet and Larry Sheridan. I learned many practical details from a young locksmith, Stephen Ball, who was sadly killed in a road accident before this book reached its final form.

I have used some pseudonyms – Geoff Derr, Brewer,

and Mike Jesswell – where this was sensible: these men may be identifiable to those who know them well, but deserve protection from idle curiosity.

I am grateful to the Hulton-Deutsch Collection and the British Film Institute for permission to reproduce illustrations.

Prelude
The Great Cornhill Robbery

In every generation there is a robbery which grasps and shakes the popular imagination by its size and daring, one which sets the honest citizen daydreaming about that one huge haul big enough for any fantasy shopping spree, and wondering if he could ever find the nerve to carry out such a crime. The Brink's Mat raid in Boston, back in 1950, still features in books and films, while twenty-five years after the Great Train Robbery of 1963, a film telling the life story of one man who took part was a major success at the box-office. We all want to know how it was done, who did it, and what happened to the cash.

The Cornhill burglary shocked Britain in the 1860s. It came as the climax to a season of bold attacks in which thieves in London and Manchester stole thousands of pounds from premises which had seemed completely secure. John Walker, a jeweller at 63 Cornhill, was certain that he had taken every precaution against burglary: he kept his stock in a Milner's List 3 safe, described by the manufacturer as, 'Milner's Quadruple Patent (Sealed 1840, 1854, 1855 and 1859) Violence, Robbery and Fraud-resisting Safe, strongly recommended for Cash and Valuables. Doors half-inch, Bodies quarter-inch thick, wrought-iron, very strongly constructed, lined throughout with Milner's unequalled double Fire-resisting Chambers.'

Nor did Mr Walker rely on the safe alone. His shop was in a busy street, and the safe stood in a room lined with iron. As a further precaution this fortified room, and the room next door, were lit with gas whenever the premises were unoccupied, and holes were pierced in the iron shutters so that passing policemen, indeed any stroller, might see clearly into the shop. There was even a mirror arranged so that every approach to the safe was in sight.

Yet on the morning of Monday 6 February 1865, when at eight o'clock Mr Walker's assistant entered the safe-room, 'He saw at once what had happened. The safe door had been burst open, and all the most valuable portion of Mr Walker's stock . . . consisting of gold watches, chronometers, diamond rings, pins, studs, bracelets, earrings, and other kinds of jewellery, and the cash-box, containing a quantity of gold and some valuable securities, was gone.'

When the alarm was raised, crowds gathered outside the shop, and more arrived by the hour to stare at the scene of the astounding robbery. Merchants grew pan-icky, and within two days thirty local traders presented a petition to the alderman who was chief authority in that part of the City, calling for a meeting of all the local inhabitants to consider the threat to trade security, and the efficiency of the City Police. Mr Walker had lost £6000; a previous raid on a similar business in Thread-needle Street had yielded £4000; in Lombard Street nearly £10,000; in the Strand nearly £1000. Faced with these persistent and damaging thefts, shopkeepers lost their nerve – there were hurried trade meetings, anxious editorials in national newspapers, and everyone had an opinion about the causes and the necessary cures for the crime wave. To one writer it seemed that crime itself had been transformed: 'Now that the enemy applies the principles of war to the acquisition of gold and jewels it is time to devise defensive plans even more scientific than those already adopted.'

Now details of just how the crime had been committed

were becoming clear: the thieves had entered the building
during the day on Saturday by a side door which stayed
open to allow access to a number of offices. They had
climbed to an upper floor to hide until the close of
business, and Mr Walker had in fact locked them in when
he went home. In looking for a hiding-place the thieves
had been lucky to find a key which was always left on a
bracket on the landing, and they were able to lock
themselves out of sight during a last-minute inspection.
When they came out of hiding, they first picked the lock
of the first-floor premises, where they found a little cash,
then cut a hole in the floor of this office, to drop down
into a tailor's shop next door to Mr Walker's rooms.
They tried cutting through the wall into the jeweller's but
were blocked by the iron lining of the strong room. By
going down into the tailor's basement they could try
another approach, cutting up through the floor of Mr
Walker's back room close to the safe. Across a part of
this back room there was a partition which provided them
with cover, from which they could emerge whenever the
coast was clear to attack the safe. To open the safe they
used a series of ever-larger wedges to pry open the door
far enough to enable them to complete the work with a
large jemmy or lever. Six thousand pounds richer, they
left the building by retracing their steps, removed the
lock on the outside door, and made off into the night.

For all the public fear, it did not in fact take long to
capture the thieves. A reward of £1000 was offered for
their capture, adding to considerable amounts already on
offer after the previous robberies, and this may have
helped the police, but the immediate cause of the gang's
capture was a simple old-fashioned jealousy.

One of the women associated with the gang vengefully
betrayed her man, he in turn implicated others, and after
a couple of well-devised raids the police were able to

charge eleven people – burglars and their wives – with stealing and receiving. The trials of the Cornhill Robbers attracted a great deal of public attention, and broad relief was expressed that a gang which had marauded so widely was safely behind bars. This was not, however, the end of the story, and the criminal hearings were quite eclipsed by the civil case which followed.

Mr Walker, even after the arrest of the burglars, was not a happy man. He was angry to have paid good money for a safe about which many promises had been made, but which had proved so apparently easy to open, and he chose to sue Milner's, the manufacturers. This would have aroused interest in itself, but what turned this civil case into an extraordinary spectacle was that Walker chose to call as his chief witness, with the most appropriate expert opinion to offer, the very man who had broken into his safe, the freshly-convicted safecracker Thomas Caseley.

A good-looking young man, Caseley had made a strong impression on the public since his very first appearance at Bow Street Magistrates' Court on remand. Self-assured to the point of cockiness, with nothing whatsoever to lose, he made the most of his new role. His testimony was remarkable for its lightheartedness, and for the extent to which Caseley revealed the secrets of his trade.

When the case opened in the Queen's Bench before the Lord Chief Justice, on 14 February 1866, the safe itself sat in the centre of the courtroom. As everyone stared at the twisted metal, Mr Walker and his son told how they had been assured that the safe was 'thief-proof', and had therefore paid £40 for it. Plaintiff and defendant were each represented by four counsel, and there were lengthy exchanges which helped the jury to grasp the layout of the shop, and the relative positions of the safe, the mirror, and the partition. Then Caseley was called.

Although he had been brought from Millbank Penitentiary, where he was serving the first part of his fourteen-year sentence, and stood in his prison uniform with a good conduct badge upon it, Caseley gave his evidence with 'the most amusing coolness', drawing laughs with his account of the break-in. He explained how, taking care to stoop low every nine minutes when a look-out's signal told them that a police patrol was about to pass, the thieves had tested the safe by inserting a small wedge behind the edge of the door. Since it did not fly off, but held, they knew that it would be possible to force a way in.

Under cross-examination, Caseley was asked: 'You have had some experience in opening safes?'

'Yes, unhappily, I have. We have experimented on Milner's safes before. It took seven hours before it gave at all, and we then tried what we call "unlawful" means – that is, tools which we could not use in a burglary. [Great laughter.] Another took six hours to open. Two of us purchased two of Milner's safes to experimentalize upon, and we succeeded upon one after seven hours . . . The other safe was opened in six hours, with the best sort of "lawful burglar's tools", including an iron bar five feet long, jointed in several pieces so as to be carried in a small case. That was the only thing that could open one of Milner's best safes.'

Caseley described the range of bars, or jemmies, used by the thieves. The first ones were used only to widen the gap first made by the wedge. 'These bars, however, would not open the safe, they were only used to get what we call the "alderman" in. [Roars of laughter.] That is a "head bar", which would open any safe. The smaller bars were called "citizens". [Laughter.] These names were used to avoid the real words; it would not do to be heard in the streets talking of crowbars. [Laughter.]'

As Caseley was about to step from the witness box, the Lord Chief Justice commented, 'It is a pity you did not turn your talents to better account.'

The convict retorted, 'It is a pity the police did not let me.'

Caseley had been a frequent player in a Judge and Jury Club, a sort of drunken debating society popular at the time, in which revellers would meet to match wits. He had used the pseudonym Counsellor Kelly. The *Daily Telegraph* published an appraisal of his performance which virtually amounted to a dramatic review: '. . . a keen wit, coarse in quality, inexhaustible in quantity, that bubbled up like bad petroleum; a fine dramatic instinct, infinite readiness, surprising fluency; the instinct of an actor for effect; the craving of an orator for applause; the complacent delight of an artist in flattery – these were a few of the characteristics that struck every one who saw "Counsellor Kelly" on his trial.'

The outcome of the case was a further loss for Mr Walker, as the court did not share his view that a safe could be expected to protect for ever, in an otherwise unguarded shop, his six thousand pounds' worth of stock.

All the attention given to the burglaries, and to Caseley's casual dismissal of the security offered by safes, transformed the public view of safes, and the safe industry itself. For every hundred light and inferior safes sold before the Cornhill raid not ten were sold after, as customers realized that an impressive appearance was no guarantee of strength, and became knowledgeable enough to distinguish the shoddy from the sound. This is of course exactly what the reputable safemakers had wanted to achieve with competitions, and law suits against counterfeiters, but they were less pleased with another result of the case. Security had now become a very visible big business, and new inventors and entrepreneurs were drawn into the trade – in little more than a year, thirty-six new patents were granted for what their creators called improvements in safe and lock design, and a new round in the contest between thief and safemaker had begun.

PART ONE

The Box

1

Stronger and Stronger Boxes

When wealth was measured in head of livestock, or the size of crops, it was held secure by the strength and guile of its guards. When mankind decided that some metals and stones had a value beyond their usefulness, the new riches were more easily carried, or carried away, and open to a new threat. Wealth could now be lost not only to bands of rustlers, or the armed men of an invader or a usurper, but to thieves within a tribe or nation, thieves who might melt and rework gold and silver, or recut stones to conceal their theft.

In many lands the new forms of wealth were more than mere currency. The costumes, decorations and possessions of royalty and religious leaders expressed authority. A pharaoh had no need of purchasing power, but risked utter downfall if his symbols and totems were lost, or even soiled by the people. To leave them under simple human protection was dangerous – guards might pilfer, or at worst betray the owner to his enemies. In civilizations whose building methods and materials allowed it, first attempts were made to construct treasuries and vaults: more than 3000 years ago Rameses III of Egypt had a treasure temple built, and the ancient Greeks stored the wealth of the state behind great bronze doors.

These were great civilizations, but they were not empires: when they came to dominate their world the Romans needed a form of wealth that was accepted across their territories, at an understood value, to trade in goods and to hire people. They could pay off their important allies and creditors with the old wealth of land

and produce, but for everyday use they needed cash. They too built treasuries, but to trade, to conquer and to govern they had to be able to transport wealth, and to protect it from the peoples they had conquered. We know that they made chests of wood and cast iron to secure their cash and smaller valuables, for the state and for its powerful governors and merchants.

It is at first remarkable to find that they used a design which looked like the bullion boxes in Western movies, the ones that the baddies always steal from the Wells Fargo stage, but in fact the size and shape of both were dictated by what they were made to hold, and how they were to be carried. Coin and bullion are very heavy, so the box had to be strong enough to bear the weight of its contents: given the materials available, this meant the box could not be large. The boxes also had to be strong enough to withstand simple force, but there was a working limit set by the weight that men could carry. Boxes that were too heavy would be more likely to be dropped in transit, and it was risky to make boxes so large that a couple of loyal men could not drag them to safety in an ambush or emergency.

Small strong chests were popular for the next many centuries because they could be carried easily, transported by horse, camel or elephant. National treasuries might be built of stone, yet when kings and princes went on campaign, or moved about their realms, they carried with them not merely funds for their expedition, but the emblems of their power. When merchants went to the Orient for silks and spices, or north for furs, when the conquistadores brought back the gold of the New World, they carried the chests we remember from every cartoon of eye-patched pirates, every story of buried treasure: thick planks bound with iron.

This chest design worked well enough to be retained

even when the wealth was to stay in one place, but it grew in size and became more elaborate. The bulk and style of the chest represented the standing of the owner, until the grandest among them reached the limits of practicality. When the weight of the lid with all its elaborate lockwork required enormous strength to lift, and was dangerously difficult to control while closing, it became much more sensible to turn the box on its side, and replace the troublesome lid with a hinged, swinging door.

The very first safes were thus no more than an upright form of the strongbox or chest, each made to order from a hard wood, then lined inside and out with iron plates screwed or riveted in place. External hasps were still occasionally used, but the layered construction permitted the makers to shield boltwork, and there was a steady move from padlocks to internal locks.

Strongboxes which we would recognize as safes were first manufactured at the end of the eighteenth century, to meet the needs of a new age. It was a time of discovery and progress: steam power was freshly harnessed, the American and French revolutions had transformed international and national politics, and economic power was shifting from the landowners to the mill-owners, from the nobility to the ironmasters. These may seem to be very grand themes, far removed from the making of compact metal boxes, but without them safes had no place.

Safes were not a radical invention, and nothing in the technology used to make them was far removed from the materials and skills used for a hundred other products. The vastly important change lay in the need, the market requirement, for secure storage for wealth.

While the rich were also the truly powerful, it was not difficult to protect the wealth itself. If a man's economic standing was measured not in cash but in land, he had no need of massive physical security. His possessions, even his income, would very largely be in properties and commodities difficult to store or to steal – land, grain, produce of all kinds. When we want to describe a person as rich, we judge their value in cash, by the numbers of units of currency they possess – millionaire, multi-millionaire, billionaire – but in past centuries there were only a very few whose wealth, power and influence was measured by their ownership of coin.

There were bankers and merchant adventurers but only in a very few cities; ordinary traders and the professionals, successful lawyers and physicians, might be paid in coin but when successful they were quick to translate their wealth into conventional forms which carried more prestige – usually land. Even goods which could easily be carried away were at little risk: the wealthy had servants, even private armies, to stand permanent guard over their bodies and their goods. Only a king or an enemy in war could seize their property. There might be pilferage within a household but this was easily discovered, and criminal strangers were rare. Even a stealthy thief faced extraordinary difficulties in keeping his crime secret in a society in which each man knew most of his neighbours. Sudden affluence, or an attempt to dispose of rare and costly goods would be swiftly discovered; flight was slow and very dangerous, punishment ferocious.

For centuries those few people in England who held large amounts of cash, the merchants, placed it with the Master of the Mint. Since the Mint was then a part of the Tower of London their money was powerfully protected from thieves, but the traders' confidence was very severely shaken when in 1640 Charles I requisitioned £200,000 from their bullion deposited in the Mint. Some merchants decided that they might as well keep their money themselves, others lodged cash with goldsmiths: since they had of course to provide safety for their own stocks and cash, goldsmiths were regarded as reliable custodians.

At this stage they were not bankers in the modern sense, since they had no permission to invest the deposits, but merely held them as separate, sealed packages. The depositor would receive not an amount equal to his funds, but the very same coins he had lodged. Only late in the seventeenth century did some businesses pool depositors' money and offer 'joint bonds' instead of a simple receipt, and invest the cash in a form of early unit trust. Others advanced money – to farmers whose crops would not pay until later in the year, for instance – some met the need to exchange currencies for international trade by holding stocks of foreign coin. Add all these functions together, and banking had been invented.

Banks took in cash and issued their own substitutes in the form of bills of exchange, drafts and notes of various kinds. Most large banks also issued their own banknotes in large denominations, which would be accepted just as long as the bank itself was seen as healthy; cheques were at first too restricted and expensive to be popular. Only at the end of the eighteenth century, at a time of gold shortage, did the familiar small banknotes appear for the payment of wages and for retail trade.

All these paper forms of wealth carried risks: forgery was much more common than theft, despite the fact that forgers faced the death penalty, and banks were often tempted to issue many more notes than they could cover with their gold reserves. Any public suspicion that a bank could not redeem its notes would cause a run which would ruin the bank, all its depositors and anyone who held its notes – despite this, banks not only overextended but speculated wildly in dubious businesses.

It all had to end, and in 1825 there was a serious
financial crisis and a collapse of credit; people became
suspicious of the way many country bankers did business,
and in particular of paper money: '*A guinea it will sink
and a note it will float / But I'd rather have a guinea than
a one pound note.*'

The ballooning in the circulation of paper wealth may
have been foolish, but by creating the illusion of affluence
it propelled trade: even if many businesses were founded
on credit which was flimsily supported, some would
prosper. The history of this expansive phase can be seen
in the Georgian building developments in many British
cities – the new houses were homes for a new class. This
class did not own landed estates nor exquisite works of
art – their wealth was in anonymous, easily traded cash
and financial paper. This mattered not only because of
the way in which they gathered and accumulated their
wealth, but in the way they spent it.

As the numbers of people who could buy expensive
goods increased, shops and businesses grew to provide
them with ways to spend. Jewellers, furriers, all the
purveyors of personal luxury; tradesmen to provide for
the not-quite-so-wealthy all the services which the old
rich had obtained from their own staff. The new spenders
bought foods which the old rich would have produced on
their own estates; the markets for clothing and carriages,
for housing and horses, expanded enormously, and all
fed with cash.

As this cash made its way around the system, it
accumulated. In banks and businesses, within households, it would stack up. There was official money, the
notes and coin issued by national and commercial banks,
but equally negotiable were the documents – stocks and
shares, bonds of all kinds – which represented the owner's
stake in the economy. To display his wealth, the owner

would not fling wide his window and spread his arms across the land he owned, but produce a stack of paper or a note of his deposit in a bank.

All this paper needed protection, and was lodged in safes. The safe was not an invention, in the sense that the steam engine, the spinning jenny, or the seed drill were inventions. Nothing in the technology, with the possible exception of the newest locks, was fresh or unfamiliar. The essential design was exactly what a blacksmith would make if asked to provide a strong cupboard or closet. No vast factories were built in those early years to make the new safes; the work was contracted out to large numbers of small workshops in which traditional metalworkers built boxes to simple specifications.

The new safes, to serve the new market, were sold with a fine Victorian gusto. Extravagant claims were made for boxes carrying splendid and fanciful names, competition between manufacturers was by our standards brash, advertising mixed bragging with aggression and a deal of blatant dishonesty. The customers were usually small businessmen, distrustful of their own employees, unsure about banks, quickly alarmed by reports of theft, uninsured and easily ruined. It was an age in which product names were as grandiose as architecture, and who could fail to be impressed by George Price's 'Improved Quadruple-Patent "Royal Climax Champion"'?

Safemakers took competition on to the streets and into the fields. In the early days, in the fight to make their reputations, manufacturers and their agents were always quick to reach the scene of a burglary, trying to make a sale to the victim, but also keen to get their hands on the remains of the old safe. If it turned out to be one of their own, they would hide it, but if it had been made by a rival it would be placed on display, might even be taken from town to town on a cart.

Confident safemakers staged public tests of their boxes, always an excellent way to get the sort of coverage which would have cost a fortune as paid advertising. Long before the press conference and the photo opportunity, safemakers found ways to give reporters copy which would reach around the country. They placed their safes on enormous piles of coal or timber, and before the local mayor, or a jury of notables, locked money or documents into the safes, and lit the bonfire. The crowds would buzz as the safe was hauled from the embers, opened with a flick of the key, and the triumphant safemaker extracted the papers intact.

When spectators wearied of fires, manufacturers offered explosions. Safes were loaded with gunpowder and blown up, to show how strong the demonstrator's boxes were, how robust his locks, and how feeble his competitors'. One bang might not impress, but Chatwood, the English safemaker, himself set eight successive charges, from one ounce on up to a pound of gunpowder, and was rewarded with notices in the press congratulating him 'on the success of his invention which renders gunpowder utterly useless for the purpose of opening safes made on the escapement principle [Chatwood's design which allowed the powder to fall away, within the safe, from the lock where it would do damage].' This demonstration passed off safely, but one of the more sinister reasons for the press interest was that just three years before, a small child had been killed by a piece of flying iron at a safe-blowing demonstration.

With the demonstrations came more and more public challenges. In 1865 Chatwood threw down the gauntlet to his customers: any purchaser could have forty-eight hours, using any kind of burglar's tools, even gunpowder, to attack the safe, and should it be opened Chatwood promised to give £100 to any charity. To upstage this,

Chubb tried to secure the temporary release of a safe-cracker from prison to perform a public attack on one of his safes. After Hobbs' defeat of the Bramah Lock, a patent lock that was supposedly impregnable, and his success in the British market, a rivalry grew between British and American safemakers, a cutthroat commercial competition which reached a climax at the Paris Exhibition of 1867, in what became known as the Battle of the Safes: patriotic teams doing their utmost to break into each other's safes in a race against the clock.

Safemakers kept a very careful eye on safe attacks and the ways in which they were reported in the press. Sales staff and agents were required to investigate local crimes in their areas and make a report back to the company. The commercial advantage was plain – if a representative called to see the victim of a crime, and could persuade him that his own company's safe would have resisted the burglars, a sale might be made on the spot. A letter would be sent back to company headquarters giving details of how well a particular safe had performed, and anything learned about the equipment and techniques of the safecrackers. This was commercial common sense, but these agents would also try hard to make sure, by befriending and rewarding local reporters or police, that if a competitor's safe were broken, the brand name was quoted, but any failures of their own make were well hidden.

A longhand note by George H. Chubb, headed 'for my information only; not to be made public in any way' tells us much about both his methods and preoccupations and those of his adversaries.

On Friday March 27th 1874, saw the Deputy Chief Constable of Manchester, who shewed me the tools taken from the burglars lately captured at a jeweller's shop in Manchester – there were a number of tools, a very complete set, but none very highly finished; among them was a very neat and small screw-jack, about three inches high, capable of lifting a heavy weight; also an 'alderman', several small crowbars or wrenches made of the best steel, some rose drills tempered to a good straw colour, a number of skeleton keys and instruments apparently to smash the works of the locks, a very tiny oil lantern (the only light they used), wads to deaden the sound of hammers, chisels, wedges, etc. I was told that the men were a gang that had opened no less than fourteen safes in Birmingham and the neighbourhood, and all were captured but one man who contrived to escape; unfortunately he is the cleverest of the lot – Since the rest had been sentenced to fourteen years' penal servitude, they have been very free in telling all they know; and it seems that all their tools are made by a man in Birmingham well known to the police, who cannot however find any actual proof against him – He charges enormous prices for these tools, and recently made diamond drills for this gang worth £200; burglars merely tell him whose safe they want to try, and he gives them the requisite tools. No attempt is ever undertaken by them until they have 'weighed' the place and know all about it – One or more safes at Birmingham that had steel over lock, they opened by softening it with a blowpipe; in one case, getting the gas from the bracket by an india-rubber tube, and in another taking portable bags of gas with them. The only time they failed was with one safe that had Spiegeleisen instead of steel, and they say that they could not go through that at all. The mode generally adopted was not wedging but drilling down on the lock. The deputy chief constable thinks that there are no safes better than Chatwood's; has not seen any of our best quality but knows two of Chatwood's that cost £800. Thinks the enormous thickness of his doors a very good protection, and has heard of one case where the owner of one of Chatwood's safes lost his key and had to have safe *planed* open at the back, which took a day and a half. Although some of Chatwood's keys are six inches long, yet by the plan he has of removing the bit, the bit may be carried separately from key.

As far as he knows, this gang never tried one of our

Safes; he will enquire and let Mr Codde know – will be happy at any time to give us whatever information he has.
  George H Chubb

XX A gentleman [Mr Barker] told me that a friend of his had a Chatwood key in his pocket in a railway accident and it was driven in near one of his ribs.

In the rivalry of the time even a horror story of a hazardous key would have been useful to the salesmen.

There were other public relations problems which worried many makers; any one safe might continue in use for dozens of years, and there could be great embarrassment if a burglar with a new technique opened one of a company's old and obsolete models, giving the maker the tricky job of disowning a product with his name on it while reassuring buyers about his latest line. Just as troublesome were the fraudulent safes and the outright fakes. The basic design of metal box was simple enough to be made in the smallest workshop, each business using only simple hand labour to assemble bought-in stocks of metal frame and sheet. These might be sold under the maker's own name, often with fanciful and extravagant claims, but it was also very common for safes to be made to order for retailers who would add their own nameplates. Construction quality varied from workmanlike to downright shoddy: it was very easy to conceal poor materials and handiwork under the final coats of paint, to fill with ineffective materials and to give false comfort to the purchaser by fitting an expensive reputable lock in the cheap thin shell.

Few of the small independent firms were capable of making their own locks, and it was much more effective to buy in good locks as needed and then let the name of the lockmaker feature prominently in advertising. Some relied on public ignorance even further by deliberately copying the external designs and trademarks of reputable makers, or even transferring a maker's plate to a repainted secondhand box. Safemakers instructed their agents to be vigilant for these fakes, and were swift to sue any forgers they found. Few products were so dependent on the maker's good name – Sir Charles Rolls said when he joined with Royce that he wanted his name to be attached to a product that would stand for excellence among cars just as Chubb represented the finest locks.

The fakers were defeated in the end not by lawsuits but by design changes which also drove out of business many respectable but small-time manufacturers. For as long as safes were made up from simple flat, straight stock it required very little in the way of workspace or capital to produce them. All the cutting, welding and riveting could be performed with simple inexpensive standard tools. Only the larger companies could heat-treat the bigger panels, but no more than conventional blacksmithing was needed for small safes, and in any case the customer was unable to see and test the hardness of a casing for himself. The bent-corner models which were devised at the end of the nineteenth century were much more difficult to produce, since the sheets of iron and steel had to be worked cold if they were to keep their strength, and this demanded large and powerful hydraulic presses. The extra investment in premises and equipment required to produce modern and competitive safes had the immediate effect of raising prices. This permitted some undercutting by the old small manufacturers, but they could not expect to stay in business for long. Buyers learned that a safe with square corners was a product which was cheap in every sense.

The customer did well in those years, able to choose what he needed from among the products of a smaller but competitive number of manufacturers who fought each other for trade, developing fresh solutions to each burgling challenge and eager to carve out specialized markets for themselves. Some had models which were favoured by banks, others were regularly entrusted with sensitive Ministry contracts or were well regarded in particular trades.

There were still some makers of inexpensive boxes which sold to small businesses, but the larger firms now offered a remarkable range of products and services. The surviving major companies were both mass producers of locks and boxes selling for a few pounds and vault constructors with a place among major civil engineering contractors. It was almost as if watchmakers, washing-machine manufacturers, architects and shipwrights had all found a common cause. There was also a bespoke element, since any customer could specify modifications to standard products, like the jewel merchant who insisted that a mirror be fitted within his safe so that he could keep an eye on any customer during the vulnerable moments when his back was turned to reach his stock.

The gap between the weak companies and the strong was further widened by the two world wars, when the foundries and presses of the larger firms, combined with their expertise in hardening and forming, helped them to win contracts for armour plate and other war materials. In the first years of peace there were major programmes of replacement and re-equipment, to make up for bomb damage and counter the challenge of the safecracker, but a gap widened between the companies that adapted well and those which failed to reinvest.

The whole industry had to face the problem that their product was a success: the materials, the shape, the mechanisms were all good enough to need no major improvement. Safecracking became rare enough to disappear from the list of workaday business worries, safes were good enough to last for at least twenty or thirty years (my bank branch has a safe that was made in the early 1960s, though a more recent alarm has since been fitted), and when the big customers had completed their replacement programmes, the market was bound to shrink dramatically and permanently. To stay in the trade at all the strong safemakers bought out the weak, not to gain plant or workers, or even to lay their hands on the odd useful patent, but to merge the customer lists.

The remaining companies have closed factories and automated the survivors; they have brought in industrial designers to tempt buyers with more attractive boxes which would look good in modern premises. Research and development continues, and manufacturers are genuinely proud of the state which the safemaking art has reached.

They have made stronger safes to meet tougher demands, and tested them more thoroughly – a maker may well utterly destroy thirty or forty prototypes of a new model. Once the basic design has been agreed and put into production there may still be changes which help to preserve the security of the model. Thorough thieves have bought and stolen new safes to learn about the internal arrangement of lock, boltwork and re-locking devices, so safemakers may well move these in the course of a production run, while maintaining the same external appearance. Since the safe must not only defeat the burglar but provide ready and reliable access to the user, each of these modifications has to be tested to make sure that ordinary functioning is not threatened – sales would certainly be lost were a model of safe notoriously vulnerable to attack, but the market would be equally unforgiving if a maker gained a reputation for safes that refused to open at the start of a working day.

Given the banality and crude simplicity of most safe attacks, the level of caution shown by many safemakers smacks of overkill. They test with the most exotic, military-style configurations of explosive, use cutters supplied with quantities of gas which would almost never be usable by working thieves, and attribute to their enemies a level of knowledgeable cunning which would flatter the real-life thief. The result of all this effort is that safes are rarely opened, yet this has helped to ruin the market for good-quality safes. The customer reasons not that he must buy one of the good new safes, but that since safecracking is now a rare crime he need buy no more than basic protection, adequate defence against fire and pilferage.

The better safemakers have outdistanced most of their market, and safemakers have told me glumly that they fear a fresh outbreak of safecracking once criminals realize just how flimsy some new cheap safes can be. If the only thing preventing the return of the full-time safeman were the strength of the box, they might be right, but most safes now hold little worth stealing. The very same factors which led to the invention of the safe – the ways in which wealth is used and stored – have changed once again to make it redundant. We have learned how to hide our cash from harm, and invented ways of storing and transferring wealth without bags of coins and wads of banknotes.

2

The Arms Race

'They keep coming up with new gimmicks to try and get ahead of us, and we come up with gaffs to beat their gimmicks!'

These were the words of an American safecracker, but might as easily have been said by any safemaker or locksmith of the last six generations. The first safes had been opened by adapting traditional burgling tools to make the best of the thieves' strength with levers, drills, hammers and wedges. The safemakers' responses could be just as crude: new much-vaunted, much-patented methods of fixing together the plates of a safe were often no more than adaptations from carpentry – comb joints, dovetails, extra fillets at the corners.

Then came waves of genuine innovation on both sides. Steel was hardened, making hand tools obsolete; the first considered use of explosives brought changes in locks and boltwork; combination locks and time locks, nitroglycerine and electric fusing clashed in a war in which, like many a military campaign, victory demanded cunning as well as strength.

The best surviving account of this long campaign is in the boxes themselves. The shape, the mechanisms, every feature of a safe from the alloys used in the casing to the composition of the paint has been made or chosen as a defence, a counterattack, or an attempt to gain a tactical advantage, and each can be read and interpreted.

Examples of early safes have earned their place in museums, but many more are in common daily use, kept because the veterans have served their owners well, and there is no very obvious reason to throw them away. Only a small proportion of all the safes ever made and sold have been attacked by burglars or fire, and to the great frustration of at least six generations of salesmen, businesses have kept their old boxes, next to the new models they have bought for higher security: some owners have copied the example of a man who kept his old box for odd papers, but left it unlocked, and tied a notice to the handle asking burglars not to cut or blow it.

In researching this book, I have seen in use safes from every decade back to the middle of the nineteenth century. None of the old ones held valuables or cash, but were kept because they were part of the company's past, and pleasing to the eye. Although they are cumbersome, safes and parts of safes are also now being collected and traded; a rare or interesting one may be worth more money than any sensible person would keep in it.

So to study the history of safe design, there is no need to visit museums; with ordinary powers of observation and a basic knowledge of design features the story can be traced, as each generation of safes was improved to meet new dangers. There's no handy dating procedure as simple as the hallmarking of silver, but it is quite easy to make sense of the external signs of a safe's construction and age, which are much more easily memorized and classified than those of furniture or porcelain. Insurance companies have issued staff with simple guides to help them assess the strength of safes, and we can borrow some of their simpler rules.

When looking at a safe, start with the simplest question – does it have any sharp, square edges? The more of these, the earlier the box. If all a safe's edges and corners are square, this shows that it has been made by riveting flat sheet metal onto an angle-iron frame, a method used in the nineteenth century to make what were then regarded as good safes, but later only on the very cheapest later models. A maker's name may have been painted on, and most brands carried their trademark on a distinctive metal plate with a name and trademark – usually brass, later chromium plated. Not all these names represented separate manufacturers, since many distributors and important retailers have had safes made to their specification and sold them under their own name.

The brass plate on the front may not always be a true indication of the origins of the safe. Makers of cheap and shoddy safes found it easy, from the earliest years, to counterfeit the plates of better safemakers, or to remove genuine items from broken safes to apply to their own. If you should discover that you own a safe which is a fake, do not despair. The ways of collectors are strange, and as in other fields a rare counterfeit may be more valuable than a common original.

Occasionally you may come across safes with the same external squareness, but made from the thickest of plate, half-inch or so, and with the plates dovetailed together. This was a very effective defence against the use of a wedge or lever, and was a technique used in the best safes. Perhaps it is found so rarely today because the customer who needed that higher degree of security, and was prepared to pay for it, was more likely to replace their safe with a later, better model when it became available.

A more common reinforcement, from about the turn of the century, was to wrap around the safe, at the front and rear edges, a reinforcing band intended to prevent peeling of the sides, top and bottom. If the band were not wrapped over the edges of the back plate, this remained vulnerable, and if the plates on the sides were too thin, they could still be ripped in the sections between the bands – it was generally accepted that mild steel more than 1/4-inch thick could not be ripped in this way.

This was the end of the first phase in safemaking, in which the original box design had been refined and strengthened, but was vulnerable to a number of new forms of attack. Improved technology seemed to be providing safecrackers with weapons which would give them domination of the battlefield, enabling them to launch a successful attack anywhere they chose.

To discover the state of the safecracking art at the end of the last century we don't have to rely on the memoirs of villains or policemen, the publicity handouts of the safemakers, or the excitement of newspaper reports: we can rely on an official United States Government report. Congress became so concerned about the skill of thieves that they passed an Act 'to enable the Secretary of the Treasury to appoint a Commission of scientific or mechanical experts, to report on the best methods of safe and vault construction, with a view of renewing or improving the vault facilities of the Treasury Department'.

One engineering journal called this 'an amateur burglar Commission, whose lack of professional skill was partly compensated by favourable conditions for nefarious attacks on standard types of safe', and there can have been few civil servants enjoying their work as much as the stalwarts who battered, burned and blew their way into safes during this investigation. They didn't even have to limit themselves to the more discreet methods of the burglar, since their brief required them not only to consider the risk from thieves, but what might happen if a mob chose to attack a government deposit. This meant that when pretending to be cracksmen at pains to limit the noise they used just three ounces of nitroglycerine, but as fake rioters they could indulge themselves with a dynamite charge weighing close to ten pounds.

The very publication of the report provided the reader with full operational details of how the experiments were performed. The descriptions were full and precise, a veritable Consumer's Guide to techniques. Need to know how long it will take you to peel a safe? Unsure whether to wedge or drill a safe apart? The Commission had the answers: '. . . the wedging off of sheet after sheet is found a better method of attack than drilling. A single uninterrupted night's work sometimes gives entrance into the heaviest of safes. Your Commission have seen a large and well-built safe thus practically destroyed by four hours' steady work, using no other tools than a heavy sledge, cold chisels and the wedge.' So, if you were considering an expensive investment in fancy equipment, save your money; if you've already bought too much to carry, spare your back and speed your getaway by leaving the inessential gear at home.

Perhaps all that hammering seemed like too much hard work, but you were unsure about how to set about using explosive. Let the Commission guide your thoughts: 'By the use of glazier's putty [the gap between door and frame was sealed from] about the middle of its height down to the bottom, and for a third of the length of the crack along the bottom of the door; nitroglycerine was poured into the crack until 3 oz had entered' – I do hope you're taking notes of this recipe – 'until 3 oz had entered and it had begun to drip from the lower side of the door. It was then fired.'

But did this work? 'The result was the complete destruction of the lower part of the door, the serious injury of the whole upper portion, and such general disruption that the entrance of the safe by the use of the

jemmy was made easy.' How about the noise? 'The sound
of the explosion was not very startling.'

If you are keen to know the saving in time over the
wedging method, take comfort from the Treasury figure
– blowing took just seven minutes. Possession of hand-
written notes containing information about safecracking
methods had always been prima facie evidence of criminal
connection and intent; now the well-informed thief could
turn aside suspicion by spending a couple of bucks on a
report that he could respectably carry under his arm
down Main Street.

The conclusions of the Commission were largely those
of all the makers, breakers and thieftakers – given time,
all safes could be opened, and by a variety of methods,
except for one innovative design. Only the Corliss safe
resisted them, to become the only strongbox to win
government approval: it was a cannonball design and
posed the next great challenge to safecrackers. Cannon-
balls were made as the name implies – by casting the
body of the safe as a sphere, instead of assembling flat
sheets into a cabinet, the designers were able to eliminate
all the vulnerable corners and edges which safemen had
learned to attack. The whole casing could be made of a
hardened steel which would be very difficult to cut, rivet
or weld if made as separate panels, and a circular door
aperture machined from solid metal was both stronger
and a more accurate fit than a cornered frame made up
from separate pieces. Although a sphere is not an efficient
shape in which to store conventional rectangular boxes,
the design remained supreme for almost a generation,
until makers learned how to work the better alloys,
and to manufacture rectangular boxes to comparable
tolerances.

Even without official proof, safemakers were conscious
that very few of their designs were capable of delaying a

skilful burglar for long, and they were resourceful to the point of eccentricity in thinking up new defences. Improvements in materials helped greatly, but the physical design was at least as important. Manganese steel, for instance, was a greatly improved defence against cutting, but if used as a simple substitute for earlier steels it remained vulnerable to a nitroglycerine attack. This liquid explosive was capable of penetrating a gap no wider than one 500th of an inch, and in such small quantities still had the power to blow off a door.

To seal the gap around the door some manufacturers had taken to fitting a rubber or fibre strip, but if this were first attacked with acid the gap that was left was even larger than it would have been had there been no strip fitted. The answer lay in improving the fit of door to frame, and here the round door had clear advantages over the ordinary square-cornered fitting, since a circle could be more accurately machined than four sides which must each be both tight and truly square to the frame and the other sides. Like the stopper in a glass decanter, the circular door could even be ground into its seating.

There was another obstacle to that final perfect close fit. On a conventional hinge, a door swings in an arc around the pin of the hinge, and some of the edge closest to the hinges must be shaved away to let it go home. The answer, developed and used in the United States long before British safemakers could be persuaded to change their designs, was to use what is known as a crane hinge. In this design, the door was hinged to an arm which in turn was hinged to the box, and the effect is to allow the door to fit into the aperture like a bath plug rather than a gate – straight in rather than swinging in.

With crane hinges, devices could now be fitted onto the door which would apply pressure to tighten the fit of door to frame even before it was locked – in pictures of strongroom doors we can often see a strong shiny horizontal bar, which looks very exposed to attack, but in fact serves only to carry cams which press the door into its seating before the locks proper are applied.

One design of door allowed both locking and sealing, and that was taken from a shape used in the breechblocks of large guns. The door was a large plug carrying a screw thread into which slots had been cut – an interrupted thread, as it is known – and when inserted into a matching hole required not more than a partial turn to draw tightly into place. This principle was used in the Corliss safe, the model which satisfied the Senate Commission, and therefore became the official Best Buy. Inevitably, a way of cracking the Corliss was devised, but not via the door.

Those rules of thumb which the insurance companies use to assess the worth of a safe are useful in identifying older safes, and are the best guide for any modern customer casting an eye over the new and secondhand safes in a showroom. Only safes with the rounded edges of a twelve-bend design, or a modern model with all its edges welded, will resist forcing apart by wedge or lever. The thickness of steel is important: many a safe rated only to resist fire will have walls one sixteenth of an inch thick, which represents just two minutes' hard and noisy work with a hammer for a thief. There are impressive-looking boxes with combination locks, sold in do-it-yourself shops for use in the home, which are at this level.

Though gelignite is almost never used these days, the insurance firms know that steel less than a quarter of an inch thick is also too flimsy to withstand an explosive charge, since it cannot withstand the internal pressures created, and there is little point in relying on a relocking device if the casing itself has been split apart.

Beyond a quarter of an inch thick, the steel will not

only be resistant to explosives, but proof against ripping. To defeat any form of drilling, the nature of the steel is as important as its gauge, and any reputable manufacturer will at the least defend the lock with an extra layer of hardened metal. Steel more than an inch thick is regarded as drillproof. Since plates this thick cannot be bent with ease by the manufacturers, such a thick wall will be made up of several thinner layers of different alloys chosen to resist attacks by drill and torch, and provide resistance to high temperature.

The overall weight of a safe should be more than eight hundred pounds, which is usually enough to prevent the box being carried off – if the body is made of quarter-inch plate this means a safe of ten cubic feet or more – though the extra precaution can be taken of bolting the safe to the floor or wall.

One part of a safe which is usually beyond reproach is the lock, since any combination lock, or a key lock having seven or more levers, is regarded as unpickable. The way to find the number of levers is usually to count the steps on the key, and deduct one: the final step is the one which actually withdraws the bolt, each of the others acts on a lever. Less easily assessed are the internal locking devices which act against explosive and burning attempts, and since no sensible salesman will allow you to dismantle his stock to examine them before purchase, you'll have to take his and the maker's word for it.

For anyone thinking of buying a box, the degree of protection offered by a good modern safe is greater than ever, and the level of genuine knowledge and expertise of the older established manufacturers and dealers is very impressive indeed. If they have a fear, it is not that the arms race with burglars will begin again, but that complacency may tempt customers to pennypinch, and buy a box which gives too little protection for their needs. It is worth remembering that safecracking was defeated not because safes became impregnable, but because owners stopped keeping too much money in them.

This brings the story of the conventional safe up to date, but safemakers have been resourceful, sometimes to the point of eccentricity, in thinking up new defences. Many schemes depended on moving the safe in some way – down, round or sideways. Normally a safe is required to stay fixed in one spot, but an idea which has been revived successfully down the years is the safe which sinks like a lift from one floor on which it is accessible, down into a doorless, windowless well, beyond the reach of thieves. It was first used in the middle of the nineteenth century while conventional vault design was being developed, and the idea can still be very useful where the contents of the safe are to be on public view by day, but must be secured at night. Just such a mechanism has been installed to protect the original copies of the American Declaration of Independence, Constitution and Bill of Rights – the glass case in which they are kept on view sinks beneath the Exhibition Hall of the National Archives into a discreet 50-ton vault whose walls are fifteen inches thick, behind doors weighing five tons.

It seemed to some inventors, professional as well as amateur, that a safe should be mounted so as to revolve. How could a safecracker apply leverage, or introduce explosives, to a moving target? This idea was revived several times, and a version in the 1930s which was a favourite project of one English safemaker had the extra embellishment of a reflector on top, so that a light beam directed on to it would be made to flash eight times a minute, the idea being that a patrolling policeman would know that all was well for as long as the light continued to flash. An alarm was also triggered if the safe should stop rotating. A prototype was built and placed in a

London showroom window where it attracted much attention in the Press, but no orders.

The safemaker was very frustrated that few of his colleagues, and none of his customers, shared his enthusiasm for the spinning safe, but there are obvious practical drawbacks, not least that a massive safe demanded a massive base and a powerful motor, and would always be expensive to buy and maintain, apart from being as potentially dangerous as any revolving mass of several tons. Storing heavy gold bullion, for instance, would have required a great deal of care if the whole rig were not to be placed lethally out of balance.

There were no real grounds for believing that this spectacular safe could have stayed inviolate. Safes on public view have been opened many times, a cunning thief would have devised some way of providing that reassuring flash of light, and one man claimed to the showroom staff that he could open a revolving safe with an oxygen flame. 'But you cannot as it won't stand still.' 'That would make no difference to me: I should sit on top and go round with it.' I have been unable to find any example of a successful, and dizzy, safecracker using this approach on any of the versions of the revolving vault.

Sinking safes were meant to drop out of reach; spinning safes to defeat attack; the sliding safe was designed to hide itself away. I have found no manufacturer's specification for the device, but a strange design which reached production was found by one American safecracker. Though only four feet high, the safe was all of ten feet wide, and had two doors. The outer safe was fire-resistant, intended mainly to protect the books of the business, but within it, as was customary with American safes, should have been a stronger compartment in which money would be kept. The safeman was perplexed – when he had opened all the doors, he had found no inner box, but he was sure that he had seen something sliding quickly sideways as the last door came open. Indeed, the designer had intended that, like a compartment in a conjuror's box of tricks, the spring-loaded money box would seem to disappear. Only because the mechanism was not quite quick enough was the trick discovered, and the secret safe blown.

Almost as popular among inventors as tricky safes, and as poorly received by paying customers, were boxes which not merely resisted burglars but contained booby-traps which would counterattack. A safecracker called Eugene, who wrote his memoirs in 1952, had rueful memories of a safe that fought back: 'Up in Wisconsin, in a laundry, we punched the safe. I reach over and open up the door. When I do I get me a great big whiff of tear gas right in my snoot. You see, what they had hanging in the gut-box [inner safe] was a phial of tear gas. That money stank for four hours. If we'd have got caught we'd have been a dead pigeon.'

Bleary Eugene was the latest, but one of the luckiest safemen to encounter a box that bit back: tear gas was benign compared with some older devices. Early in the seventeenth century the Marquis of Worcester had pondered why a locksmith should not build into his lock a mechanism 'so constructed that if a stranger attempt to open it catches his hand as a trap catches a fox, though so far from maiming him for life, yet so far marketh him that if once suspected he may easily be detected?'

In the Middle Ages chests were built which contained a trap for the unwary thief – having opened the top he would be faced with a tray which apparently bore no lock, but had three holes by which it might be lifted out, each hole conveniently the size of a finger. Each hole was in fact the entrance to a spring-loaded trap, with toothed jaws ready to bite into flesh, to grasp the thief until he was discovered. Every variety of vengeful lock has been suggested, to fire darts into burglars, stab them with dagger blades and hurl pepper into their faces.

These days a burglar savaged by a booby-trapped box might make more money by suing the safeowner than by robbing the safe, and our countermeasures are less blood-thirsty. As I was writing this manuscript a magazine article brought news of the latest gadget: for a couple of hundred pounds any safe can now be fitted with a device which, once bolted to the internal roof of the box, is ready triggered by movement of the safe or heat from any kind of cutting torch. If it is set off, it releases clouds of dye which will permanently stain anything within the safe, and the thief too.

3

Wood and Iron, Steel and Plastic

The first strongboxes were made of wood, the very latest prototypes have a plastic shell, but the history of safes is a story of metals in defence and in attack. The properties of these metals have given safes not only their strength but their shape, and of all the metals it is iron which has dominated. Cast iron, wrought iron, iron combined with carbon to make steel, this steel in turn combined with manganese, laminated with copper, heated to cut and heated to resist the blade. A new understanding of metals changed the industrial world, and came to the aid of the makers and breakers of safes: for them this was no abstract science, but a vital part of the contest.

For centuries iron was made by heating iron ore with charcoal, to make a spongy mass which could then be hammered into shape for swords and ploughshares. Applying a bellows to blow air through the fire, a technique which the Egyptians had used in making copper and bronze, made the process much quicker, and in the fifteenth century furnaces were built which had bellows to blast air through them, taking the iron to the point where it would melt and could be poured as a liquid.

This new cast iron, or pig iron, could not be hammered – it shattered under the blows – but it had the great advantage that it could be moulded into any required shape, time after time, and furnaces fuelled with charcoal could turn out useful quantities, several tons in a day. The limit then became the availability of charcoal, with forests falling to meet the demand. The next break-through came at the beginning of the eighteenth century when Abraham Darby succeeded in smelting iron with coke, a cheaper and more controllable process which made possible large-scale production of pig iron.

There was now an iron industry, producing a uniform and reliable product at a price which made the metal useful. Casting in iron allowed mass production of parts to close tolerances. Engineers and architects could pre-fabricate bridges and buildings (most famously the Crystal Palace), replacing many of the skills which had been used at a construction site with expertise in the factory.

Cast iron was strong under compression, but much too brittle to resist hammer blows, and was used for only the cheapest and most fraudulent strongboxes and safes, but the pig iron now cheaply available could be refined further in a process known as 'puddling' to provide the much more useful wrought iron. Puddling was a hot and demanding process which used small furnaces to remelt the iron, and iron oxide and other substances were added to remove unwanted carbon, silicon and sulphur. The more pure the iron, the higher the temperature needed to keep it molten, and the hard work of the process came in dragging out white-hot spongy lumps of iron and hammering them to beat out the impurities within.

The end product was wrought iron, a much tougher material which could withstand stresses and knocks, which could be hot-rolled or forged into plates and strips ready for the user to assemble as he wished. This was the metal that the first safemakers needed, and it served them well until the middle of the nineteenth century.

Like other engineers, safe manufacturers knew that though iron was good, steel would be better. Steel is no more than a very pure form of iron, to which the maker has added just those other elements, in very precise proportions, which will give the metal the properties he needs. It was not a new metal, but had only ever been made in small and expensive quantities until Henry Bessemer came along. In 1856 Bessemer announced his invention of a process to make steel, still regarded as an exotic material, for just one seventh of its previous cost. His method, of blowing hot air through molten pig iron, was at first seen as enormously dangerous, and there was little trust in the steel itself. One railway engineer, offered steel as a material for railway lines, exclaimed, 'Mr Bessemer, do you wish to see me tried for manslaughter?'

With fine Victorian confidence, Bessemer went ahead and built in Sheffield a works which would soon turn out nearly one million cheap tons of steel each year. Engineers could make use of the combination of strength, resilience and workability which makes steel essential to the lives we now lead.

The raw materials of change were just iron and carbon. Simple steel is pure iron with just a very small amount of carbon, and it is the proportion of carbon in the metal, and the effects of heat upon it, that give different grades of steel their properties. Less than one quarter of one per cent carbon gives us the mild steel from which car panels, ship plates and other large, easily worked and flexible sheets and strips are made. Just a little more – four tenths of one per cent – and we have already doubled the strength of iron on its own: we are approaching the range of steels cast to make machine parts, or cruder tools.

With more carbon, there is more strength at first: with one per cent the steel becomes three times stronger than iron, but further increases will produce a steel which is more brittle, more vulnerable to blows and stretching, bending and twisting. It is now a harder metal which can be finely sharpened to make scalpels for surgeons and saws for lumberjacks, tools for every trade. Increase the carbon still further, beyond 2.5 per cent, and there is another change – we now have cast iron, reasonably strong and hard, which can be moulded easily to make vast quantities of a single item.

The ways in which the molecules of iron and carbon combine vary according to these proportions but also according to the heat to which the alloy is subjected. The simplest demonstration is what happens to a simple steel needle.

As bought, the needle is tough and will spring back to shape under all ordinary loads; if it is heated to a bright red and then cooled very quickly in water it will be harder, but will snap easily. A similar needle heated to the same temperature, and kept hot for a short while, but taken from the flame slowly and allowed to cool gradually, will bend and stay bent like a soft wire. This needle can be restored to its original springy strength if it is first heated to a bright red and cooled rapidly like the first needle, then cleaned and reheated to no more than a straw colour, then allowed to cool slowly.

To these processes which are applied to the whole workpiece, the engineer can add surface treatments, which use heat and the presence of other materials to increase the amount of carbon (sometimes with nitrogen) at and just below the outer face of the metal. The result is a metal which has the general strength of a low-carbon steel, but which presents a surface which resists wear and is much more difficult to drill or cut. A term often used is 'case hardening', the case being that outer, often thin layer on the surface of the metal produced by the process. The safemaker George Price built his business on the quality of the hardened sheets of iron used in his products.

The final important way for the metallurgist to produce particular qualities in his steel is to make what is called an alloy steel, by adding further elements which will help the processes of heat treatment, or give special extra properties such as strength, hardness, springiness and resistance to wear. The alloy steel we know best is stainless steel, made in many varieties, but usually with chromium and nickel to give the metal its great resistance to corrosion. The figures 18-8, found stamped into cutlery or used in the description of containers from beer barrels to kitchen sinks, are the percentages of chromium and nickel in the alloy. Stainless steels are unusual in that they perform best when they contain no carbon, and special techniques are used to reduce the carbon content as much as possible.

In 1882 an alloy steel was discovered which was to prove enormously useful to the safemaker, when Sir Robert Hadfield discovered that a steel containing one per cent carbon and thirteen per cent manganese could be made very tough indeed by heating to 1000 degrees Centigrade and quenching in water. This steel performs in an odd but useful way – as poured it has a structure which is only moderately hard, but any attempt to cut or abrade the surface will produce an intensely hard and resistant layer at just the point of attack. Manganese steel has been put to use wherever it was important to prevent sawing, drilling or filing, from the bars on prison cells to the shells of safes.

The safemaker, like any other engineer, tries to choose the material which will serve him best. His requirements are not unique – many designers want a metal which will withstand heavy impact, and resist cutting, abrasion and heat and all engineers would prefer to work in a metal that can easily be formed – but the perfect safe would require all of these properties, not just at specific points of wear but across its entire exterior surface and at points within the safe where lock and bolt mechanisms need further protection.

The sudden cooling which makes iron hard also makes

it impossible to bend or work without the risk of fracture. Safe designers often used two kinds of metal, placing tough on top of hard, but in the 1860s Chatwood the English safemaker was the first to devise a better way of making this sandwich of metal: he took two cold sheets of softer but tougher iron, and then poured molten metal between them – it chilled on contact to become very hard, so that a drill point which penetrated the outer skin would flatten or shatter when it hit the hardened middle layer. This was much stronger than simply riveting the metals together, and was only bettered when larger machines were made for working large amounts of steel.

Then it became possible to sandwich high-carbon steel by welding and rolling it between layers of iron or mild steel, this combination bending as readily as simple mild steel. Cutting was carried out after hardening, to make sure that the dimensions remained stable and accurate, using special emery wheels.

Sandwiches helped in other ways. Steel resists cutting, but is vulnerable to a gas flame, and many attempts have been made to develop an alloy or a combination of layers which would give protection against a torch. One of the simplest has been to place sheets of copper between the steel plates; this works because copper is an excellent conductor of heat and prevents the steel behind it from reaching its melting point. Copper itself can be cut or torn with ease, but its use forces the safe burglar to stop his torch work and reach into the jagged, extremely hot aperture he has made in the steel to try to tackle each copper sheet in turn. The greater the need for security the more complex a sandwich of different materials could be put together; each layer served a separate purpose, the total effect of which was to increase the time taken to broach the safe.

A cross-section of Chubb's Extra Heavy Triple Treasury Door shows ten separate strata: from the outside in the safecracker would first have to penetrate a sheet of five-ply drill-resisting steel, in which two very hard layers of steel which are drill-resistant but brittle are protected against blows by a sandwich of three layers of softer but tougher steel. Next comes a deep layer of anti-blowpipe material (a form of concrete including hard mineral chips) with an I-section steel joist embedded into it. Beyond this is a layer of a robust but expensive Siemens steel, a sheet of copper, another five-ply layer, and a slab of Chubb's Special Alloy – their proprietary alloy steel for which great claims were made. Between two more layers of Siemens was a final layer of five-ply, and the very last protection for the lockwork was described as an Anti-Concussion Spring Diaphragm Plate.

No metal can exist which is forever proof against heat, but the safemakers were able to develop alloys with very high melting points, which were impervious to drill and explosive. When attacked with a torch they tend to choke the flame, and even to explode and spit in ways which make the cutting task more unpleasant and difficult. A layer of metal in a crystalline form, usually Spiegeleisen, would be incorporated; this would not lose its hardness on being cooled. If an attempt were made to drill it while it remained hot from a blowtorch, the drill itself would lose its temper immediately; the cutting edge would be lost and fail to penetrate further.

If heating and sudden cooling – quenching – hardens steel, reheating with slow cooling can reverse the process and make the steel soft enough to cut. Applying a source of heat such as a flame is one way of achieving this, but the friction of drilling can take the temperature high enough to achieve the same result. The effect of the drill is then a combination of simple cutting and de-tempering. One way to defeat this sort of attack is to use a steel exotic enough to require unreasonably high temperatures to soften, but it has also proved effective to provide a layer which will carry any heat away so quickly that the softening temperature cannot be reached, and for this an alloy of beryllium and copper has often been chosen.

4
Fillings

For the safeowner whose premises burn down it is not the quality of the lock which matters, or the ability of the casing to withstand a high-powered drill. When he stares at the waterlogged ashes he has to hope that the filling within the safe walls, a component which he has never seen, has proved good enough to preserve his cash and his paperwork.

No part of a safe has to be taken for granted more than that layer between the shell and the lining, but upon it depends almost all of the fire resistance of most boxes, and now much of the thiefproofing too. The purpose of the filling between the inner and outer casings of a safe has principally been to resist the transmission of heat, to allow the contents to remain cool even when the whole box is caught in a building fire. Like the burglar, heat can never be resisted indefinitely, but must be kept at bay for long enough to give a reasonable chance of survival.

For a long time there was a market for safes in which the whole casing was intrinsically fire-resistant. We are used to the idea that a safe must be made of metal, but often protection against fire was more important than a defence against thieves, and wooden safes with just a thin iron cladding were still popular for a hundred years after metal safes were invented. If the wood was soaked in a chemical such as alum it did not burn, and was able to retain enough moisture to make steam which would cool and preserve the contents of the safe. The good reputation of the better wooden safes such as the American Delano was not enough once the effective metal models could be mass produced cheaply: then the buyer could have both kinds of protection in a single purchase.

The reason wooden safes worked so well was that their construction easily satisfied the basic requirements of a fireproof layer. To be effective, fillings had to be of the right material, in the right thickness, and to be distributed evenly around the inner shell, so as to leave no gaps through which heat could be transmitted. For a metal safe to protect well, each of these specifications had to be met, but the customer had to take a great deal on trust, since he could measure none of these factors by looking at a complete safe, and was unable to spot poor construction and outright trickery like one maker's fillings of garden mould, complete with resident worms.

The principle behind older fillings was the same as that used in flasks made to keep drinks warm or cool: not a vacuum, but a layer of contained air which would make a poor conductor of heat. That air could be trapped between the relatively coarse chippings of sawdust, with the wood itself a feeble conductor, or in even smaller cells within and between the particles of a mineral filling.

Some of the materials which are poor conductors, such as charcoal and sawdust, will burn. Sudden combustion was to a degree prevented by compressing the fillings so as to limit the amount of air within the casing, and in this way even quite inferior safes would offer brief protection, but it was usual to give the sawdust a chemical treatment. This usually consisted of a salt which would contain water within its crystals, releasing it at high temperatures as steam. Asbestos was used, and fire clay; slag wool, or silicate cotton, which was rather like modern fibre glass; cement and plaster of paris, either dry or mixed with water and poured to set in place. Most economically, safemakers would use the waste products of other processes, such as cinders, ashes or slag. An unlikely link was made between safemakers and the producers of soda water and other fizzy drinks, who poured acid on to marble chippings to make the carbon dioxide which gave their products their bubbles. This process left a fine white powder which made a good insulator since it was inert and trapped a useful volume of air.

Many reputable safemakers chose to use a material many millions of years older than these industrial by-products. In mining land which has once been under the sea, strata will be found of silicates composed of fossilized algae – diatomaceous earth – which has the happy property of inhibiting heat transmission, since each particle is a minute air cell. Once it had been removed from the ground, this earth was treated to remove any traces of organic matter, and dried very thoroughly to remove moisture absorbed from the atmosphere. To gain the extra protection of a material which was not moist, but which held water to be released under heat, the earth was mixed with pure crushed alum.

By the first part of the twentieth century even cheaper safes were acceptably effective, and used a standard simple sand filling, mixed with sawdust, alum and soda. Experience had shown that cedarwood sawdust, which would absorb more moisture, was preferable to common sawdust of pine or deal. A good safemaker would also take steps to compress the filling with pressure and vibration; air within the mixture would reduce its effectiveness, and at worst the filling could settle leaving the top section of the shell quite hollow and empty. An alternative, which could be built easily into the walls of a safe or a strongroom, was to produce slabs in which the sawdust and alum were bound together under pressure by kaolin or gum.

Any additive which generated or released water helped to control temperatures, and there was one fabled case of a pair of cashiers who hid bottles of beer in the safe during a Christmas celebration; their boss locked the safe, and they feared discovery but were saved by a fire which destroyed the building – their bottles burst, and the beer protected all the banknotes and certificates in the safe.

The physical strength of the safe, its capacity to resist blows and pressure, was safeguard against not only theft but fire. No filling could be effective if the case itself had been distorted or split. Heat alone could do this, or a fall through the floors of several stories as the boards gave way under the safe's great weight. The heat which safes had to endure when buried in hot ashes was often more destructive than exposure to flame itself; the prolonged cooking effect could render every piece of paper inside brittle, ready to fall into dust at the first touch. Too many firemen and safeowners tried to open safes before their inner temperatures had dropped to safe level – the first inrush of air onto hot papers brought them to flash point, and they would burst into bright flame before the owners' horrified eyes.

As with every other feature of safe design, the fireproof quality of each competitive model was shouted in the market place, and contests held to prove the claims. One of the best and silliest tales was the legend in the safemaking Chubb family of an argument which broke out between a Chubb and a rival manufacturer, which could be settled only by a public trial of their products. A great fire was built and the two safes put into it, but just before the safe doors were closed a live chicken was thrust into each. Five hours later, a full three hours after the safes had reached red heat, they were drawn from the fire and allowed to cool. The rival safe was opened first, and to Chubb's dismay the chicken jumped out, clucking a protest, and scuttled away. Even worse, when the door of the Chubb safe was opened the chicken inside had perished – the poor bird had frozen to death.

Testing is no longer a matter of building a bonfire; makers have installed grand furnaces, large enough to put any safe through sequences of temperature rise and fall which can mimic the course of any likely fire. The concrete-like filling developed to resist gas torch attack is of course just as effective against fire, and all the layers in a safe can now be relied upon to combat both attack and accident. The buyer of a modern safe will be asked a number of questions which help the maker to select a suitable safe. The site will need to be considered: if it burns, what temperature will be reached, and for how long? This will mean a review of the structure and any features such as timber frames or plastic cladding, and the goods and equipment stored there, with special attention to products such as paint or potentially explosive chemicals.

The likely maximum temperatures can then be foreseen, and provision made for any special local risks; sometimes the answer may be to put the safe somewhere else, rather than install a much more expensive, better-defended model. The length of time for which protection will be needed can also be broadly predicted by looking at the amount of combustible material, and assessing how quickly a fire could be brought under control – how good is the sprinkler system; is the building next door to a fire station, or on a remote hillside?

Finally, the acceptable internal temperature can be calculated: ledgers and other paper items must be kept below the point at which, although not actually burned to ashes, they would be reduced to fragile, crumbling uselessness. Precious metals, diamonds, and more recently the discs and tapes which store magnetically the computer data on which companies depend, will each set working limits for the designer and govern the choice open to the customer.

5

Raising the Alarm

If a safe is a way for the property owner to gain strength, an alarm gives him extra senses, watchful round the clock. The very earliest alarms were made of flesh and blood, not wires and bells: the dogs around the encampment which barked, or the beasts that stirred to warn of the approach of attackers or intruders. Most famous were the geese said to have saved Rome from the Gauls in 390 B.C., and geese are still in use in Scotland, as sentries guarding a billion pounds' worth of Scotch whisky. On one site covering forty acres, patrols of Chinese geese protect twenty-five million gallons of the spirit, tended by an official goose-keeper; a goose survives for thirty years and so has a longer useful life than the wiring of most electronic systems.

Burglars had their own ways of limiting the risk presented by dogs. Produced in evidence against two nineteenth-century burglars were the written prescriptions they had kept: 'To Kill Dogs. – A little liver cooked and some choloroform mixed with it.' This provoked a heartless laugh in court. 'A little liver cooked and some aniseed mixed with it. Let the dog smell it, and it will not bark.' Laughter, again.

A recent and bizarre example of animal protection came during a rebellion against the Philippine government of Mrs Aquino, when insurgents sneaking up on a police barracks stumbled upon a pet kept by the commandant, and in panic betrayed themselves to the guards: Colonel Adam Jiminez was very fond of his seven-foot crocodile.

The fearful owner can place his faith in human guards, but they may betray him or shirk their task. It is notoriously difficult to be vigilant through all the nights when nothing happens and to avoid a regular and predictable pattern which a thief can learn too easily. For this passive menial work the pay has never been enough to guarantee fidelity – guards have plenty of time to compare their wages with the wealth they are protecting.

The ideal might therefore be a device, or a system, which will unfailingly warn the owner of any attempt to rob him. A string tied to ankle or wrist before sleeping and elaborate contraptions of wires and cranks and bells were all tried in their turn, and the use of electricity as a way of providing a warning was explored even before there was a reliable source of power – the first alarm company was founded by the American Eldwin Holmes in 1853, six years before the first electric battery allowed current to be stored. By the 1880s the major safe manufacturers were designing and patenting electrical bell systems which might be built into safes, though it seems that relatively few orders were received. More commonly a business needing an alarm would hire a local jobbing electrician; using standard wires and relays, switches and contacts he would install the most ingenious ambushes and traps he could devise.

One nineteenth-century safecracker was bemused to find a number of very comfortable seats set out within a bank he was raiding. 'When I saw an upholstered rocker or an ordinary chair left with such insistent convenience, that alone was a sufficient indication to me . . . that all was not right. And again, when I saw a chair left, as by neglect, in front of the vault door, there was sufficient reason in that for entertaining suspicion . . . Upon making a careful examination of these chairs, I discovered that they were all cunningly attached to the burglar-alarm system. Be sure that we met the mute, though pathetic appeal from these appliances to make ourselves comfortable with a stolid disregard.' Of another alarm connected straight to the police station he wrote dismissively that, 'I could cope, handily, with it, for I had only to pass the word along to the First Precinct police station that I was ready to "pull off" the trick, and my friends there would put the wire out of commission.'

In London, New York and other large trading centres, it became too burdensome for the police to provide a line to every business wanting one. Central bureaux were set up to receive alarm signals and alert the police, but the most usual arrangement was, as today, an external bell intended to attract the attention of a passing patrol. Merchants who lived close to their businesses could have a bell wired at their bedside, and one New York jeweller who invested in such a system in the 1880s was able to rise, dress, and take a cab to his shop in time to interrupt a couple of rather lethargic burglars. They must have been ill-informed as well as slothful: other thieves must have been quicker to grasp the basis of the new alarms, since by 1887 it was already necessary to provide circuits which were proof against cutting and bridging.

Many of the components of modern alarm systems were first conceived of a couple of generations ago, but the path of progress was not always straightforward. In October 1911 the London *Daily Mirror* reported the invention of the Trusty Alarm Box, which 'growls like an angry mastiff for hours and hours if any unauthorised person lifts it up . . . [When triggered] the electric circuit is connected and the hammer hits the inside of the box thousands of times a minute, setting up a resonant growling noise like no other sound in the world . . . The feeling when one was picked up . . . was most uncanny . . . It growled and growled, filling the room with the noise and sensation of the presence of a large and angry dog.'

More conventional electrical alarms were being built into the very fabric of all large and important new vaults. The wiring of alarms which used trigger contacts was now embedded in the concrete of the walls to prevent tampering, and following a fresh principle, the vaults were lined with electrified mesh and panels to become capácitors. Any intruder would cause a shift in the frequency of an oscillator in the circuit, tripping a relay and so triggering the alarm.

A cruder way of alerting either a proprietor or the police was to place a sensitive microphone on the premises, and to run a line to the owner's home or the police station where an amplifier would relay the least sound. Alarms are intended to give peace of mind but any merchant who bought such a system, trying in the middle of the night to make sense of strange noises coming down the wire, must have lost hours of sleep.

A new invention promised a better remote warning which used the telephone system: a conventional alarm could now be connected to an apparatus which would not only trigger a bell but make an automatic call to the police. This new machine had a small gramophone – turning at 78 rpm, of course – and the internal components of an ordinary telephone, linked by wires and levers, and all contained in a transparent case. The owner arranged for a recording to be made of an announcement reporting a break-in at his address, and this disc was placed on the turntable; if the alarm were triggered, a mechanical finger dialled 999, and when the call was answered, the arm on the gramophone was lowered to play the message: very crude by modern standards, but certainly as effective as the other links in the alarm system.

All this was much too costly for the ordinary trader, but a simpler device which reached the market in 1928 greatly impressed the *Daily Mail*: 'In a room of mystery in the West End of London, whose secrets have been closely guarded, I yesterday saw in operation what will be a new terror for burglars – the invisible ray which sets alarm-bells clanging when anyone crosses its path.' The use of an infra-red beam is now commonplace in household alarms but the magical effect remains impressive, and a beam which opened a door was still the most popular exhibit in the Children's Gallery of the Science Museum fifty years later. This use of infra-red radiation was claimed as a British invention, but a challenge came a couple of years later from an American alternative at the other end of the spectrum, when an engineer from Westinghouse proposed the use of an ultra-violet beam, and was able to demonstrate that the infra-red given out by an ordinary flashlight could be enough to fool the infra-red sensors in use. An alternative to invisible light was inaudible sound. Ultrasonic transmitters and receivers can be used in much the same way as infra-red beams, though some operational disadvantages have made them less popular.

Most alarms are attached to entrances, to be triggered when an unauthorized person tries to break in. It is possible, however, to make the whole room or vault an element in the alarm, using what is known as the pressure differential system, which maintains the air pressure within the room at a different level to that outside it. Any hole made by a thief cutting through the floor, ceiling or walls will change the pressure and set off the alarm.

The air pressure within the room is controlled by a fan, which creates a known pressure inside. The alarm is triggered by a diaphragm, a flexible panel which has one face into the protected room and one exposed to the ordinary atmospheric pressure outside; for as long as the difference between the internal and external pressures is within a set range the diaphragm stays in balance, but if any attempt is made to break into the room, the air pressure within will rise or fall, the diaphragm will move, and the alarm will be set off. The change in pressure within the room does not have to be very great, no more than the differences caused by a change in the weather, but the system is very sensitive indeed and will respond to the cutting of a hole of just a few square inches in the wall of a storeroom of 30,000 cubic feet.

Air pressure was used as long ago as 1870 to monitor a large well-safe (a safe which sank at night into a deep shaft). The designer provided that the pressure would be measured and displayed outside the building in a tall glass tube containing coloured water, which would not only show that an attempt was being made to reach the safe but even from which direction the attack was being made.

One method of protecting safes was to place them within cabinets which were connected to alarms. The cabinets were usually made of plywood and had no strength to resist attack, but were easier to wire up than a whole room. Thieves learned how to cut into these cases to manipulate ordinary wiring, but it was easy to install an air pressure system which could not be defeated in this way, and needed no more than a two-inch blower to protect a cabinet large enough for two or three safes. These outer cabinets were effective, but now it is common for alarm components to be built into the safe itself, with circuits hidden within the casing, contacts ready-fitted on the door and frame, and sensors attached to the lock to detect an attack; the buyer of such a safe simply connects it into the building's alarm system. Staff as well as valuables can be defended by a feature built into modern combination locks – if the person opening the lock is under threat he can, in turning the dial, trigger a silent alarm, rather as an airline pilot has ways of secretly notifying ground stations that his plane is being hijacked.

From the burglar's point of view alarms became nuisances rather than absolute deterrents. Rarely would a building have alarms which prevented all access, since the cost of fitting and maintaining a total system is high, and the likelihood of false alerts increases with each added feature. The thief's best approach was usually to spot the contacts and wiring and then contrive a route which would avoid them, perhaps through a roof or an unprotected route from another building. Once inside, he could make his way to the central control box and set about neutralizing the circuit. If he feared a well-hidden silent alarm, he had only to make sure that he had a place to hide outside the premises and retreat to it rapidly, waiting out of sight to see if a police patrol arrived.

Defeating the very best alarms by skilled sabotage has tended to be a specialist task. For the most intricate jobs an outside expert called a 'bellman' could be brought into the team, but it was not too difficult for an experienced burglar with the right friends to learn enough to neutralize an average alarm, and then the person within a team who seemed to have the best knack would keep the role. Either to cut a wire, or to place a connection to bridge a pair of wires, was rarely difficult, and the simplest physical solution was often enough: '[He] spiked that dangerous contrivance by the simple method of gumming the open space between the base of the bell and the gong. Then he filled it with fine bird sand.' Time and again countermeasures were developed: early alarms used a circuit which was normally open, that is, current flowed only when it was triggered, and this could be beaten by finding and cutting the wire; the closed circuits which followed had to be bridged. The first version of the infra-red magic eye was triggered if a torch were shone onto it, switching on the lights throughout the premises, but they also went out if the beam was withdrawn, so a thief could use a torch to spot the cells.

Once the basic technical skills had been learned, a burglar needed a mixture of common sense and instinct: unlocked doors, cupboard doors left ajar, a single valuable item left conveniently to hand, could all be booby-traps ready for the greedy and unwary. Veteran safecrackers tried hard to drum caution into young or inexperienced accomplices, and had to keep a careful eye on companions whose frayed nerves and curiosity gave them itchy fingers. One of the burglar's greatest allies has been the unreliability of old alarms. Police and public used to respond very quickly to the sound of the exterior bell ringing in its box, but poor installations left without maintenance, sensors which reacted to wind and rain, and the decay of older wiring left exposed to the weather have led to so many false alarms that many alerts are ignored. Many police forces now refuse to accept direct connection of alarms because of the disruption caused by faulty equipment, leaving private security firms to provide the first response.

The security industry has lost credibility and customers and has a battle to maintain standards; after all, alarms are usually intended to replace a more expensive human guard, but any watchman who gave such unreliable service would be sacked very quickly indeed. Good or bad, an alarm can give the owner a sense of security which leads to carelessness about ordinary precautions. Why be so fussy about the keys when all the doors and windows are protected anyway? Why send a patrol round if the telephone link will report a break-in automatically? Thieves who were confident about their ability to deal with circuits came to rely on this factor. By the 1960s English safeman L. J. Cunliffe was confident enough to say, 'The gaff had to have a burglar-alarm before we would consider it a proposition. It mattered very little whether the alarm was an automatic one linked to the bogies, or a plain straightforward bell system . . . mess up the works and walk in.'

Locked In

All the materials for a horrid tragedy are supplied by the details of an accident which occurred on Friday to a Dundee workman. He was engaged in putting up a large safe, and getting inside, incontinently shut the door, which has a self-acting lock. Fortunately for him, the key was at Birmingham, and was sent off in response to a telegram so that he was not more than 30 hours inside. But could anything more hideous have happened than the chance that he should have had the key in his own pocket and the door have had no aperture? Writers of the realistic dramas of today might make good use of the situation.

The Globe, 8 December 1884

It is among the commonest of mishaps, as the Automobile Association and any jobbing locksmith will confirm, to be stuck on one side of a locked door while the key remains on the other. This is frustrating, often embarrassing, and can leave the ordinary citizen very uneasy when he sees how casually and quickly a skilled stranger can get into his car or home.

With the development of formidable large safes and vaults, it was inevitable that some unfortunate souls would be trapped inside. For the claustrophobic, what could be more terrifying than to be locked within such a strong, airtight, lightless, seamless tomb? Newspaper reports played upon the terror with fine Victorian relish. Deaths were almost unknown, but even where the body has survived, the spirit may have been destroyed by fear. A man rescued after hours trapped in the vault of the City Hall in Philadelphia was described as emerging 'a raving lunatic . . . terribly weakened by his shrieks and

his struggle for air' and a New Jersey bank clerk was said
to have been found 'unconscious, his face and tongue
blackened, his hands bleeding, and his boots in rags from
frantic kicking against the walls of the vault'. Nor was
this always the result of accident: in the course of robbing
the Dexter Bank of Maine, it was claimed that a robber
called Sam Perris – Worcester Sam – murdered a cashier
called Barron by cold-bloodedly locking him into a vault
because he refused to divulge the combination of the safe
within the vault. Barron died before he was found the
next day.

Again and again the public was invited to share the
fear and desperation of the unfortunates behind the
impregnable door, but some of the reports may arouse a
worldly curiosity. In just one year, 1920, there were
almost identical cases in Berlin and London in which two
colleagues, male and female, were trapped together, but
their reasons for being in the vault in each other's
company were not immediately clear to their employers,
nor dwelt upon by the newspapers. (The London couple
seem to have been the luckier – they were provided
through a narrow chink in the door with 'sandwiches cut
very thin'.) Another case which had unexplored comic
possibilities arose in Stockholm during the long investigation which followed the death of Ivar Kreuger, the
industrialist and prodigious confidence trickster: the team
of auditors sent to Sweden to investigate his affairs may
have felt they were victims of a vengeance from beyond
the grave when they spent a long time locked in his vault
with all his papers.

The potential for tragedy is real, and a lock-in con-
fronts the locksmith with his most important challenge,
and the weightiest responsibility. A New York craftsman
was once gravely puzzled when called to open a jammed
safe in a railway station office. A bungled burglary had

left the door stuck fast, and when he arrived he was accosted by a man who told him to 'watch out for the man in there'. The safe was not large, and at first the disbelieving locksmith took little heed, but when just a short while later another man came to him with the same plea he grew very concerned. When the safe was opened there was no sign of a man, but the ticket agent pointed to an urn inside and explained the town's preoccupation. A local politician had died in Florida, and had been cremated, but his ashes had been brought back for a big funeral, and the whole town was anxious that the man should be released.

Time and again the authorities have sought criminal safecrackers in an emergency, and during the night of 10/11 November 1920 the warden of Joliet, the famous prison in Illinois, received an urgent call for help. Could he provide expert safe-blowers to rescue a bank teller from within the vault of the National Bank in Ottawa, a small town some miles away? The teller, Mr Francis Carey, had been locked in by a bandit, and the time lock was not due to release for more than thirty hours because the bank had been closed for Armistice Day. The robbery had been unsuccessful – the bandit had dropped his haul of $50,000 in his flight – but there was great fear that Mr Carey would suffocate. The warden agreed that every effort must be made, and there was talk of an amnesty for the man who could perform the rescue. But when he called back, it was to admit with regret that he had only a few safe men of the old-fashioned kind, and having talked to them, he was sure that none would be of any use against a modern strongroom.

Back at the bank, despairing officials summoned acetylene torches and dynamite, and attacked the vault as best they could, shouting encouragement to poor Mr Carey. Wire services carried regular bulletins on their progress to newspapers across the land. At last, late in the day, their labours had cut and blown away enough of the defences for them to make one last hot and dusty effort, and they broke through into the vault. But there was no one inside, just a note which read, 'If you'd treated me right this would not have happened.' Next day, Mr Carey emerged from hiding to surrender to the police, confessing that he had in fact planned the entire scheme.

From a veteran safe engineer comes this account of just how hair-raising an attempt to rescue a person trapped inside a safe can be:

One often sees 'cliff hanger' films of someone, usually a child, locked in a vault with the 'race against time' theme, which arouse much sympathy for the locked-in victim. After my own experiences, my sympathies are with the poor mutt responsible for getting the door open! Whilst working on the Bank of England site, I received an urgent call to go to a bank in Piccadilly, where a girl was imprisoned in a vault. So taking a few tools, which included a crowbar and a sledgehammer, I hailed a taxi and, together with a hefty labourer, arrived at the bank. There was considerable panic because, as it was explained to me, the girl had been imprisoned for nearly two hours and there was some doubt about how long the air would last.

At this stage a brief description of the vault would not be amiss. The door itself weighed 4 tons, pivoted on roller and thrust bearings, the walls were 2 feet of reinforced concrete with an inner steel lining. The frame of the door was fitted with a rubber insert which made it watertight and, incidentally, airtight. When the door was open, a wandering lead was taken from inside the vault and plugged into an outside socket. This was to ensure that when the door was closed, there was no live wire inside the vault which might cause a fire. It was this wandering lead which had caused the trouble. A junior of the bank, seeing a young lady entering the vault, had, for a joke, given the door a push to give the girl a fright. Previously,

I have mentioned that doors of this weight swung very easily, and this door encountered the electric lead, severed it, and in effect arc-welded door and frame together.

Obtaining a crowbar and after sustained efforts, they finally broke the handle off the door and only then decided to get some expert assistance. I immediately telephoned our depot and told the storekeeper to remove a handle from a similar door and send it, together with another sledgehammer, and a couple of men by taxi. Having little knowledge of how long the air would last, I did however know that people in times of stress used more oxygen than if they were relaxed. So we shouted as loud as we could to get the girl to lie on the floor close to the door, hoping she could hear us. After getting the new handle fitted, I was able to use the crowbar to obtain leverage and at the same time the men belted the frame with the sledgehammers to try and break the weld.

I became very worried after an hour of sustained effort with no progress and could see that I would be in a very difficult position if our efforts did not succeed. So telling the men to take a rest, I telephoned our head office, got the general manager on the line and told him to get a compressor and pneumatic drills up to me at once, as I was going to break through the wall. His reaction really amazed me. He started to tell me about the cost and also the difficulty of getting this equipment at short notice, and was it really necessary? I really lost my temper and told him that a girl's life was at risk and if he didn't comply with my requests he could bloody well come up and take charge himself as I was leaving. He agreed at once. I then told him to send at least two more men in a taxi as the men I had were exhausted.

By now the girl had been imprisoned for over five hours, so I asked the bank manager to get a doctor who might advise us about the consumption of oxygen. He agreed that we had been on the right track in advising the girl to lie on the floor.

We had resumed our labours with sledgehammers, and just when the compressor gang arrived, I detected a slight movement in the door. With renewed efforts, assisted by the new arrivals, we finally succeeded in opening the door. The girl was in a very distressed state of shock, according to the doctor, who immediately ordered her to hospital. Personally, I wasn't feeling at all that good myself, so went off to get a meal. When I returned to make sure the door would close perfectly, there was a great feeling of anti-climax. The manager casually remarked that I had certainly made a mess of the paintwork!

6

Vaults

A strongroom or vault is in principle a very large safe, but with every element in its design and construction greatly exaggerated. The walls, the doors, the locks and the defensive system of alarms have to be made resistant not to a weekend's work by semi-skilled thieves, but to an extended and cunning assault by the sort of resourceful, patient and skilled thief who may spend months seeking and exploiting any weakness, then put to work a large team using a variety of high-powered tools. If the stakes are high enough thieves will go to extraordinary lengths, as we shall see in the section on pages 238–43, which tells the story of the greatest vault job of them all, the Nice raid of 1976.

Where there is any risk of major riot or insurrection the vault designer has to protect not merely against the stealthy burglar but against the strength of attack which a mob might be able to make, a mob which might bring uncommon equipment and skills. The more volatile the politics, the more robust the defences; in countries where an uprising could have military support, and possession of the reserves is as vital as control of the television station, a fortress may be needed.

An example which shows the lengths to which a major nation will go to protect its wealth can be found in Paris. In the 1920s France held vast amounts of gold – more than £400 million, twice the reserves held in Britain, and the men in the Bank of France who ordered the excavation of the new vaults had to bear in mind the recent history of powerful military threats from beyond the

frontiers, the advances in technology during the Great
War, and startling evidence from Russia and Germany of
the dangers of internal struggle.

The siege of Paris during the Franco-Prussian War was
still remembered by many citizens, as was the advance of
German armies in the early stages of the First World War
which had placed the capital within range of enemy
artillery. Bombing by aeroplane and the use of poison
gas were now established military techniques, and the
way in which disaffected armies could combine with
civilian revolutionaries in Germany and in Russia had
scared Western governments badly.

Paris was vulnerable to invading forces, and it might
have seemed sensible to choose a distant spot which could
be easily defended and erect a stronghold, as the United
States did at Fort Knox. Politically, this was unacceptable
– to remove the wealth of the nation from the capital
would betray a lack of confidence. Instead, the vault
designers were resourceful and used natural features as
well as manufacturing skill to make the very best of their
brief – under the buildings of the Bank of France they
discovered not only strata of solid rock through which
they drilled but also the course of an underground river,
and they elected to dam the waters and lodge the entire
vault beneath a vast subterranean lake.

The vault they built covers no less than two and a half
acres, under a roof supported by 750 massive pillars. It
can be reached only through a series of vast steel and
concrete doors of differing designs – one is a section of
revolving cylinder, another an enormous plug on an
electrically-driven trolley which runs on rails to set it in
place. The final doors cannot be opened from outside,
but only from within by the garrison which stays underground to guard the reserves of gold and securities lodged
there. The vault was designed not only to contain the

wealth but to provide a workplace under bombardment, and has its own set of electrical generators, a supply of clean air (against gas attack) from a secret source, fresh water from the underground river, and kitchens ready to feed two thousand staff and guards from stocks held permanently underground. In all, this was as clever a design as any section of the Maginot Line, and was of course to suffer the same defeat, not by assault but by encirclement.

A vault can be kept small if the contents are mostly gold and paper, but the number of citizens who needed high security created a market for vast safe deposits: chambers in which a large number of smaller, separate lockers would each serve one customer. Renting a box was more effective than having a safe at home, and cheaper than any domestic safe, which could not offer even a fraction of the security of the large, strong, patrolled and supervised vaults.

First to open in the United Kingdom was the National Safe Deposit in Queen Victoria Street in the City of London. It took seven months to complete, and contained thirty-two separate vaults, arranged on four floors which began 40 feet below street level. Within outer walls 13 feet thick, the vaults were assembled from layers of sheet steel. Each had a massive door a foot thick and weighing five tons, but without a conventional lock; the doors were opened and closed by hydraulic power, drawing on a reservoir or cistern above the vault. At night this entire system was disconnected, and the pipework so arranged that any attempt to reconnect the supply would instead cause a flash flood of the entire vault. The combination of concrete, steel and water was designed to resist attack by explosives, drilling, or any other physical means. To protect against simple assault an armed guard was mounted at all times, and they could not merely fight off an attack, but trigger a flood to prevent robbers from using force or hostage-taking.

The popularity of the safe deposit idea was such that the largest in London, in Chancery Lane, was several times extended until it held about 40,000 separate lockers and drawers within it, serving not only City firms and individuals, but large numbers of jewellers and diamond merchants whose businesses had traditionally clustered in nearby Hatton Garden. Each box has two locks – the subscriber keeps one key, the other is with the staff who thus monitor the use of any box. Subscribers' keys get lost, but have been returned by finders as far afield as Buenos Aires and Cape Town – one was even returned by a mountaineer who came upon it while climbing the Matterhorn.

Across the Atlantic, strongrooms were no less impressive. One British safemaker reported:

The best and heaviest strongroom that I visited there was one in which the walls were five feet thick of reinforced concrete and steel. The circular door weighed 250 tons, and you could easily swing it with one hand. It was fitted with Combination Locks and Time Locks. It was built in a Sub-Basement, and the bank above it took up the entire block with its own armoury, water supply, and its own police force, and it was victualled for fourteen days. At the four corners of the building, out in the street, were four big bronze statues of Liberty and other forgotten American Gods, and connecting these statues to the Bank were underground passages, so in the event of attack, or of mob rule, access could be obtained to the statues, and the plinths taken down, machine guns could be brought into action.

When the French started construction of their vault in the 1920s, they had prepared for the known hazards of war. A generation later the risks have grown to include nuclear bombs, while the treasures to be preserved are not only items of immediate cash value, but records without which entire corporations would perish as utterly as if their capital had been stolen. Modern security vaults are used to store microfilm, magnetic or optical forms of data storage, and the computers which can retrieve all this information. Extortion by threatening to destroy or corrupt company records is an under-reported but potentially very profitable crime, and there are legendary examples of the damage caused by employees with grudges.

Every major company now takes steps to create secondary records, and the space required for such archives has led to the use not only of purpose-built vaults but fortified mine workings, even abandoned underground railway stations. The first commercially important vault of this kind was probably the one under Iron Mountain in New York State, created in the early 1950s against the nuclear threat. By 1955 a disused Bath stone mine in Wiltshire had been converted to offer similar security. Chosen to be remote from any strategic area, the Wiltshire mine runs between 100 and 150 feet underground, and gives 70,000 cubic feet of storage space, protected by airlocks and a vault door of the kind used in important bank strongrooms. Inside, the developers divided the space into insulated damp-proof cubicles of steel, aluminium and vulcanite into which any tenant might build such further security as was needed. A company might choose to rent an area and install a strongroom to their own specification.

Crime and war are not the only threats against which companies will choose to use strengthened vaults for their records; in Japan every major corporation has planned against the predicted risk of earthquake in the Tokyo area by establishing remote headquarters far from the capital, complete with duplicate records and ready to function at very short notice. Only in Japan has the strength of a commercial vault suffered an explosion of atomic force – the strongroom of the Teikoku Bank in Hiroshima was only three hundred yards from the centre of the bomb's blast, but survived unbreached, and the bank was rebuilt around it after the war.

Most safes are standard models, produced on a fairly large scale to a few basic patterns. Customers assess the strength and quality of safes needed to protect against a reasonable level of risk, make one or two individual choices – colour, perhaps, or type of lock – and await delivery. At the other end of the scale, any large vault is a major work of civil engineering. To protect its contents it must be strong and heavy, massive far beyond the ordinary requirements of a building's foundations and needing protection from water, subsidence and other natural enemies as well as human predators. It has special power requirements – there must be a supply of electricity for lighting and alarm circuits, but great care must be taken in providing power within the vault in case of electrical fire. At stake is not merely a building, but the future of the company or institution should its records or assets be destroyed.

Since a vault has to serve its owners for several generations, and repair would jeopardize security, the design and the quality of construction of a vault must be as nearly perfect as possible from the first. It is possible to add a vault to an existing building, or to replace an existing strongroom with an improved version, but this is even more demanding than to erect the entire building upon and around a new vault. Either way the task can take years.

The security of early vaults often depended more on the fact that they lay underground than on the materials and construction methods used – they commonly used no more than thick conventional brickwork, with at best a sheet iron lining. Builders might have particular bricks which they favoured for their hardness, but any such construction was vulnerable once the first brick or block of stone had been removed.

Though bricks could be broken or prised apart, they were useful and flexible prefabricated parts, and a logical next step was to use the same method of assembly but improve the components. The American Hough and Harper vault of the 1880s used chilled iron blocks, each weighing between 1700 and 10,000 pounds and having dovetails ground into its edges. They were assembled onto massive granite and concrete bases, and 'bound into a homogeneous mass' by steel rods. Floor, ceiling and sliding doors were all assembled from similar blocks to form a vault which did not need to be buried but could be taken piece by piece to stand within an existing building. Unusually it had only a triple-clock time-lock, which was set not into the door but into the inner face of the wall. Although this vault design was impressively resistant to drilling and dynamite, no design which depended on simple iron could withstand oxy-acetylene attack, and in less than a generation it was obsolete.

The wall of a vault is constructed according to the risks to be prevented. If fire is the only enemy, brick walls eighteen inches thick will probably be good enough if sealed by a fireproof door. As this can never be a serious obstacle to the thief, concrete is used, but this has its own disadvantages: it must be carefully compacted, and in the thickness required to make a vault wall, may take more than a year to dry thoroughly. During that time nothing can be stored which might be damaged by moisture, and to build in a ventilator shaft is to introduce a serious gap in security. One German bank was raided simply by sending a small burglar through the single oversized ventilator installed in its vault; subsequent designs used several smaller tubes, but even when these have been contrived so as to give no opportunity for the use of explosives they are unsatisfactory.

The reinforcement of concrete has been of great concern to designers, who have the aim always of using materials which are intrinsically strong and resistant in forms intricate enough to frustrate the thief. No protection is ever permanent, but if the thief can be forced to change his method of attack frequently, his task can be made too long-winded. A thief wants to make a hole in the wall only large enough for a single person to enter the vault, and can spend a great deal of time in research and preparation, but he must always complete his task before he can be discovered.

Simple concrete could be breached much too easily with pickaxe or drill, so chippings of hard stone were included in the mixture. At first granite was used, but when the source of supply favoured by British manufacturers ran out, a type of shingle quarried in the Midlands proved a good substitute. Not quite so hard, it nonetheless had a greater resistance to power drill attack, since the secret of defeating drills lay not only in presenting a hard surface, but in forcing the drill to deflect and break. The smooth, rounded surfaces of shingle did this more effectively than the flat faces of granite chips.

Concrete is conventionally reinforced with steel for structural strength and rigidity, but the mild steel rods used in ordinary construction while strong enough to help a building to carry its own weight are too thin, too widely spaced, and too easily cut to present a significant extra obstacle. The first modification made was to use lengths of railway track or I-shaped girders, set like a close fence into the wall. This made heavier work of cutting the steel, but had the drawback of weakening the concrete: since the bars did not interlock with the concrete, nor trap it within a framework, it was possible to strip away the concrete and reveal all the steel at the same time for cutting. A better solution was to set two lines of rail, between which concrete would be retained, but mere thickness of metal was never enough; a thinner bar which presented only an edge, and which could not easily be chipped free from the concrete, was much harder to cut.

These standard stocks were eclipsed by a twisted bar developed especially for vault use, each bar made of two kinds of metal with mild steel wrapped around an anti-blowpipe metal core. Gas cutting gear was almost as quick to cut through thick stock as thin, so an arrange-ment of the bars which would complicate the task was as important as the stock itself. A successful early version was a 'mattress' – intertwining steel spirals – first erected on site for concrete to be poured around it, and then used to provide the skeleton for prefabricated blocks which could be kept in stock and shipped for assembly as needed. Prefabrication was to become the norm for all ordinary vaults, and a single British maker installed about two thousand of this kind during the postwar improve-ment in bank security.

Manufacturers did not learn only from attempted thefts. They have always tried to stay ahead by testing their designs, and this splendid description by one British safemaker of the 1930s has survived:

To test the wall properly, and to get at its real strength, one has to do what is called an unlimited test, that is to say, the burglar may have access for as long as he likes; there are no watchmen; he can make as much noise as he likes, and use anything he wants provided he does not use sufficient explosives to blow down a whole building, which would defeat his own ends. In this one we started with rock drills to get through the concrete, and the man kept on until he had a hole about 2 inches in diameter right through the concrete, when he came to the steel; then he got his oxygen flame to work . . . is a very difficult thing to work in a confined space; after a time he gave it up and said he could not go any deeper unless a series of holes were made and the whole of the concrete broken away. Then the next operator came on the scene . . . he was really a most anxious looking and inoffensive man with a black felt hat, and in a small bag he had two pounds of nitro-glycerine, part of which he proceeded to put into the wall. Actually he put half a pound of nitroglycerine in, and it was ignited with an electric spark. The damage done to the outside of the wall was not very much, but [inside] it blew away great blocks of concrete, and entirely separated the concrete from the face of these joists. The lesson we learned from this was that reinforcement is most desirable in the concrete, but it must mix intimately, so to speak, with the concrete itself . . . you must have a number of surfaces if possible, which would bury themselves into the concrete and form a perpetually recurring obstruction to the man who is trying to break through.

The best reinforcement uses bars which form a kind of basket-weave with each other, and manufacturers offered many alternatives, from a flat bar with interlocking tabs to coiled steel rods which entwined with each other. This approach is sound enough to have lasted to this day, any extra security being gained by adding extra layers. The thief is now confronted, within the small hole he is trying to make, with a large number of pieces of steel which he must cut, but each is locked firmly into its concrete setting. The very last layer to be breached is usually a box made of solid metal plates. These may be dovetailed together for strength, with no rivets or bolts, so that once the concrete has set about them they cannot be dismantled.

Into this bunker-like shell, deep and thick and strong,

locks, which must all be activated at the same time by separate keyholders.

It is normally prudent to conceal lockwork from view, to avoid giving the slightest assistance to a potential thief, but safemakers are usually confident that no attacker could penetrate a vault door, and may give way to a little vanity. Since the main door may well remain open during the working day, placing the inner face of the door on public view, some manufacturers display their craftsmanship by revealing the lockwork through a plate of glass with their name and device engraved upon it. To prevent casual entry while the door is open, yet allow the free passage of air, an inner gate is also fitted within the frame.

One unfortunate consequence of the size and the tightly accurate fit of vault doors is the increased chance of a seized door – a lock-out. It is not uncommon, for instance, that soon after a vault has been installed a settlement in the building distorts the door frame very slightly, but enough to jam the entrance. This can be corrected by excavating, jacking and repacking with steel and concrete, but how can a bank reach its deposits during this work and, even worse, what if there is a person trapped within the vault? The cause of lock-out may be much less impressive – one safemaker had to free a door held by no more than 'a great accumulation of dust and a much-compressed cigarette', a jam which could only be cleared by pushing the door open from within.

A large modern vault will have not just one door but two. To provide a margin of safety for anyone accidentally or maliciously locked into the vault a second much smaller door is usually provided. This is intended only as an emergency exit, and is no larger than is needed to allow a person to pass, but must of course be built to the same standards of security as the main door. To gain access to the vault with the cigarette-jammed door the safemaker had to climb to a hatch set eight feet from the ground; not all secondary doors are so inconveniently placed, but they should be far enough from the main door to be unaffected by the event or factor – subsidence, or an explosion – which has caused the original lock-out. Vault makers complain that secondary doors are neglected, left without maintenance or regular testing, and thus even more likely to jam than the main entrance. Even though it is small, an emergency door is still hugely expensive, and makers now recommend the use of two full-size entrances which allow the business of the company to be conducted whenever there is a problem with either door.

To alert anyone who might remain inside as the door is closed and the locks set, many safes have automatic devices which sound a warning alarm during the door-locking procedure, and should an unfortunate customer or clerk still be caught they will now find a reassuring, battery-powered lamp which allows them to find an emergency telephone and read a set of clear survival instructions. They will be told how to unplug a ventilator, to open oxygen valves, even spread chemicals which will absorb carbon dioxide; above all they will be urged to keep calm.

Time is a crucial factor in both lock-ins and robberies, and regular guard patrols now ensure that neither captives nor thieves will spend weekends unseen and unheard inside a vault. A successful vault theft is now much more likely to be the result of inside help than months of tunnelling. In 1987 the Knightsbridge safe deposit in London was robbed at gunpoint, and a haul of £30–40 million in cash, jewels, drugs and precious metals taken from 121 safe deposit boxes. The managing director of the safe deposit company, a Mr Latif, had himself been handcuffed and questioned by the robbers.

When the news broke, two very experienced vault engineers, living a hundred miles apart and acting quite independently, made telephone calls to their local police forces to say that they were quite certain that the theft was an inside job. Neither man seems to have been taken seriously, but more than a month later Latif was one of the men arrested for the robbery, after gang members had had time to sell gold, drugs, and currency, and buy a black Ferrari Testarossa for £87,300 in cash.

Brothers in Crime

Enterprising thieves have taken labouring jobs in vault construction gangs in the hope of finding a design fault or building in a weakness to be exploited later. One of the most daring attempts to compromise a vault was made in Copenhagen just before the Second World War, and defeated only by chance when two mechanics working late on the construction of a new bank interrupted a pair of masked intruders. The workmen had returned to the site to disconnect the electricity supply when they heard a deep clanging sound, footsteps, then a warning shouted in German, and had stumbled upon the two masked men. After a scuffle the intruders broke away and fled.

The police were called and at first it seemed that this must have been an attempt to steal some of the valuable surveying instruments kept on site, but face-masks seemed unnecessary for such a petty crime. Equally, there seemed little in the empty strongrooms of an unfinished bank to attract the sort of serious criminal who would cover his face. When morning came, the strong-room doors were examined minutely, but even with the help of enlarged photographs no trace of fingerprints or violence could be found. Still unexplained, however, was the workmen's belief that they had heard a metallic sound. Since there had been two important safecrackings in the city recently, the police decided that the safemakers must be called in for a full inspection, not least because they were now sure that a false key had been used on a basement door to allow the intruders in. An experienced locksmith arrived, and began meticulously to study each part of the installation. Not until the strongroom doors had been completely dismantled did he discover what the mysterious men had accomplished.

Eight of the tumblers within the door lock had been removed, filed down carefully and precisely so that they no longer functioned, then replaced. The effect of this was that although the correct legitimate key would continue to work without difficulty, and with no indication of tampering, only a very simple key would now be needed to open the doors. Further, the locksmith reported that the work must have taken at least ten hours of concentrated effort, not including the removal of the back of the vault door, which itself had been so very carefully carried out that no evidence had been discovered even under the most minute scrutiny. All of this pointed to a level of skill and a depth of knowledge that would normally be restricted to legitimate craftsmen, and it was the luckless locksmith himself who came under suspicion at first. Fortunately for him, the police were thorough enough to take microscopic photographs of the filed surfaces in the sabotaged mechanisms, and to compare them with the man's past work: the techniques were plainly different, and the police began to consider other suspects.

Their thoughts turned immediately to a pair of Germans, brothers called Swartz, who had been suspected of a tunnelling raid on a bank in Berlin two years before. They were known to have entered Denmark – a police officer had come across an irregularity in their papers but had been able to take no further action; they had been suspected of two recent and very professional raids on a jeweller's safe and the strongroom of a tobacco company; a check had already been ordered on residents of Copenhagen who had arrived only recently. During this earlier investigation the police had learned of a young hotel receptionist called Kirsten Borgmann who had been greatly impressed by the attractive free-spending visitors, and was infatuated in particular with Max Swartz.

A permanent watch was kept upon her, and when she was seen in a nightclub dancing with a man who matched Max's description, a full alert was declared. The taxi which the couple used to go home was followed to an expensive suburban villa which was swiftly surrounded. It was a house which had been divided into apartments, and the owner protested that all her tenants were very respectable, including the Lodz brothers – two nice young German photographers who used one of their rooms as a studio, another as a darkroom.

When the police burst in, they found Miss Borgmann posing near-naked in front of a large studio camera. The brothers were outraged, and protested loudly, but when they were confronted with the policeman they had met when they were travelling as the Swartzes a scuffle broke out. Both men were carrying guns, and a search of the darkroom uncovered not only a large quantity of pornographic photographs but a collection of burglars' tools, and a well-hidden tube of toothpaste. Inside the toothpaste was a page torn from a diary belonging to Ernst Swartz, bearing a sketch of a complicated lock, but this was not the lock of the bank vault, nor did a pair of wax impressions in the same hiding-place appear to have any connection with that work. Another of the city's new buildings, Shell House, was to include a safe-deposit, and when a precautionary check was made there, locksmiths found that the doors had been doctored as cleverly and as thoroughly as those of the bank vault. The Swartzes had been busy there too, and the sketch and impressions were a part of their Shell House caper. As they pieced together the whole story, it came as no surprise to the police that these meticulous international crooks were better qualified than most: Max had trained as a chemist, Ernst as a locksmith.

The Swartzes were convicted and sentenced to many years in prison, but when the Germans overran Denmark they were listed for transfer to another prison, and during the journey they were both shot by their German escort; the official account said that they were trying to escape. The war also provided a final irony: Shell House became the Gestapo headquarters, and when it held a group of Danish Resistance workers who were to be executed the Royal Air Force staged a low-level bombing raid to demolish a part of the building and free the prisoners. This sortie carried the code-name Operation Locksmith.

PART TWO

The Lock

7
Tumblers and Keys

A safe should be a strong box secured with a good lock. A box may be strengthened by giving it thicker walls and adding reinforcement to seams, corners and hinges, but the creation of effective safes had to wait until better locks could complete the defences.

Whatever the design, any locking system has just three parts. The bolt is the bar or hook which moves to perform the locking, strong enough to withstand any expected attack. Between the bolt and any attempt to withdraw it is an obstacle of some kind, which may be the mechanism of a mechanical lock, the circuitry of an electronic control, or the discs within a combination. For a long time the only common key was a piece of cut metal, but it can now be a memorized number or a plastic card bearing a magnetic strip.

There have been mechanical locks for more than four thousand years. An Egyptian key, fully three feet long and shaped like a toothbrush with wooden pegs for bristles, might not be recognizable to a modern householder, nor the huge keys with curved blades which were carried for wealthier Greeks by trusted (and muscular) slaves. The Roman use of iron and bronze allowed them to make much smaller, neater devices; they had learned new and important lessons about how to use a spring to return the bolt, and how to make the keyhole smaller to resist picking. Roman keys have survived where the locks have long been lost to rust, and it has been possible to picture the mechanisms they had been cut to fit, including the earliest form of a design which was to last for more than a thousand years – the warded lock.

The obstacle within a warded lock is a set of circular fences – a key cannot turn unless it has slots which will fit over and between the fences. Locksmiths added more fences, and devised a more complex shape for each, so that for a perfect fit the key would have to be more and more elaborate. Not that the lock was made first – for the traditional locksmith who wants to achieve a precise functioning fit it has always been the rule to make the key first, and then to adjust the mechanism and tolerances of the lock.

The designs of lock and key were intended both to demonstrate to the user the security offered by the lock, and to put on show the craftsmanship of its maker. Only the rich needed the most secure locks, and only the rich could afford the cost of the weeks, even months of intricate skilled labour which would go into each piece. For his fee, the locksmith would deliver a handsome, even a beautiful lock, and a key that could be carried and handled with great pride of ownership. Even so, these locks were rarely secure, since the conventional warded design might foil the pilfering servant, but offered no defence against a thief with a little knowledge.

This is as far as the story went for hundreds of years. There were a few skilled men making locks, and a small number of thieves with the expertise to defeat the conventional mechanism. For as long as locks were expensive, bought and used only by very few people, most of them wealthy enough to have a staff of servants, the limitations of the warded locks mattered little. Many a street door carried no lock, not because there was no danger of theft, but because it was simply a duty of the staff to inspect callers before admitting them. For the less well off, a lock good enough to keep out the opportunist sneak thief was all that was needed. There was a similar change for business premises: rich merchants could afford to hire permanent watchmen, but there were many smaller concerns who could not afford extra hands, or paid too little to keep their loyalty.

It was the growth of the middle classes which created a new demand, in the late eighteenth and early nineteenth centuries, for better defences. Just as in modern times car theft has grown simply because there are many more cars on the streets, housebreaking became profitable with the expansion of the cities, rising to an early peak in the 1780s.

Presented with new and rewarding targets, criminals were spurred to develop fresh techniques, including lock-picking, and the enemy of the warded lock is the skeleton key. This is an expression much misused, to describe almost any key found on a thief, or after a theft to explain how a thief made his way in and out. In fact a skeleton key is, as the name implies, a key which has been cut to its simplest. Bypassing all the elaboration needed to fit round and through all the wards of a lock, it has a very simple shape, often a thin L or a Z which will miss all the fences within the lock, and apply pressure on a spot which will throw the bolt.

The working burglar soon found that a remarkably small number of these skeletons would open almost every domestic lock, and if he had none to fit, he could swiftly make one. In his pocket he would carry a set of blanks, of varying shapes and sizes, which he would first use to learn the shape required by the wards. Having found by rapid trial and error the blank which most closely fitted, he covered one of its faces with a thin layer of wax, inserted the blank and turned it gently to press against the wards. The imprint left upon the wax told him enough: from another pocket would come a small saw and a set of files, to cut away all surplus metal and leave that important skeleton.

The Bramah lock was the first to resist picking, and its story is told in the next chapter, but much more important than its overcomplicated design was the spur it gave to other lock inventors. As with any innovation which sells, the new lock encouraged other designers to enter the market, to compete on efficiency, extra features, and price. There were oddball inventions and ineffective ones, but the best designs were both technically and commercially successful. We know now that the winner was the lever lock, simple and strong, in which each step on the key tilted a separate brass plate – a lever – until all the plates were aligned, and no longer obstructed the movement of the bolt. It has been a very adaptable design, which in a simple version might use only a couple of levers when fitted to desks or drawers, five levers for good protection of a street door, and nine or more for very high security on a safe door. The most famous of these products has been the Chubb lock, which introduced a version of the lever mechanism in the early 1800s which is still found in the front doors of millions of British homes. It tells us a great deal about the households of the time that those first Chubb locks sold well because they would tell the lockowner if any attempt had been made to pick it: their extra detector lever was a check on the honesty of the household servants.

The lock was good enough, and profitable enough, for the Chubb family's business to expand from lockmaking into the new growing trade in safes. They did not at first have to make the safes: the design and the techniques needed to assemble the box were simple enough for them to be made in small workshops, fitted with Chubb locks and nameplates, then delivered to the company. Chubb locks were supplied to other manufacturers, and since they were recognized as among the very best designs on the market, they earned two kinds of accolade: the public came to rely on the name as a guarantee of quality, and dishonest makers and traders copied the design or simply applied false Chubb labels to inferior products.

The products of other successful manufacturers were also faked, and the reputation of the entire trade was put at risk when newspapers reported that a Chubb lock had been picked, or a Price safe broken open. It became very important for the companies to check, and usually disprove the stories, and to stage their public demonstrations and tests.

Now that good locks would not yield to picking, thieves switched their attention either to physical attack upon the box, or to the ways in which they might obtain a working key. The craftsmanship which had been used to make a skeleton key could be used to make accurate duplicates from the original, which might be borrowed with the help of a corrupt servant or obtained by a trick; either way, the most common way to cut the copy was to work from an impression. Criminal keymakers had learned to cut keys from their wax impressions of the lock interior, and it was a simple matter to adapt the technique.

Wax was the most common choice, but any medium that would take an accurate sharp impression would serve as well – a pliable cuttlefish bone was the favourite of some. One cunning burglar discovered that a confidential clerk in a broker's office was fond of gambling, so he joined him at cards, and making an excuse about wanting to open a desk, managed briefly to borrow the clerk's keys. On top of the desk was a sheet of blotting paper that had been saturated with water. The burglar pressed the key into it and carefully preserved the paper, and from the impression he later gauged the thickness and the pattern of the key.

The technique of making a useful impression can be rehearsed so that only the briefest handling of a key is needed. One pair of thieves in the 1950s used a degree of dramatic skill: one dressed in the uniform of a chauffeur while the other put on the morning coat, striped trousers and spats which were then the customary clothes of the prosperous doctor. They would choose a spot on the street where a chosen victim must pass, and stage a polished act in which the 'doctor' would berate his 'chauffeur' for his idiocy in leaving behind the keys to his instrument case. Turning to the victim the doctor would explain that it was absolutely vital that the case be opened for his next emergency call – did he by any chance have a key upon him which would open the locks on the precious case?

Eager to help, the victim would offer his own keyring, and with just a little fiddling the chauffeur would contrive to open the case. Once the chauffeur had made impressions, the keys could then be returned with profuse thanks, and only when his safe was opened some time later would the victim understand what had really happened. The tricksters were caught in the end by a jeweller who had second thoughts about having handed over his keys: he notified the police, a watch was kept on his premises, and the thieves were snatched with ease.

The long-term success of such a method might seem to depend on being so very ordinary in appearance that the victim would have great difficulty in providing a description many weeks later, after the theft had been carried out. The doctor and chauffeur might seem a little obvious, but the most foolhardy man to approach his victims in public must have been the illicit keymaker John Bernasconi. Bernasconi's legs had been amputated when gangrene set in after an accident, and he drove an invalid carriage; using this to gain sympathy he accosted the manager of a travel agency and borrowed his keys, making an impression of the door and safe keys in modelling clay while an accomplice distracted the victim. Nearly a month later five hundred pounds' worth of travellers' cheques and foreign currency was stolen, and at first the manager made no connection with the loan of his keys in the street, but more than a year later he casually mentioned the legless man to the police, and Bernasconi was very quickly identified.

The technique is simple in principle but the ease of making a key, even from a very clear impression, must not be taken for granted. The tolerances in a good, unworn lock are very tight, and it is common practice with all but the crudest locks for the manufacturer to make keys first, and only then to assemble the levers of the lock to fit. There certainly are and have been exceptionally skilled men with the talent and acquired skill to fabricate good working copies of keys from no more than a series of careful observations: the author worked in an English prison for some years, and was given the customary warnings at the beginning of his service, with instructions to keep keys tightly secure, never allow them even to be seen for long.

To make the risks clear, the officer in charge of security displayed a collection of confiscated keys, made from plastic and metal, each made accurately enough to stand a good chance of operating locks. However, the scale of the risk was then explained – of the 50,000 prisoners held across the country, just half a dozen were said to have the necessary skills to turn out such effective keys. Even among those few none has been quite so remarkable as Mark Shinburn, a German-born American crook of the 1880s. Shinburn was on one occasion obliged to spend a night in a hotel with the policeman who had arrested him. As a precaution the officer handcuffed himself to

Shinburn, but by morning the prisoner had picked the lock on the cuffs (apparently using a small piece of steel which he had concealed in his mouth) and escaped.

Shinburn could obviously pick locks, and had the mechanical skill to duplicate keys, but he was by no means the aloof craftsman – his special and daring method was to sneak by night into the bedrooms of bank officials, to draw the keys from their pockets as they slept, and make wax impressions on the spot. A quick thinker, Shinburn was once interrupted in the middle of a job, at the point at which he was replacing a keyhole plate: one small screw was missing, and Shinburn improvised by placing a small piece of wax into the screwhole, and indenting it with a fingernail to look like a screwhead. This cool attention to detail was, ironically, his downfall – when he was arrested, a search of his clothes turned up the missing screw, embedded in a ball of wax. This remaining wax in his pocket was of course a perfect match to the wax in the screwhole and this unusual forensic evidence was enough to convict him.

If picking was impossible, and a duplicate key could not be obtained, thieves would try to destroy the lock or to displace it so that it would no longer retain the bolt. The simplest approach was to push a strong steel rod into the keyhole and hit it hard with a hammer; any lock that was not firmly attached or braced would fly off, and the thief had only to insert a wire and pull back the bolt. This was a very noisy method, and safemakers learned how to reinforce the lock mountings, but clever burglars switched to using a new and cunning tool called the jack-in-the-box. This small device was attached to the keyhole and held a threaded bolt which was driven into the lock with a long spanner so that it applied a force of tons, until with a single explosive sound the lock was parted from its mountings. For a while the press treated this tool as if it were the ultimate secret weapon for safecrackers, which must have boosted the profits of the craftsmen in the West Midlands who made and sold them, but lockmakers were quickly able to introduce a simple change which foiled the attack. From now on the plate at the back of the lock against which the jack-in-the-box pressed was made deliberately weak, to break away leaving the lock mechanism safely in place.

Gunpowder was also an ally to the burglar, who would blow a charge into the keyhole with a small bellows, light a fuse, and blow the lock apart. Safemakers tried three main countermeasures, which can be summed up as more metal, less metal, and a lump of wood. More metal meant strengthening the lock, but this was not successful; less metal involved making holes, or leaving gaps in the lock so that powder would drain away within the door to burn without explosion or explode far from the lock itself. More promising was to limit the amount of powder which could be detonated within the lock. It was the wood which provided the most lasting solution; lock casings had been large, with only a small proportion of the space inside occupied by working parts, with enough room left for a substantial charge of powder. If that space were filled with a shaped, close-fitting piece of wood, the thief could not blow in enough powder to destroy the lock. The wood was literally a stopgap – designers made sure that later models would always use a smaller case and arranged the mechanism to leave no unwanted voids.

At this point, about 1890, the development of the conventional keyed lock reached a stage which was very little short of perfection. The number of levers could be increased, and internal modifications would make it even less easy to pick; some locks included shutters which closed off the keyhole to prevent tools from reaching the mechanisms, but the principles remained the same. After a phase of great inventiveness and competition, the victorious companies were satisfied to consolidate their markets, refine their products, and find more economical ways of turning them out. Other designs have been produced and sold, either as genuine new inventions or merely to bypass patents, but none has proved to offer any advantage important enough to make the lever principle obsolete.

The Picking of the Bramah Lock

The time was right twice for the Bramah lock. When it was invented, the world wanted a lock which would surpass the overelaborate but still vulnerable locks on the market, and Bramah provided it. In the 1780s there had been a wave of housebreaking, and the public wanted not only a good lock, but reassurance and a restored sense of security. Joseph Bramah, one of the very first industrial heroes, 'the first mechanical genius of his time and . . . the founder of the art of tool-making in its highest branches', could give both.

His claim, his promise to the worried householder, was that his lock was unpickable. The design did not depend on wards, so a skeleton key would not work, nor was it likely that any one Bramah key would fit another lock, since there were 479,001,600 potential variations. This range did not come at the expense of impractical bulk or weight in either lock or key, and the very idea of security shifted once and for all from massive, physically impressive locks to smaller but exquisitely made precision fittings. Smaller was now better, and although the locks were still made by hand, they were industrial products made by the thousand rather than expensive gilded masterpieces. The new middle classes could afford them for their modest homes. Bramah locks were modern.

For two generations the Bramah represented security in the popular imagination, even though other excellent designs, simpler still and just as effective, were now on sale. In the window of the Bramah premises in London stood the very best advertisement to new customers and reassurance to old – from 1787 a lock was on display which carried the caption:

> The Artist
> who can make an
> Instrument that will pick
> or Open this Lock, shall
> Receive 200 Guineas
> The Moment it is produced.
> Applications in Writing only.
> Bramah's PATENT locks.
> CAUTION.
> The Public is Respectfully Informed
> that every LOCK made by BRAMAH & Co. is Stamped
> with their Address
> 124 Piccadilly

Through sixty-four years in which the safe industry began, grew, and gained the respect and reliance of its customers, the lock in the window stood unopened.

The rivals to Bramah, in the bold Victorian spirit of commercial swashbuckling, were also to throw down the gauntlet to the lockpickers. Pursuing an official prize of £100 Jeremiah Chubb offered his lock for a team of legitimate experts to pick – they failed, but in a prison hulk close to the Chubb factory was a trained locksmith who had turned to crime. He heard of the contest and begged to be allowed an attempt on the lock. Chubb heard of this and saw the potential for publicity – he offered £100 should the man succeed, and the government offered a pardon.

Chubb was confident. He provided the convict not only with a full set of tools, and a generous supply of key blanks, but even a lock similar to the one which had to be picked, so that the man could learn how it worked. Watched by a guard of soldiers, the prisoner spent ten weeks at the task, then conceded defeat. Chubb was delighted, and promptly staged another stunt – one of his locks was attached to an engine which would turn a key, rapidly locking and unlocking it, inflicting more wear each hour than a lock might suffer in a lifetime. After 460,000 locking cycles the lock was removed and stripped – every part, and the key, were examined. Apart from a high gloss on a few parts, no sign of wear was seen, and when it was reassembled the lock worked as sweetly as ever.

Across the Atlantic, fastened to an iron chest in the State Bank in Boston, The Newell Parautoptic Lock was also to defeat allcomers. Newell first offered $500, and required candidates to agree to pay him $200 should the lock be damaged. As one after another failed, Newell raised the prize to $2000, raised his time limit from ten days to thirty days, and was even prepared to offer a further thirty, then sixty days, if the picklock could establish some success.

This may seem like a generous allowance of time, but Newell's lock had a key with twelve separate steps which could be removed and rearranged in any order, and the challenge to the candidate was to put back the scrambled steps in the form which had been used to throw the lock. Taking just one minute to dismantle the lock and reassemble its steps, and working every hour of every day, it would have taken no less than 1082 years to run through all the possible combinations. Newell kept his money.

By the middle of the nineteenth century the commercial atmosphere was hotter, the pace much faster. Inventiveness alone was no longer enough: competition was savage, and public contests were an easy means both of discrediting competitors and giving a boost to the product. London was regarded as the main arena for lockpicking contests and in New York, an ambitious locksmith called A. C. Hobbs, who had already scored several public successes in picking locks, was planning a transatlantic trip.

His first steps were discreet: he obtained a selection of the best locks then on sale and satisfied himself that he could pick them with ease. In a bold move that threw down the gauntlet to British lockmakers he visited Chubb's and chose from among their stock a six-lever detector lock, the latest version of the design which had defeated government experts. He picked the lock on the spot, quickly and with apparent ease. Chubb's refused to admit so sudden a defeat, protesting that Hobbs had merely been lucky; that there must have been a fault in the lock, which Hobbs had exploited – anything but the simple truth that the American had found a way to defeat their product. They were trying to protect their commercial position, but by such a crude dismissal they provoked Hobbs, who also detected a flavour of British haughtiness. He posted a public notice that he would once more pick a Chubb lock, before an impartial committee of both Britons and Americans – further, he would open the lock within thirty minutes. Hobbs not only opened the lock in twenty-five minutes, he was able to use his tools to relock the door in just seven minutes. In dismay the Chubb company was forced to alter several features of its design, but in the meantime Hobbs had decided that he was ready to take on the Bramah lock.

When Hobbs presented himself in Piccadilly the Bramah staff were unruffled, and simply set out the terms under which the attempt must be made. Again a committee was appointed to ensure fair play, and the lock was mounted so that Hobbs would have access only to the external keyhole; the key was sealed into a pouch which was kept by a member of the committee. Hobbs was permitted thirty days in which to make his attempt, and he might use as many hours of each day as he wished. Hobbs himself asked that a strap be fitted over the keyhole, to be opened and closed only when Hobbs was working on the lock, as a precaution against tampering.

Once he had set to work, Hobbs appeared to follow no regular pattern, working on some days for no more than a half-hour, occasionally putting in a full day, and then not arriving at all. Both Hobbs and the Bramah company regarded the attempt as splendid publicity. They welcomed the close attention paid to his work, and the heated speculation about the outcome, in the press and on the street. By the end of the month he had visited on just ten days, for a total of little more than forty-four hours, when he called for the attendance of the managing director and a senior locksmith of the company, and announced that he would make his attempt.

Coolly Hobbs opened the lock, then closed it. Opened it and closed it repeatedly. The immediate response of the Bramah men was to declare that Hobbs must somehow have damaged the mechanism of the lock in a way which must invalidate his attempt, but Hobbs asked that the key be unsealed and used, and it worked perfectly. The prize was his, and even in defeat the Bramah lock had given good service to the lock industry by drawing so much popular attention: citizens who had previously given no thought to security had been exposed for a heady month to the technical debate, had even wagered on the outcome of the attempt. Hobbs was a hero, and went on to establish in London a very successful lock and safe business which capitalized on his exploit. The other companies in the field could hardly begrudge him his success, since he had by his feat encouraged a tremendous growth in the market for all their products.

The techniques which Hobbs used in opening the Chubb and Bramah locks were elaborate and painstaking, and relied upon his years of experience in his trade. No common burglar would ever show such an understanding of the task, possess such skill, or enjoy such comfort and leisure in which to work upon a lock, so the banker and the householder could be led to an even stronger belief in the value of good quality locks. The fact that Hobbs was American tended for the next several years to give products from the USA an extra cachet, and American companies were not slow to use this advantage to import and sell large numbers of locks and safes. Many were of inferior quality, and most were built to the American pattern which placed fire resistance above security from theft, which enraged British manufacturers and prompted a fierce war in the market place. Public contests were held, tempting newspapers to cartoons, learned discourses and headlines such as BRITISH INVINCIBLES versus YANKEE IRONCLADS (this for a famous international battle between the British Chatwood and the American Herring, with a neutral team of Germans given the work of breaking each). On the whole, the objective tests tended to prove that British safes were better at withstanding attack, but these events were often surrounded by angry accusations of sharp practice on one side or the other. British manufacturers were incensed when locksmiths used American locks on British government contracts, furious when they found that heavy import duties protected the American home market from British locks. On the other hand American production was much more mechanized and efficient, innovations such as combination and time-locks showed that the Americans were better at encouraging and promoting new ideas, and the workforce appeared to work harder. This may all sound familiar, and in fact the controversy was amazingly similar to the prolonged argument about British failure to compete after the Second World War.

Buyers may have become confused about the merits of particular locks and troubled by the arguments about patriotic duty, but they readily absorbed the message that a strong modern safe was the best way for a business to look after its cash. British, American or Continental locks and safes were bought as never before.

8
Dial-a-Crime

The combination lock has become the very symbol of security. The dial has a mystique which a key cannot share, in part because combination locks are associated with large safes and vaults containing real wealth, and perhaps because of the reactions that the locks provoke. Faced by a locked door with an empty keyhole we accept that the way is barred, but a dial tempts the fingers, and we can't resist an idle twirl, a throw of the wheel just to see if we can hit the lucky numbers by chance.

The practical choice between a key lock and a combination lock is not easy, and for ordinary purposes is as much a matter of custom and prejudice as of operational need. The American market favours combinations, the British keys, and the French often fit both kinds of lock to the same safe as double security. Combination locks were quick to find favour in the United States and on the Continent, but took generations to be accepted in the United Kingdom, much to the frustration of safemakers who saw their advantages.

Each type of lock has shortcomings: keys can be lost, stolen or copied; combinations betrayed or forgotten. If security is compromised, it is always easier to alter a combination than to fit fresh levers to a keyed lock. Keyed locks are also much more easily understood, and though it is hard to convey in words the function of every component in a combination lock, the basic structure of the mechanism is not too hard to visualize.

Combination locks contain a stack of discs, spaced along the central shaft which runs through the middle of each in turn. Each disc carries a peg, and when the dial is turned the peg travels round, and will engage with the peg of the next disc. The dial is connected only to the first disc; all the others are moved by the action of the pegs on the discs – the first acts on the second, the second on the third, and so on. The discs are therefore set in reverse order; the dial is turned to nudge each disc into alignment so that only when each of the others has been set will that first disc be in place.

There is a notch, a section cut out of the edge of each disc, technically called the tumbler gate. When all the notches are aligned, a bar is able to drop into all of them at once, and the lock can be released: so long as just one disc is out of alignment, the bar cannot drop. In the very earliest combination locks the bar rested on the edge of the discs at all times, and it was certainly then possible for anyone turning the dial to sense the gaps and turn the knob until he felt least friction or resistance and try to open the lock. One of the most inventive lockmakers, James Sargent, even managed to automate this process with a spring-loaded device bearing a dial, a kind of very sensitive micrometer, which could be applied to the handle.

This very early weakness in combination locks is the basis for all those film scenes in which the sensitive fingertips of the safeman allow him to manipulate the lock, but it was recognized over a century ago and steps were taken to prevent so simple an attack. One method was to cut extra notches in the rim of the first disc, none so deep as to allow the bar to fall into place, but each enough to mislead the ear or the touch of the burglar. The discs are often made of brass, and some early burglars found that if they attached a high-speed drill to the shaft of the lock to spin the discs against the edge of the bolt, the metal of the disc was soft enough to be worn down, eliminating or at least minimizing the shallow false notches.

The best solution was to keep the bar clear of all the discs while the numbers were being dialled, only allowing it to fall into place once the last number had been successfully set, and this is now universal. A modern burglar may turn the dial as much as he likes, and may sense contact between the pegs within the lock, or variations in friction between parts, but none of these is useful to him in learning the combination.

Before these improvements, one cunning team in the nineteenth century made a comfortable living over a period of fifteen years because they were skilful but not greedy. They developed a way of manipulating the tumblers of common combination locks, by drilling an inconspicuous hole and probing with a knitting needle. Their cunning, if the tale be true, lay in taking only a small amount on each occasion, which threw suspicion on the employees in the firm or bank that they had raided; one policeman's account of the gang's work stated that many clerks in the offices which had been burgled were suspected, and 'not a few were unjustly incarcerated'. Perhaps, but the degree of patient self-denial demanded doesn't quite ring true: to burgle regularly for a decade and a half, and take the risk of a heavy prison sentence every time, for an income that might as easily be obtained by working, cannot have been a sensible way to make a living.

A more authentic technique from much the same period, and one whose use is substantiated by other sources, was to secrete a piece of paper behind the dial of the combination, in such a way that when the owners operated the lock, marks were made upon the paper which could be interpreted and the combination learned. Thomas Byrnes, an American policeman who enjoyed a close and possibly corrupt friendship with a lot of crooks, attributes this innovation to 'Shell' Hamilton, a member of the Mark Shinburn gang.

If the safe owner has a poor memory, life is even easier for the thief. A safe salesman will point out that a four-tumbler lock has 100,000,000 combinations, and that if a nimble-fingered thief could manage to set a new combination every ten seconds through a 40-hour working week he would need more than 130 years to work through every possible permutation. This is not only an obstacle for the thief, but a major problem for a forgetful owner, and it is very common for safe numbers to be noted – they can be pencilled or scratched, or written on scraps of paper left in places which often prove to be as convenient for the thief as the owner. At least one burglar is known to have made a comfortable living without ever having to attempt a physical attack on a safe. He simply had a keen eye for possible places in which the safe combination would be recorded, and told police that much the most successful single expedient was to look at any convenient box of file cards: there, under the letter 'S', he often found the combination neatly written out.

Even if they don't leave a visible record, safe owners seem rarely to follow the makers' advice to choose random numbers and change combinations frequently. Harry King, the American safeman, 'soon found it to be the prevailing rule among cashiers to use figures easily divisible. For example, a train of numbers selected would be four, sixteen, and thirty-two, or twelve, twenty-four and thirty-six.' Having established that the first number on one vault lock was twelve, the safe burglar who made this observation said that he was able to open the door within five minutes, having worked through the more obvious sequences until he found the right one. Many safes are simply left on the combination which was set on delivery from the factory, a simple 10-20-30-40 or some such, and of course the experienced thief has made sure to memorize or note the numbers used by each manufacturer. Other locks are set to memorable figures which might be discovered by any thoughtful thief, such as a personal telephone number, or an anniversary. One locksmith used to try first with numbers associated with the hobbies of the safe owner, and reported success using 9-18-36-72 with golfers, 4-13-26-52 with bridge players.

It was said that Allied intelligence officers wanting to open German safes during and after the war found it was worthwhile to start by dialling Hitler's birthday; across the world in Los Alamos, where the first atomic bombs were made and tested, a physicist called Richard Feynman (later a Nobel prizewinner) made lockpicking and safe-opening his hobby during the isolated months of research. On a hunch, Feynman guessed that a colleague would have used a mathematical constant in setting his locks, and using the base of natural logarithms (2.71828) opened nine cabinets: 'I opened the safes which contained all the secrets to the atomic bomb: the schedules for the production of the plutonium, the purification procedures, how much material is needed, how the bomb works, how the neutrons are generated, what the design is, the dimensions – the entire information that was known at Los Alamos: the whole schmeer!' Just in case this seems improbable, forty years later the staff in the British nuclear weapons establishment were using *pi* as the basis for their combinations, and even more obviously locked each store of radioactive material with digits based on the atomic weight of the contents – Uranium 235, and so on.

Resourceful thieves may try to make an educated guess at the full number, but the first step is commonly to work through the dial step by small step trying the handle each time. This can work because the last person to use the safe has failed to turn the dial through one full revolution – this makes the safe easier to reopen next time, but also makes life much easier for the thief.

Safeowners may not be so conveniently foolish as to leave the number sequence in sight, or to leave the door only partly locked, but they can still unwittingly provide all that a safecracker needs to know, by allowing themselves to be seen in the act of opening the lock. A veteran locksmith told me that he had greatly worried one bank manager by striding to his safe and within a couple of minutes dialling the correct numbers. As he was installing the safe, the locksmith had realized that its door would be in plain sight from a window across the street, and had kept watch from there as the safe was used. He could not read the numbers, but could easily distinguish the sequence of turns to left and right, and the relationship between the numbers, thinking of them as points on a clock – perhaps ten o'clock, then six o'clock, and so on. For convenience, locks are commonly set to fives – 15, 25, 35 – or tens – 10, 20, 30 – and some sequences are avoided. Many a lock will open even if the numbers have been imprecisely set: where the correct number is 15, neighbouring numbers such as 14, 16 and 17 will work on a poorly-assembled or well-worn lock. By using this knowledge, and trying a number of starting points in turn, the locksmith had been able to hit on the correct numbers quite quickly.

Thieves have used observation very successfully – one American burglar hid himself above the lowered ceilings of a large supermarket and then a department store. The supermarket job was completed by stealth, but when he and an accomplice were about to be discovered in the store, they broke through from their hiding place and turned the job into a straightforward stick-up. In Toronto a burglar exposed himself to rather less risk by parking his truck opposite a supermarket, fixing a telephoto lens to a movie camera and making a film of the safe being opened for the day. By studying the results he was able to make a very accurate guess at the combination. If it can't be seen, a dial might be heard: there is a reassuring sense of precision in using a mechanism which gives out sharp clicks, and some years ago several Continental safemakers made this a feature of their combination dials. I was told the tale of a French consul who was startled when a visitor to his office strode to his safe and opened it – his guest was a locksmith who had heard the clicks made by the dial during opening and memorized them.

Much the largest and most enterprising of the burglaries to depend on observation was the 1974 raid on the Bank of America in London's Mayfair. This started out as a plan for a sneak theft, a quick grab at available money by men who would be concealed in the bank and try and get into the vault before the final locking at night. This would be possible because the team had an inside man, working on building maintenance, who could provide information about the security arrangements, and impressions of the keys to outer doors in the building. These were very useful advantages but, despite several attempts, the men never found an opportunity for the final dash from their hiding place to the vault door.

Reluctant to turn away from such a valuable haul, the team changed its plan and became more ambitious. The keys would still be very useful, for gaining initial access and reducing the work to be performed, but the final assault would now be more conventional, a direct attack on the vault by cutting through the doors, even though this would require the alarm systems to be put out of action. By keeping an eye on the bank, it had been found that security was at its weakest in the early evening, so a swift method had to be found which would make sure that the job was finished before the security guards made their regular night patrols. The thieves saw that extra men would be needed for the job, and decided to go for the contents of the safe deposit boxes as well as the bank's cash. The greater rewards seemed to justify a more complicated plan and further division of the haul.

Drilling looked like the best way to tackle the vault door, so the thieves took advice about the best spot to penetrate the door, obtained a couple of electromagnetic drill presses, and ordered special drills from a source who would ask no uncomfortable questions about their unusual length. Even the late discovery that there were computer staff still at work in a room above the vault did not deter this attempt, and it very nearly came off, until a drill bit broke, and time was lost hiding from bank staff who occasionally wandered too close on their way to make cups of coffee. The team had to withdraw empty-handed, and this time they had left evidence of their attempt.

The two failures were disheartening for the thieves, but they took courage from the fact that they had not come close to discovery and arrest, and over still more months a third plan emerged. The bank had repaired the drilled door and changed the locks and combinations, yet the inside contact was confident that something could still be done, so the gang looked at the possibility of using a thermic lance to cut through the doors. This would offer tremendous cutting speed, but would generate heat and smoke, and as a precaution the inside man was told to check the air ducts and ventilation systems.

He reported back, and included the information that he had found a false ceiling downstairs by the vault, and suddenly one of the team realized what might be done. In *Third Time Unlucky*, Pryce claimed that the brainwave was his: 'At last through all the careful and intensive planning here we were, being presented with the biggest break of all . . . I asked him whether there was any chance of someone hiding in the false ceiling, and if it actually stretched as far as the door itself.' The inside man found that he could hide above the vault door, and through a tiny hole, using a pocket spyglass, he had a clear view of the combination locks on the vault door. To take advantage of this, a man would have to hide there to watch the unlocking procedure which happened at the beginning of each working day. In the meantime, ways had to be found to defeat all the locks up to the door of the vault. Disguised as electricians, members of the team took a good look around the bank, and doctored one of the door locks by removing the tumblers so that any Yale key with the right profile would now fit to open it.

The space in which the watcher on the vault had to hide was very small, no more than eighteen or twenty inches high, and he would have to stay in place for at least nine or ten hours. A water bottle was provided, and some sweets; if he needed to urinate, he would use a plastic container that he took in with him. His other equipment included a cradle which would comfortably take his weight and relieve any stress on the false ceiling, and the trusty spyglass, which had been put to an impromptu test by reading gin bottle labels across the bar of a pub.

The bank's unlocking procedure required the manager to set one combination, and the assistant to set the other. Since the watcher could not risk making a noise by shifting his vantage point this meant two sessions of watching, from slightly different angles, but the task of recording the numbers was made much easier because the new locks which had been installed after the drilling attempt were giving the managers trouble, and they always went through their numbers slowly and with great care.

Now the gang had everything they could need for a smooth entry. Just after six o'clock on the evening of 24 April 1975, about fourteen months after the original plans had been made, eight men in dark business suits entered the bank. The bank doors were opened with keys and the vault with the combination; two men stayed on watch, but the rest were able swiftly to gather up the bank's money and start on the safe deposit boxes.

Pryce described the frantic plundering: 'When we got into the vault, we scooped all the money there into large sacks which we had hidden in our cases. Then we started "caning open" the deposit boxes. They were like small safes and we "caned" them open using small but powerful jemmies . . . There were boxes absolutely chock-a-block with pound notes and francs and dollars, and there was gold this and gold that alongside piles and piles of diamond rings, bracelets and necklaces.' They also found guns, including a machine pistol, documents and photographs which would expose prominent, identifiable people to blackmail, and at least a million pounds' worth of travellers' cheques which they thought too difficult to handle. By nine o'clock the team had opened about ninety of the boxes, and realized that they could carry no more, but as they started to leave, one of the rearguard noticed a bank employee making a phone call, and in a brief panic three late-working bank staff were taken at gunpoint and left tied up near the vault door.

The getaway went smoothly, and the thieves had completed the theft of more than eight million pounds, and earned a place in the *Guinness Book of Records*. When the truth about the crime began to come out, and Buckley the inside man was in custody telling how he watched the operation of the locks, the police and the bank were very worried that he might be lying to protect another employee, or to draw attention from some other weakness which had allowed the combinations to be revealed. The three insurance companies which had given the bank cover faced enormous losses, and their liability depended on how much inside help had been given. In the end, the only way to satisfy everyone was to take Buckley back to the bank so that he could demonstrate what he had done: he found his way back to his hiding place and while bank staff turned the dials he had no difficulty in shouting out each number in turn.

Eyesight is much more useful than touch or hearing when it comes to learning the secrets of a combination lock, despite all those movie safecrackers. Buckley had his spyglass, but he could see only the dials; when small portable industrial X-ray equipment became available which could be taken on site to find weaknesses hidden within metal structures and pipes, there were enterprising crooks who realized that they could use the same technology to look at the notches in the discs of a combination lock; spies and government burglars have also been equipped in this way. Apparatus of this kind gives a choice of methods – a set of photographs can be taken which can be examined and interpreted later, but there are also occasions when the kit can be used to watch the internal movements of the lock directly on a screen, and the door can be opened straight away.

As always, the new method of attack could be foiled. The discs of a lock spin freely and do not have to carry a load heavy enough to demand the use of very strong or hard materials. It is therefore possible, in applications where the goods or documents are precious enough to require maximum security, and there will be regular maintenance, to use discs made of a material such as a plastic or a mixture of fibre and resin which will be

effectively transparent to X-rays. It is almost impossible
to set an X-ray machine at a level which will penetrate a
thick, dense door and casing, yet give a useful image of
the discs and their notches.

The years of development, testing, and improvement
have made the best modern dial locks very effective
indeed. Fitted to grand vaults they protect the wealth and
secrets of nations, but there have also been hundreds of
nuclear devices whose main protection against tampering,
and therefore against accidental or deliberate discharge,
has been a mechanical combination lock.

Less exotic than missiles or bombs are atomic demolition munitions or ADMs: these devices are heavy but
hand-portable, intended to be planted against fixed fortifications or obstacles – as crude as the conventional
satchel charge, but vastly more powerful. From the MK
45 Mod 1 of 1959, to the B54 of which a couple of
hundred probably remain in service, there have been
several generations of United States ADMs, with explosive power ranging up to the equivalent of 15,000 tons of
TNT. The latest models require just two men to carry
and operate them, and the risk of an ADM in the wrong
hands provokes the worst kind of nuclear nightmare. The
very nature of the ADM, and the use for which it was
designed, rules out control by the fragile and complex
electronic interlocks used in other weapons: protection
has been entrusted to a good five-number combination
lock.

The cinemagoer may be wondering why a combination
lock is so highly regarded, when he has seen them opened
time after time on the screen. In researching this book I
have not met anyone who has opened a modern combination lock by sensitive manipulation of the dial, with or
without listening to the action of the lock. I have not met
anyone who has seen it done, or who has known anyone

who could do it, or who has investigated a crime in which
the technique was used.

On the contrary, every locksmith has been at pains to
tell me how foolish the public must be to believe the films
and books in which such a method is described. 'It can't
be done.' 'I've been a locksmith for sixty years – I've
never come across a single case . . .' 'Look . . . here's a
lock – you see, there's simply no way that . . .' Only one
professional, of a younger generation, admitted that he
was very intrigued by occasional references in the trade
press, and wanted to believe that it was possible, in the
ultimate test of a locksmith's knowledge and skill. Like a
birdwatcher who would sell all to find a single example of
a species assumed extinct, he wanted to believe it could
be done, longed to meet just one person who had done
it, and who could teach him to do it. He wanted this, but
never expected to find it; after all, the official records of
safe burglaries, which show how many times explosives
were used, or physical force, don't even contain a cat-
egory for manipulation.

If manipulation just does not happen, it is intriguing to
trace just how the myth was created, and why it has been
kept so vigorously alive; even today, anyone asked to
mime a safecracker has only to cock an ear and twiddle
an imaginary dial in midair. The origins are clear if we
recall those first combination locks in which there was a
mechanical connection, a contact between the discs and
the bar within the lock which held the bolt. It was possible
to turn the dials, while applying pressure on the bolt
handle, and sense the movement of part on part. With an
understanding of the mechanism, a skilled person might
interpret these minute changes and find the combination.

Manipulation worked, and it might have been profitable for a thief to set about acquiring the sensitivity and
skill. After all, it was probably easier than picking a good

keyed lock, and had the advantage that there were no incriminating tools to explain away if he were arrested.

But we have already seen that lockmakers were quick to respond to so obvious a challenge – within fifteen years of the first dial locks going on sale, they had learned to eliminate the mechanical link which made manipulation possible. Locks of the earlier design must have remained in production and on sale for some time, if only to avoid payment of royalties to the new patent-holders, but it is hard to imagine that any box more secure than a basic fire chest would have carried a manipulatable lock by the turn of the century.

Even if he knew how, no working thief would have spent precious time on the job twiddling a dial. Most combination locks, however clever their internal design, were physically weak and could be opened within a minute by hitting them. One solid hammer blow was enough to drive the lock spindle into the case, leaving the handle free to turn.

Maybe the idea of manipulation would have faded a hundred years ago had it not suited both sides in the perpetual contest to keep it alive. Both locksmiths and safecrackers found it very useful that the public, particularly safeowners, should believe in manipulation.

For the safemakers this was one more hazard which they could emphasize to potential customers in trying to persuade them to replace their old equipment: they could say with absolute truth that their locks were proof against the most sensitive criminal fingers, that not one of the safes carrying this lock had ever been opened in this way, without ever having to point out that this was also true of every other combination lock on the market.

Experienced locksmiths knew how to make good guesses at a combination, using the numbers set at the factory, birthdays and the like, but they had an abundance of reasons to let the client believe that they had opened a locked-out safe by manipulation. It helped to preserve their professional mystique and justify a fee, and it was certainly diplomatic, if the owner had left a note of the combination in an obvious spot, not to draw attention to his folly. But also it seems that it satisfied a mischievous streak of showmanship to fling wide the safe door as if by magic – and what magician would reveal the secrets of his craft?

There were many thieves who were helped by the myth. If a safe had been opened without violence, the safecracker might well have used a method which would work again if undiscovered – an inside worker who betrayed the combination, or a clever scheme for observing the lock in use – and nothing would be more helpful to a second attempt than for the victim to put his success down to an exotic skill. If the newspapers and police declared themselves baffled by the mysterious ease with which the thieves had been able to reach the loot, so much the better.

The final element is supplied by the media which used the image of the listening safecracker. The safecracker as hero – Ronald Colman as Raffles – was no ruffian, and used a gentleman's soft hands to carry out his crimes. He certainly didn't take off his white tie to sweat with a crowbar, or take an undignified dive behind the furniture while his fuse burned down to the explosive. In just a few seconds of screen time the crime was over and done with so that he could go back to being his witty raffish self.

A more realistic version of safecracking could bring all sorts of problems for a film director: to show too much authentic detail might amount to a lesson in crime, and to obscure it could well look odd and artificial. To insert a safecracking scene into the middle of a film, unless it was as fully developed as the capers in *The Asphalt Jungle* or *Rififi*, could hopelessly slow the pace of the action, and a common solution was to give a compressed, almost token version of the crime at the beginning, even before the titles. Real safecracking methods are not always easy to film: big explosions are much more fun for audiences than discreet safecracking charges blown under a layer of mattresses, while any form of gas or electric arc-cutting will cause lighting difficulties, and the heat, flame and smoke of a thermic lance attack would put the entire cast and crew at risk. All in all, it's much easier to settle for yet one more manipulation.

There remains only the single example of a reputable author who claims to have seen safes manipulated open, and his claims need a careful examination. Willis George, a former officer in US Naval Intelligence, later the OSS, had in his search team 'a safe expert, able to open any safe by manipulation'. This paragon used the classical technique of listening and applying pressure to the handle, a method whose 'success depends on a delicate sense of touch, keen hearing, and a specialist's knowledge of the way a concealed locking mechanism works'. In his memoirs George described three successful safe openings, and no failures, with each job taking twenty minutes or a little longer, but gave no technical details about the strength of the safes.

Do these three rare examples establish that manipulation can be done? All the safes opened were American (when the OSS went to work cracking safes in Europe they relied upon explosives), and may therefore have been of the low-security fire-cabinet type; the time taken was enough for a reasonably adept locksmith to run through a selection of the combinations he thought most likely, especially since he often knew the type of safe he would be facing, and had time to check on factory settings. It could be that the author responsibly chose to leave out details of any physical measures such as drilling tiny wire-sized holes which would have improved the odds enormously.

The time has come for a revival of the great Victorian safecracking contest. It will need a sponsor rich enough to lodge a large amount of money in a modern safe on prominent public display. There it can remain, earning no interest, ready to be claimed by anyone capable of manipulating the dial without artificial aids beyond a stethoscope. To recover some of the costs, television rights can be sold, and to make the whole enterprise even more appealing there should be a grand bonus for a successful candidate who looks like David Niven.

9

The Invisible Locks

So far, we have looked only at the locks which can be seen from outside, and used at will to open and lock a safe, but fitted into the door of any good quality safe are locks which are quite invisible and have neither key nor combination. Even if the user of the safe is aware that they exist, he will probably have only a skimpy understanding of how they work. These are the relocking devices, which come into action only when the safe is attacked, triggered in a number of ways according to the method used by the safecracker.

The hidden locks respond to the heat of a blowtorch or the jolt of an explosion either by making it impossible to use the ordinary handle to pull back the bolts, or by throwing extra bolts which are not controlled by the handle. There are two distinct kinds of device, called active and passive relockers: active devices are engaged each time the safe is locked, and when triggered they retain the bolts with an extra locking bar, or disconnect a link in the system of levers which pull and push the bolts. In either case, the safe is now locked even against a legitimate user who has the key or the combination, and will remain locked until the safe is penetrated by someone with a precise knowledge of how to defeat the relocker. Passive devices have exactly the same effect, but use their own separate bolts so that even if the thief succeeds in withdrawing the ordinary bolts, there remain some which cannot be reached.

Any relocker is a last-ditch defence intended to have a drastic effect, to make it impossible to get into the safe cleanly and quickly by making each remaining bolt a separate obstacle. Even a skilled safe engineer who knows exactly where to cut or drill into the casing may have to inflict such damage on the safe that it can never be used again.

Clearly any trigger has to react quickly and reliably to an attack, but it must never be so oversensitive that it causes an inconvenient and expensive lockout. Triggers must be able to survive years inside a door which is wrenched open and slammed shut (and active devices are also subject to the stresses placed on the locking system to which they are attached), yet perform faultlessly on the one occasion when they are needed. They cannot be complex or delicate assemblies.

In a passive relocker which protects against a burning attack the vital component is simply a piece of wire, looped at the end of a steel cable which detains a spring-loaded bolt. This wire, known as a fusible link, has more than enough strength at room temperature to hold back the bolt, but if the safe is heated past a known level the link softens, weakens and is broken by the power of the spring. Against explosive attack, another simple part is commonly fitted – a sheet of glass which will shatter if subjected to the jarring of a blast. Like the wire, the glass is connected by cables to a spring-powered bolt, and it is common to place the glass on the outside of the lock, so that any attempt to drill into the lock will also break the glass. The same principles are used, but in a reversed sense, to trigger active relockers; here the spring's action will tug a vital section out of the system which transmits movement from the handle to the bolts.

These are not the only ways in which a relocker may be operated, but any system still in use will be comparably simple. As always, there were thieves who learned or discovered measures to overcome relockers, particularly when the designs were still being refined. With some earlier devices it was possible to apply hand or spring pressure on the handle which would throw back the bolts before an active relocker could work, and safemakers had to speed up the response or change to a passive defence. More subtly, some safemen found that on certain safes, having cut or blown a hole, they could push in a wire to pull back the bolt.

Safemakers fitted internal obstacles to block such manipulation, and some also made sure that the installation of relockers was varied during a production run so that no single technique could guarantee success. The purpose of the relocker is to add a final and enormously time-consuming obstacle, and its effectiveness depends on forcing the thief to waste time trying to overcome it, so even now that there are very few safecrackers, manufacturers are always discreet about the types of relocker they use, and the pattern of installation.

There is another kind of concealed lock which cannot be operated from outside, but it was not invented to defeat safecrackers – it is a precaution first of all against hostage-taking. By the 1870s the new materials, new box designs and new locks were making it difficult for the safe burglar to make a living. Although small safes were still easy prey, banks and large businesses had invested in vaults and large modern safes which resisted attack too well. The easiest method of reaching the loot was now to seize the person who could open the safe, the manager or owner, who could be forced to provide a key or turn the dial of a combination lock. Instead of taking the risks of a daytime holdup, the thieves carried out their raids at night, forcing a way into the owner's home after dark with the greatest show of force, determined to break his will, empty the safe, and make their escape before the alarm could be raised in the morning.

The unhappy key-holder might be menaced directly, or a threat made against his family. It was not unknown for the robbers to come prepared to inflict physical torture, right in front of the safe, with thumb-screws, red-hot irons, finger-nail removers and tooth extractors all used. Every newspaper report of an outrage helped to scare the next victim into yielding more quickly.

Bankers bought guns to keep under their pillows, and tried to organize extra police patrols, but a fresh invention promised a permanent solution. If an extra lock were fitted which was controlled not by a key or a combination dial but by a clock, the door could be impregnably sealed overnight, and such a time-lock would be enough to make attempts at kidnapping and hostage-taking worthless. No matter how intimidated, a captive would have no power to open his own safe.

This may have been an invention which began as a concept rather than a workbench prototype: Dickens described, in a short story called *No Thoroughfare*, a heavy oaken door in the office of a Swiss notary in Neuchatel, a door thickly studded with nails but having no handle, bolt, key or keyhole. It was described as having a clocklock made by the Perrin Brothers, which not only locked and unlocked the door, but had the force to swing the door open and shut. What makes the story tantalizing is that it was published seven years before the first known sale of a time-lock: no one has discovered whether Dickens used his imagination or had seen for himself a single early prototype of which all record has since been lost.

Patents were granted for a number of timelock designs, including a rather odd one which relied on the slow leakage of liquid between two chambers within the lock, but it is generally agreed that the first commercially successful model was the invention of an American,

James Sargent, who patented in 1873 an initial design
which integrated one of the combination locks made by
his company with two clock movements. The lock he
fitted for his first customer remained in service for more
than forty years at the First National Bank in Morrison,
Illinois, and despite early fears that the movements must
seize or fail, this first lock was replaced only because a
larger vault was to be built.

By 1893 there were at least two thousand time-locks in
use, and all the important features of time-locks were
present even in the first designs: they were mounted on
the inside of the door, and could be wound up and set
only when the door was open; from the outside they
could not be reached or manipulated by the thieves or
the owner. Reports of the new lock spread quickly, banks
and businesses advertised their latest defences with prominent notices to warn off thieves, and hostage-taking
ceased to be profitable. There is a tale that a cashier who
was snatched from his home and dragged to the bank
saved himself from assault by telling his captors that a
time-lock had just been fitted to the vault door.

'Listen,' he said. 'You can hear it ticking.' Even had
one been fitted, it is unlikely that the clock movement
could ever have been heard through such a thick door,
but like the courtiers who clearly saw the Emperor's new
clothes, the bandits were sure they heard something. 'It's
no use, boys,' their leader is supposed to have said,
'here's another six weeks' job gone to hell.'

The risk for the safe-owner was that the lock would
fail, leaving him with a locked, unopenable safe. The
reliability of any one clock mechanism may be good, but
any failure would mean a costly and lengthy cutting or
burning by locksmiths; to apply two clock mechanisms,
each capable of opening the lock, was a sensible safeguard, and in large, strong vaults three and four movements are fitted. For the most urgent emergencies, such

as major fires, locks occasionally had a secret combination, unknown even to the safe-owner, but which could
be obtained from the manufacturer by telegraph; this
may have been an attempt to reassure some customers
who feared a lockout, but by undoing the very purpose
of the lock it was an extra hazard, and seldom used.

Most ordinary locks are hidden within doors, their
working parts encased for protection. Although made
with great craftsmanship to very fine tolerances their
elegance of design has to be concealed. Time-locks are
different, an opportunity for the lockmakers to turn out
attractive designs which will persuade the customer to
buy not only because of their effectiveness in action, but
also their appeal to the eye. Brass cases, machine-turned
steel components revealed behind engraved glass panels
with bevelled edges, decorative curlicues and embellish-
ments are all common. Even cynical locksmiths speak
admiringly of good time-locks; collectors covet them, and
where the rarest example of a clever and functional lock
may be tucked into a drawer, a handsome time-lock will
be out on display for anyone to admire.

Time-locks do require some care; they need to be
wound up, set and generally treated with respect. For
some users the visible complexity of the lock is still
daunting and mysterious, and one safemaker has told
how he had to use great persuasion to convince a customer to fit one, only to receive a complaining phone call
soon after. 'We never wanted the wretched time-locks,
and now we cannot get into our strongroom.' For a while
the safemaker was puzzled, until he realized that this was
April, and the first day of daylight saving – the lock had
simply remained set for one hour later.

Escapology

This book is in the main the story of those who tried to make their living by the use of unusual skills to penetrate safes from without, but a very few have done even better by working in the other direction.

> J R PAUL
> Locksmith and Safe Expert
> 11 Ray Street
> Farringdon Street, E.C.

Dear Sir

I have in my possession a GENUINE OLD BURGLAR-PROOF SAFE, weighing about 8cwt, which will easily hold a Human Being.

I would like to know whether (you being locked up inside this Safe), there is any subterfuge by which, with your knowledge of locks, you could discover a method of escaping therefrom – WITHOUT DESTROYING OR INJURING the Lock or Safe.

If you would care to make this attempt in private you can do so at any time at my Works; but should you wish to do so Publicly, I will bring the Safe to the Euston or any other place you may designate, at your convenience.

I am, Sir, Yours faithfully,

J. R. Paul

Mr Paul wrote his letter to the most famous escapologist of all time, Houdini. In reply, Houdini published the letter on a poster, with his reply:

Houdini accepts the above Challenge, and invites Mr Paul to
BRING THE SAFE
to the

EUSTON PALACE
ON
Friday Evening next, December 4th, 1908
when he will make an attempt to perform this
UNHEARD-OF FEAT
in the SECOND HOUSE

The publicity worked well, and the staff at the Euston Palace of Varieties at King's Cross in London were turning away eager custom long before the curtains parted to reveal to the house a formidable safe. Wearing only a dressing gown and a bathing costume, Houdini came out beyond the footlights to tell the house that they were about to witness a dangerous undertaking which might fail, since a man could not breathe for long inside the safe.

From the audience he drew a committee which included a well-known local doctor and a representative from the safe company who held the only key to the safe; they looked over the safe inside and out until satisfied that it was the genuine article.

Taking off his dressing gown Houdini now declared that he wished to be searched and examined medically before attempting to escape from the safe. The doctor agreed to carry out these checks, and went along with a suggestion from the escapologist that he be examined inside the safe, with the door half open, under the supervision of another committee member as umpire.

All three emerged: the doctor announced that it was impossible for Houdini to have concealed anything about him, and that there was nothing strange within the safe; the umpire agreed. Houdini shook their hands and walked into the safe, which was locked by the committee. A large screen was drawn around the safe in such a way that no one could approach it without the knowledge of the audience. Around the screen were attendants who had been instructed to ask for the key only if they heard a series of knocks, which would be a signal of urgent distress. Fifteen minutes passed, and the audience was still eager; after half an hour the house was restless, and some cried out that the safe should be opened. After forty minutes there was an appeal to the management to bring the whole enterprise to a halt, but just five minutes more and the screens were drawn aside – there stood Houdini, still in his bathing suit, and quite free. Behind him the safe was securely locked, and the committee could find no clue as to how he had been able to escape.

The escape had in fact taken Houdini just fourteen minutes, according to a note he made later on a copy of the poster, and had depended on two manoeuvres. First, Houdini had insisted that the safe be delivered the day before the show; this had seemed a fair condition, and the safe company had been happy to agree, but Houdini had his mechanics use that time to open the back of the safe door and modify the lockwork. The lock could now be operated from within by the use of a small three-pronged key.

The passing of this key was the second important step. Houdini did not have it when he went on stage, the honest doctor did not find it because Houdini still did not have it – only by the final handshake with the umpire was it passed to him. The umpire was an accomplice who wore the tiny key clipped to a ring on one finger. With this Houdini was able easily to open the door, slip out, and spend a half-hour reading a novel as the tension beyond the screen was rising.

Houdini was the most famous escapologist in history and as a part of his act claimed to be able to open any lock passed to him from the audience. He was very intrigued by the history of locks, and made a friend of the notable locksmith Charles Courtney, whom he occasionally approached to do work for him. Even with

Courtney he maintained a magician's secrecy, but the locksmith began to suspect that he did not in fact pick all the locks he was given. When he brought in locks and asked that some of the inner works be removed, Courtney began to work out how many of the stage effects were achieved. He later wrote:

> To be sure, I asked a friend to send up a lock in which the shackle was pinned to the case and the pin so well concealed that it would be impossible to see. Then I sat in the front row and watched. Houdini apparently pulled the shackle open but sent the lock back closed. I noticed that whenever the lock was a very cheap one, he unlocked it, showed it to the audience, and returned it opened, but if it was a good lock, he always returned it closed. He didn't pick the good ones; when he got one that he couldn't master, he palmed it, substituted a similar one, opened it for the audience to see, palmed it, and returned the original one unopened. I knew that was the way he did it, but I could rarely see him do it; his hands were quicker than my eyes.

On Houdini's death, his widow wrote to Courtney asking that he should unlock her husband's safe, since no attempt to open it had yet succeeded. The lock was unsurprisingly a trick one, so Courtney asked just how Houdini had opened it – it seemed that he had never touched it, but merely passed his hands over it. Courtney went to a local hardware store, and on his return was able to pass his hands over the lock and watch it open, to Mrs Houdini's astonishment. In his palm Courtney had concealed a magnet he had bought, and it was this which drew the shackle of the lock without making contact.

Though a part of Houdini's showmanship was to play upon common claustrophobia, the inside of a safe can seem like the safest place to be. One safemaker was approached during the Second World War by an elderly couple, regally if quaintly dressed in high Victorian style, who wanted to order a large safe. Model after model was offered, but still they asked for something a little larger until a vast double-doored safe, standing more than six feet tall and costing a thousand pounds, seemed to find favour. 'Capital!' cried the man. 'That's just the safe we want.' He called for two chairs, which were placed inside the safe. The couple composed themselves on the chairs, and asked that the doors be closed on them. When they came out they declared themselves satisfied, and placed an order, so long as it could be delivered with holes drilled in it. They explained to the puzzled safemaker that their nerves were not strong, and after a flying bomb had burst close to their home, they had decided to buy a safe in which to take shelter every time the air raid siren went off. The couple's idea was in fact one that had been adopted before – the entire Finnish Cabinet took shelter in a Chubb vault when Helsinki was under attack during the Russo-Finnish War.

In a book on crime the last word on escapology belongs with a crook and a safe engineer. Ships carry mail and valuable cargo in strongrooms, and while servicing the locks on board one vessel a young locksmith was approached by a docker who wanted to make an intriguing wager. He said that he had once been an assistant to an escapologist, and was prepared to bet a pound that if he were locked in the bullion room he could make his escape within the hour. Ship work was often performed by the most junior craftsmen, and the lock-smith was young, but he was far from stupid: remembering the cargo locked into the bullion room, and its value, he politely turned down the bet.

PART THREE

The Crack

10
Kings of Their Craft

> Cracksmen of this class head the list of mechanical thieves. It requires rare qualities in a criminal to become an expert bank-safe robber. Thieves of this grade stand unrivalled among their kind. The professional bank burglar must have patience, intelligence, mechanical knowledge, industry, determination, fertility of resources, and courage – all in high degree.

This high praise of safecrackers was written in 1886 by Thomas Byrnes, Chief of the New York Detective Bureau. It was a view of the boxman's trade which would have been accepted by the police, the press, the public and almost every working criminal for the next eighty years. Safecracking was a crime which had extraordinary prestige.

In the New York of Byrnes' time, expert burglars and safecrackers were known as the High Mob, and the *New York Times* carried a piece in 1894 which described them as 'the gentlemen Joes of the trade, who scorn small affairs, and who are regarded with the highest reverence by the smaller practitioners in private plunder. They keep step with science, and they have every new invention at their command. When the iron safe came out, they brought a steel drill with them, when the steel safe appeared, and defied the point of the drill, they imagined the portable electric battery, with which they generated intense heat that fused a hole.'

To grasp just how important it can be to a criminal to be given, and to retain, professional prestige requires a substantial leap of imagination for the ordinary citizen.

The best place to start is probably the belief, which the career thief shares with the determined salesperson, that any money in your pocket belongs in his – what you own is yours only as long as he doesn't want it, and you are smart enough or strong enough to hang on to it. This is a long way from teenage pilfering, or opportunist theft by civilians too strongly tempted, or reduced by drink, debts or divorce to the feeling that there is nothing left to lose.

This is crime in real life, a long way from film and fiction. In books and films, people kill and steal for rational, tangible rewards such as an inheritance or the removal of a romantic rival. This has nothing to do with ordinary adult crime, which is performed by people who live almost in a parallel universe, a world in which values are inverted. Civilians spend time and money trying to limit or eliminate very ordinary risks; criminals not only accept the dangers of injury or imprisonment but pursue them wilfully for gains that don't even match the average industrial wage.

The traditional name for this life is the underworld, the idea that beneath us is a society which breaks through the civilized crust by night, then dives back at dawn. The image is a racy one, romantically attractive to many, a world of secrets and privileged membership full of people bolder than ourselves, the most successful of whom become fabulously rich and powerful. The reality is that although it is an exclusive world, career crime is rarely more exotic than legitimate fraternities like the legal profession or medicine, and much worse paid. Gossip, the pleasures of inside information, and jokes and tales which are funny only to other members make all these worlds go round, and reputation matters more than mere qualification. It is even more important to choose your companions with care, and to have their trust and respect, when your liberty is at stake every working day.

Safecrackers were always full members in good standing of this alternative society. They made money, they were good organizers and craftsmen, and they went out and took risks. Among safemen, status was measured by the size of job and the degree of skill and daring required. At the top of the tree were the big bank burglars, the tunnellers and vault-blowers, and one or two skilful jewel thieves who stole from the gentry. Domestic safes were rarely a technical challenge, but traditional criminal snobbery helped – thieves seem to be among the last people in Britain to be impressed by aristocratic titles – and a genuine appreciation of the long daring and cunning of the successful burglar. Members of teams which had consistent success with business safes were in the next rank. Bellmen, efficient users of explosives, and specialists who had mastered a new technique belonged here – as an example, drill men had a very high status for a while in the Toronto of the 1960s, because they were achieving impressive results with a new device, the electrical magnet drill press.

For a long time safemen in general were seen as a little superior to bank and security van robbers who hauled in comparable loot, partly because they were of the older school with more established personal reputations, and partly because there was a broad understanding that violence was unprofessional. Then came the decline, first in the US, where armed robbery was becoming more common and more profitable and the use of insecure fire safes, easy for unskilled burglars to break open, reduced the mystique and prestige of the trade as a whole. Harry King, a retired American safeman, reached the glum conclusion in 1960 that, 'At one time boxmen were rated as the kings, but then there weren't so many kids to rip it and tear now [that] it's lost its good name. Bank robbers used to be a high-class profession, but all these kids

around robbing . . . They used to get $100,000 to
$200,000 out of a bank, now they get $3,000 or $4,000.
So that profession fell down to the bottom.'

In Britain change was already under way when the
Great Train Robbery placed major robbers decisively at
the top of the tree. The scale of everything in that job,
from the size of the haul to the length of the sentences
handed out, eclipsed even the best of the safe and vault
efforts. Many of the individual participants were well-
known, and not always greatly respected, but criminals
are as easily carried along by publicity as any other
citizen, and there was a Wild West flavour to the train
robbery which impressed them too.

If police and villains were respectful of safemen,
reporters could be downright admiring:

> We may have lost the Ashes, productivity may be lagging,
> our sportsmen may finish last in many things. But one
> made-in-Britain skill remains supreme. Our safebreakers
> are the best in the world . . .
> Why is the British safebreaker so good? One reason is
> that cracking a crib requires characteristics in which Brit-
> ons excel – skill, tenacity, stamina and patience.
>
> Peter Ellis, *Weekend*, April 1963

No working criminal has been treated so kindly by the
press as the safecracker. Murderers have inspired rage,
contempt and occasional pity, and many thieves have
seen their lives' works dismissed as petty, but safe
burglars seem to have inspired from the earliest days a
coverage more appropriate to heroes whose skills and
personal qualities are to be admired.

This seems to have been true from the earliest days of
specialized safecracking. In the 1860s George Price, the
early safemaker, promoted his designs in a book called

Forty Burglaries, in which he assembled dozens of newspaper reports and letters from burglary victims to prove
how weak were cheap safes, how superior his own. A
tally of the words used to describe safecrackers and their
deeds is revealing – by far the most popular adjective was
daring, which featured in a dozen accounts, *determined*
was used five times, *expert* and *bold* twice each, followed
by *skilful, ingenious, clever, audacious*, and *extraordinary*. Larger thefts were occasionally called *great*, or
serious, but only one was described pejoratively, as both
determined and *disgraceful*.

Can there ever have been a safecracking that was not
reported as daring? Down all the years, from Hong Kong
to Johannesburg to Toronto, the word has been used in
the first three sentences of so many reports, even when it
failed to find a place in the headline.

To banish any thought that burglary was a secretive
and shifty business, the London reading public was told
in 1913 that, 'A flavour of the romances of the Wild West
rather than of the stern realities of Central London marks
the story of a daring and successful burglary . . .'

The tools of the burglar's trade, and the skill with
which they were used had long been fascinating reading
(did not Sherlock Holmes take a pride in his dexterity
with a kit?) and each fresh and ingenious tool an object
of uneasy marvel. This respect turned to downright
admiration as the complexity of burgling increased, and
safemen transformed themselves from craftsmen into
scientists. When science was still seen uncritically as a
blessing to all the world, papers were reporting that
'scientific burglaries have not been rare in London during
the last few years' (1913) and announcing a crime in a
headline such as 'THE SCIENTIFIC THIEVES OF THE
WEST END' (1927). By 1965, when the white heat of

technology was deemed the correct temperature for progress, *The Star* was ready to set a measure on the level of knowledge needed: 'If official diplomas of merit were handed out among today's criminals according to their prowess and qualifications, then there would be a few villains about who would be Master Technicians, or even graduates in Crime Technology.' Who else but safecrackers? Nor were they ruffians: comparing the safeblower with the Great Train Robber, 'Your grudging admiration is for his craftsmanship rather than his military-style organization.'

Portrayed on the cinema screen by handsome stars, and endowed by the press with the boldness of an explorer and the brain of a Nobel laureate, who could not want one as a son-in-law? Safecrackers were almost a national asset. Peter Ellis even managed to link safemen to frustrations in British foreign policy: 'President de Gaulle is keeping us out of the Common Market. But if there is a really difficult box (safe) to be "blown" or "cut" on the Continent, it's usually a British "peterman" (cracksman) who gets an invitation to visit Europe.'

This, and the quotation at the beginning of this chapter are absurdly jingoistic, but not the only examples of the type. In a long piece called 'The Smartest Burglars in the World', published in Toronto at about the same time, the author was very keen to impress on his patriotic readership just how dreaded were Canadian safemen in the United States, and how they had been responsible for so many useful innovations in the trade: 'US burglars, *supposed* to be the slickest in the trade, only recently began using techniques that are well-established here.'

Safebreakers had to earn their prestige, and some crooks never quite grasped the techniques needed. In 1921 the Chatwood Safe Company in England used a heartless advertisement headed with a picture of seven doleful Romanians, attended by a policeman with a rifle. Under the caption: 'These 7 burglars failed to open The Chatwood Safe in 17 days!', they reprinted a letter which explains the wretched expressions on the prisoners' faces:

To The Chatwood Safe Co Ltd	BUCHAREST
Bankers' Engineers	19 March 1921
BOLTON, England	

Gentlemen,

Enclosed herewith I am forwarding you a photograph representing a band of seven burglars and the gendarme in charge. These 7 men tried on 2 January 1921, to steal the contents of THE CHATWOOD SAFE No. 32404 belonging to the Petroleum Refinery 'Helios', Societe Anonyme, in Tirgoviste, Romania.

THEY BROKE THROUGH THE WALL OF THE HOUSE, TOOK THE SAFE OUT AND TRANSPORTED IT, PER CART, A DISTANCE OF 9 MILES, where they left it for some time buried in the sand and gravel of a river bed.

THEY AFTERWARDS WORKED 17 (SEVENTEEN) DAYS ON THE SAFE, exhausting all ordinary devices of safe opening known in this country trying to open it, but beyond succeeding in breaking off the hinges and the handle and severely battering the outside of the safe and the lock, they FAILED UTTERLY in getting at the contents of the safe.

The safe was eventually found, and it took skilled mechanics a whole day to straighten out the keyhole, after which, by turning the bolts with the aid of a strong pair of pliers (the handle having been knocked off), the contents of the safe were found in perfect order.

11

Learning the Trade

No ordinary working safecracker ever began from a broad knowledge of locks and safes; he worked in a trade which usually relied on simple knowledge passed in whispers, techniques rehearsed in garages and kitchens rather than workshops or laboratories, and put into practice in the small glow of a handlamp on a rainy night.

'I worked for Dick for three years as an apprentice. My job was to go steal the dynamite and cook it up; which, incidentally, gives you a terrific headache if you smell its fumes while you're cooking it. I would steal the dynamite, take it out in the country and build a fire, get a can of water in it, cook it up, and hide it away. We just used a very small amount of it.' This was Harry King's introduction to safecracking before the Great War, when he made a slow start by doing the unpleasant chores. Only by stages was he admitted to the mysteries of his new craft. Any apprentice must learn to keep his bench tidy and his tools in good condition, and King was taught the elements of preparation. 'I would also lay on the joints that he picked out. It was my job to watch the joint for three or four nights and see when the door-shaker or the policeman would come by; what time they closed the place up . . .' Denver Dick was a demanding but generous master: 'I did all the work and he was the brains. It was quite lucrative for me as I got an equal share of the loot. He was very fair and trustworthy as far as dividing the loot.'

King's apprenticeship sounds much like that of any trade. He was lucky enough not to be exploited, but the way in which his master held back knowledge of the mysteries of the craft, when King was obviously an eager pupil, seems to show that Denver Dick's purpose was to maintain the standing of his caste as much as to provide an education.

Denver Dick was an independent thief working within a fraternity of safecrackers, and after choosing King would have been as conscious as any club member of his responsibility for a newcomer. The standing of a craftsman was important even within a single city, but when safecrackers roamed across the United States a good reputation meant that wherever he went, a craftsman could be assured of a secure hiding-place, a loan, local help to act as lookouts and drivers, and a reliable market for any valuables he might have stolen. King was being groomed not only for prestige, but for privilege.

There were other paths into the profession. Most safemen simply picked up what they could, in bars or during long conversations with other prisoners, and learned one or two techniques which would allow them to open a limited range of ordinary safes. This was a way to make a living, but no way to get rich. If a safeman was ambitious, he had to be knowledgeable and versatile enough to tackle the newer, better safes which held really valuable prizes. He had to understand the construction of boxes made by the better manufacturers and the lockwork hidden inside, then carry out his attack with whatever method or combination of methods was required.

These technical challenges of safecracking have had a powerful, even a compulsive attraction for many crooks and not a few amateurs. There is something in the male human psyche which seems to become besotted with mechanisms, from car engines to cameras or clocks, and safecracking is a crime which seems to have a similar attraction. There have been many men without mentors, without examples to copy, who spent their working and leisure hours teaching themselves the intricacies of the trade. Where better to learn the elements of safe design and construction than from the makers? The American Herbert Wilson took a labouring job in a safe factory for six weeks, then rounded out his observations with three weeks at another, memorizing all he saw until he could commit it to paper at home. He completed his studies with two months' research in the Bureau of Standards, and was then able to compile his notes on materials, mechanisms and explosives into a full manual for safeblowers.

Wilson was a professional, planning a career, but citizens with no criminal connections have been seized by the same need to learn, understand and defeat safes. In August 1949 two young Australian men were arrested at gunpoint as they were preparing to blow the safe of a cinema in Melbourne. The younger thief, just eighteen years old but clearly in command, turned out to be one of the most methodical students in the history of safecracking. He had embarked on a course of self-directed study which had included not only days in the public library but periods of work at a local explosives factory. He spent months training as a welder, and picked up more than enough knowledge to cut safes with oxyacetylene gear. He was a hobby thief, who appeared neither to have used nor spent any of the proceeds of several safecrackings, but to have stored them at home as trophies of his raids.

If safecracking is a trade which can be learned at home, or passed on by a tutor, why not teach it as a formal course? This is exactly what has happened: in the late nineteenth century one of the most successful American fences, a woman called Frederika Mandelbaum, set up the first known safecracking school – she sponsored the training of students who would then bring their loot to her for disposal.

On the very fringes of legitimacy, an academy which called itself the Wayne Strong School of Safework was established in Los Angeles in the 1920s. There is a long and honourable American tradition of vocational training, and this was a school which like many others issued a diploma certifying that the named student had 'satisfactorily completed the subjects mentioned herein as taught by our safe experts' – a list which included 'safe opening, safe repairing, and safe lock work'. So far, so legitimate; but the first diploma to come to the attention of the police carried the name Joseph Lauson, whose most recent use of his expertise had been to steal about $40,000, and he was happy to relate that his fellow-students were doing well, opening safes all over the USA.

Mrs Mandelbaum was reputed to have taken her operation over the border into Canada, and may have set the precedent for a very similar enterprise in the 1960s. A raid on a garage in Toronto uncovered a very impressive crime college – in classroom style, trainees had taken their places at tables around the room to examine the finer points of the safe doors, and learn how to handle the oxyacetylene cutting gear and drills, the nitroglycerine and the detonators. Written materials included plans and diagrams; there was even a home-made textbook, arranging the course into numbered lessons, and fully footnoted and cross-referenced.

Home study could take a different form. A Canadian office equipment company put on display two safes proclaimed to be 'anti-blow, anti-drill', and the challenge was much too tempting for a local gang of drill experts. They broke into the building, and stole just the doors from the safes on view. The very next day one of the gang telephoned the police to tell the duty officer where the doors had been hidden, and when detectives went to the spot, they found the doors – riddled with holes. This may have been the work of the same safecracker who boasted that he had even managed to break into a drawing office where he could photograph working plans for new safes, so he was ready to open them even before they were on the market.

Much the best set of instructions that I have ever seen for safecracking, a guide to blowing a safe with gelignite, was published in 1965. This is no rough duplicated handout to be passed shiftily from hand to hand: it contains thirteen fully captioned photographs of each stage involved in blowing a large safe. The reader is shown how to remove the keyhole cover, place and tamp the first charge, wire up the detonator, then drill a hole into which a second and larger charge is inserted, held within a condom (discreetly described as a balloon in the caption). The method of sealing holes with Plasticine is shown, and the use of a battery to fire the detonator. Only one significant detail is omitted, and a blank frame inserted at this stage in the procedure: the amount of gelignite required is not shown, and the frame carries a CENSORED stripe, with a laconic caption, 'Amateurs are liable to blow themselves up.' This was a sensible precaution, since the instructions were sent out to the homes of more than seven million British citizens, as a feature in the colour supplement of the *Sunday Times*.

12

The Burgling Life

A job was always much more than just the breaking of a box. Safecracking was always burglary, perhaps the ultimate form, but a virtuoso safeman would still fail if he did not have the ordinary skills and instincts of the burglar. He had to choose a target that was both accessible and profitable, to reconnoitre and plan carefully, and choose his companions with care. For the break-in itself he had to be able to neutralize any alarms and make a clean entry, maintain a careful watch, and get away without incident. Thieves say that they find targets easily, but we have always to remember that any working criminal sees his surroundings with a sharply professional eye. Just as a good actor absorbs mannerisms and accents, and an engineer understands the structure of the objects about him, the thief is aware of patterns and possibilities invisible to the honest citizen. This is not merely the lure of the unlocked window or the unguarded handbag: the good burglar perceives not only places but people. He has a nose for the police, of course, for victims and other crooks, and may have that most useful gift: a sense which helps him to use the folly of ordinary citizens.

A thief can draw a lot of useful information from amateur informants, citizens upon whose ordinary weaknesses he can play. The dissatisfied employee is an obvious candidate, and a sympathetic ear for his grievances can soon turn into a proposition. Among otherwise respectable people there are always those who lack the ability, or the courage, to carry out a crime themselves but are easily induced to pass on information which will enable others to steal. Their reward may be a simple fee, or a share in the proceeds. These civilians are probably only useful for one or two jobs, since they are commonly betraying their own past or present employers. It is even simpler to find the semi-professional informant, one of the people who live on the fringes of the active criminal life. This is the sort of citizen who sells stolen goods to workmates, family and friends, savours his small local reputation as a smart operator, and enjoys the glamour of being just a little of the outlaw. He drinks in the right pubs and bars, likes to be seen in the right company, and is even pleased to lose money in a card game if the other players are suitably notorious. If he hears that a business is slipshod in the way it protects its cash or goods, or vulnerable in any way, he will take a fee for his knowledge, but the reflected notoriety is his biggest reward.

These minor villains may well trade both ways, and give information to the police either for money or to prevent themselves from being prosecuted, so they are treated with caution by sensible thieves. Mike Jesswell, a London safecracker who tells his own story in the next chapter, preferred to cover some of the risk by taking the informant along on the job, at least as a lookout; if the job seemed promising, but the informant seemed reluctant, then he would be picked up at the last moment without notice. This was an effective safeguard not only against a police ambush, but against any last-minute loss of nerve or indiscretion which might put the thieves at risk.

Many safecrackers shared this American's view of informers: 'I usually don't accept capers from a finger-man. I go find my own, because there are so many of 'em. Because I have enough to worry about; the caper, plus the box, and getting it organized. I have enough to contend with without worrying about the person who gave this to me. Maybe the pressure's been put on him by the police department to set me up.' Allegations of police corruption are common and unreliable, but Geoff Derr, a safeman active in south London in the 1960s, insisted when I interviewed him that one of his best informants had been a local crime prevention officer – a very dangerous game for both sides.

No successful thief would let his plans depend on the raw information he was given – much of it would be no more than outdated gossip, and even informants with privileged information about the routines and security of a company would not have looked at the job with the eyes of a burglar. The rewards and the risks involved had to be checked.

The first thing the safeman needed to establish for himself was the value of the job – did enough money go into, and stay inside the premises to make the job worthwhile? This may seem obvious, but many a frustrated thief has miscalculated and made off into the night with no more than loose change after hours of hard work and strain. Some businesses such as pawnbrokers and scrap merchants keep cash on the premises at all times because they must be ready to buy stock; others need cash in hand to pay casual staff. Businesses with a regular cycle of trade were only worth visiting when all the collections had been made, such as a dairy or bakery whose vans took householders' money at the end of the week. The most conveniently regular pattern was staff payment – until quite recently the workforce in many industries was paid in cash which had been delivered to the company a couple of days in advance for the wages staff to count out into little envelopes. Even where companies had given up paying their staff in cash, pay day could be profitable – in the USA, bars which cashed the paychecks of workers would lay in extra cash at the end of the week to meet demand, and so become targets. Some businesses were attractive because they used equipment which would be helpful to the burglars, as we shall see.

By asking around, a thief could discover how much trade a business was doing and arrive at a fair estimate of the cash kept in hand, or use a formula which would provide a useful estimate. For a business like a dairy or a laundry he could simply count the vans in the yard, and multiply by a sensible sum to guess the weekly turnover. 'If it's a place that has delivery trucks, you can figure five hundred dollars for every truck they got and they'll have that much in the safe. I mean, that's the average for any kind of business whether it be a beer truck or a dry-cleaning place.' If the result of these enquiries and observations seemed promising, the watching burglar would want to know how thoroughly the business looked after its cash. There might be a nightwatchman permanently on the premises, or just a visiting patrol: safecracking is noisy, and for many teams the presence of a watchman was enough to rule the job out. If the prize were too good to abandon, the patrol had to be watched – was the security man diligent or lazy? Did he have to keep to a regular timetable, governed by a clock, or did he vary his tours? Did his route even come close to the safe? Many companies were more worried about stock pilferage and vandalism than cash security, and did not want unsupervised manual staff wandering around their offices, even to protect them. And always worth considering: could the watchman be 'straightened' – paid to turn a blind eye?

What of the premises themselves? The most promising targets were those at a distance from housing, and away from the casual passer-by. There was a small extra risk that any car loitering in such an area would be more

obvious, but equally the approach of a security patrol or
a police car could quickly be spotted. The layout of the
site was important; from the burglars' point of view, the
best place for a safe was in a building away from the
street. This observation of the target, usually called
casing, is a skill in itself, and clever watchers did their
best to be utterly forgettable. It is hardly surprising that
one British postmaster became suspicious when four
different men came to his counter, one after another,
each buying just a single one-penny stamp. He followed
them, and when he saw them all climb into the same car
he picked up the telephone; the police who stopped the
car found a full explosive kit in the boot.

Even with much more cunning it can be hard for the
safeman to keep an eye on the same place for long. Harry
King used to find that when he was watching premises he
intended to burgle he was often picked up by police; he
was also irritated by other people in the area: 'Several
times I would be swearing at some guy necking with a girl
in a car because I was trying to case the joint and he was
sitting there necking with this girl. It suddenly dawned on
me. Why not get a girl and sit in the car and neck with
her every time a policeman came by?' He found a girl
who could be relied on, but made the mistake of taking
her into the job. When she wanted to help open the box
he gave her a hammer to punch out the lock, but she hit
his hand instead, breaking several bones.

From watching outside, the safecracker would probably
learn enough to make up his mind about the potential in
the job. The next stage was to find any reasonable excuse
to take a look inside. A few minutes would be enough to
learn the layout and locate the safe, to take a quick but
invaluable glance at the internal locks, and spot any
visible alarm wiring. An inside informant might smuggle
him in – no one asks about the unfamiliar worker carrying

the other end of a long package – but even better were approaches which gave a little more time. The safeman could masquerade as a lost traveller needing help with a local map, the delivery driver with a package for another similar address, or the man asking about the job advertised in last week's paper. Any excuse which allowed him to take a look around the workshops or the yard could be helpful, too, to spot the run of the alarm circuit, and the storage of any tools or cylinders of gas which could be borrowed to save the risk of stealing or buying elsewhere.

Thorough preparation would always improve the odds, and no one seems to have taken this further than George Leonidas Leslie, a nineteenth-century gangleader who came closer to being a criminal mastermind, and a gentleman thief, than almost anyone else in this book. He retired from active crime, unconvicted, when he was just thirty-six years old, after a career which had yielded millions of dollars.

Leslie came from a brewing family, rich enough even without his criminal earnings to relish a leisured life in a Manhattan hotel suite and to mix in the politest society. He had studied architecture, and pretended an amateur's interest in the subject: this was an excellent cover when he obtained plans and drawings of the banks he intended to raid. The next step was to open an account, and to include his own observations in constructing a scale mock-up which the team could use in planning. To improve the odds still further, Leslie sometimes used his social connections to obtain a job for one of the thieves in the bank, and commission the making of any special tools for which he foresaw a need. This meticulous approach paid off in twenty years of raids, and even when he no longer took a direct part in burglaries Leslie offered his planning skills to other teams, acting as a consultant.

On the basis of all he had seen and heard, the safe-cracker would know enough not only to carry out the raid, but to determine how many helpers were required. He might need extra muscle to move a large safe out of a convenient exit, or one more lookout to cover the approaches. On some jobs it was possible to leave a car or lorry outside, freeing the driver to take on other tasks, but it was usually wiser for the driver to find a safer spot to park, then come back at a set time or in response to an arranged signal. On the day of the raid, rarely earlier, the safecracker had to assemble the equipment he would need. There are laws in most countries which impose heavy penalties for holding unlicensed explosives and detonating equipment, and stocks were always kept well away from home, literally buried from view, but even to carry simple legitimate tools by night requires a plausible justification. Gelignite was generally safe to carry, but nitroglycerine had to be moved with extreme caution even in the very small quantities needed for a single safe. Most safemen would take personal charge of the nitro, and keep the bottle tied to their own body, but for a longer journey by car some means might be found of isolating it from any impact – in one car recovered in London the boot had been fitted with a criss-cross of rubber cords, to allow the bottle to be suspended in the middle, safe even from parking collisions. Others put their faith in robust boxes lined with foam, but whatever the precautions tension must have run high.

The old-fashioned fuse which needed to be lit was not in itself a hazard, but detonators are fragile and easily set off. A single detonator might not have the power to kill, but the shock from one could easily discharge others, so the prudent safecracker would pack them carefully and distribute them about his pockets to reduce the risk.

Any cars to be used had to be stolen or bought. There

were thieves who took the chance of using their own cars or vans, if only as back-up, but this was very foolish if the registered owner had any kind of criminal record, and had no very obvious explanation for being in the neighbourhood. A common solution was to buy a cheap and disposable van, with no rear windows so that everyone but the driver could lie low in the back; one flamboyant but effective alternative was the hearse which Billy Hill, a British safecracker, used for a while.

In choosing a time to launch the raid, the safecracker would obviously pick the day of the week which would give the biggest haul, but most burglars also preferred to work when the weather was bad. Heavy rain made it less likely that there would be people on the streets who might guess what was going on, or recall what they had seen for the police. Strong winds, or even better a full storm, would help to cover the noise made in moving, breaking or blowing the safe. The first task was to reach the building, perhaps across a yard, alert for watchmen and dogs. 'Good guard dogs rarely kick up a fuss at the sound of humans,' wrote L. J. Cunliffe, a postwar English safecracker, 'and will sometimes let you right into a gaff before tearing the arse out of your trousers, but even guard dogs cannot resist cats.' Cunliffe's solution was to sound like a cat, miaowing and scratching, to draw any dog from hiding.

If all was well, the next stage was to neutralize any alarms that were fitted. If the thieves were confident that there was just a single external bell, with no connection to a phone line, it was usually an easy matter to silence it physically, even if only by levering it bodily from the wall, and damping the sound with a hug until the leads could be cut. On his reconnaissance the safecracker would have looked for alarm contacts on door or window frames, and had techniques which allowed the team to defeat them:

> We had to get the exact height from the floor at which the button was placed, cut out a tiny slit and pass through this a screwdriver which would keep contact whilst Slim bridged the wires which would inactivate the alarm . . . Slim brought out a small drill and began work, he was confident that he could loop. This means that before you break the circuit of the alarm by cutting it, which would set it off, you loop one of the two wires above the point of entry to a bypassing one of [different] resistance, joining it again below. You can then safely cut in, though you must repeat the drill every time you cross the system . . . It was a real education to watch Slim at work – it was just like a surgeon joining up.

If the team needed to put a more complex system out of action, they looked for a route which the alarm circuit did not cover, from a connecting building or through the roof. Tackling the central control box might require attention from a skilled member of the team, or a specialist bellman. This was not easy work, and teams would often take cruder measures: when it was still uncommon to install the kinds of infra-red and ultrasonic area alarms now used in many ordinary houses, alarms were often connected to simple pressure mats under carpets, and the team had to cross rooms without letting a foot touch the floor; one beginner asked an old hand how this could be done: '"This sort of screwing needs planks . . . planks is what you lay across the floor to work on in case they've got it belled. You wouldn't believe how diabolical some of them are." So we practised walking on planks, and bloody silly we looked.' Now safely within the premises, the team's first priority was to secure at least one escape route in case of trouble. This might mean breaking internal locks, unbolting doors or

windows, even making a hole in a wall or internal
partition if this could easily be done. If a passing patrol
were to notice signs of where the team had broken in,
that spot would be kept under close watch until reinforce-
ments arrived, and guarded while the police made a
search.

With a clear exit established, and a lookout posted, it
was time to look around the room in which the safe was
kept. A great deal of hard work could be saved if the key
or the combination had been left in an obvious place, and
many of the hiding places which seem so inventive to the
businessman or his clerk are very obvious indeed to a
thief who has seen it all before. The strength of the safe
and its lock might be less important than the strength of
the desk drawer in which the – labelled – safe key was
kept.

If no key or no combination came to light within the
first few minutes, the team would face their safe and
decide whether it could be tackled on the spot, or needed
to be taken away for opening. They could make an
estimate of the noise that would have to be made, and
the time that would be spent, in attacking it now; they
would assess whether the kit they had brought, or tools
found on the premises, would be up to the job.

When it seemed possible to press on, any heavy tools
would need to be organized quickly – bottles of gas might
have to be wheeled or dragged, cables run from electric
sockets. Even if it were to be opened on site, the safe
might have to be moved to give free access to the side
which the cracker wanted to attack, since some safes had
known weak spots. The safe might be dropped on its
back – the technique of shooting for space with nitroglycerine worked only when the safe was in this position.
Just to move a safe could be difficult and dangerous: a
pair of American burglars who tried to drop a large safe

were afraid of making too much noise, and while one got behind the box, the other tipped it towards him. The safe slipped, trapping the man behind, and his accomplice panicked and ran away. When the attempt was discovered the next day, the man beneath was found dead – he had suffocated after four or five hours of trying to hold it up, suffering extraordinary injury to his legs and hands.

When the box was in position, the task of opening could begin, and all the many methods are covered elsewhere in this book. At just this point, while the safe remains tightly closed, we can pause to remember that the last years of safecracking were among the busiest ever as dozens of teams major and minor, veteran and novice, went to work. One proof of just how competitive the trade had become was an example in 1957 of completely disorganized crime: two quite separate gangs arrived on the same night, at the same time, to break into the same safe.

The scene was a grocer's premises in Fulham. Moving stealthily, each team suddenly became aware of the other, and of course was quite certain that the police had arrived. Everybody froze, until it dawned on them that whoever was out there, it couldn't be the cops. A long whispered argument broke out, and a deal was struck. The safe would be removed by joint effort, opened elsewhere and the take divided down the middle: with a fine attention to protocol two members of each team carried out the box, one from each side accompanied it to a garage hideout.

There was, however, a third team in the game. The police, whose attention had been drawn to all the unlikely activity, waited until all the players had assembled for the opening of the safe, and the cutting had begun. Each gang of thieves blamed the other all the way from the garage to prison.

The unexpected arrival of police or a guard could be experienced even by competent crooks, and they would head immediately for their escape route, with a fair chance of getting away. If the job went without interruption, success or failure in opening the box depended very much on the skill and experience of the thieves: amateurish beginners were easily defeated by anything but an ancient box.

It took more than luck to open a box, but the final profit in a job was still a matter of chance. Like collectors who can still remember the lifetime bargain missed twenty years before, safecrackers I have met still recall with feeling the times they missed the haul of a lifetime by hours or days. Some had been driven to raid the same premises twice, so sure were they that the original hunch or deduction was too good to abandon.

Whether winners or losers, safecrackers went home having spent a great deal of physical and nervous energy on the task, and many could not leave without recording their feelings.

'NO GUNPLAY, NO VIOLENCE, NO HATE,' wrote the Spaggiari team after they had taken $8,000,000 from the vault in Nice in 1976. Less cheerfully, burglars who had gained little from a raid on a large Parisian grocery took out their frustrations on the stock, scoffing tins of lobster, green peas and anchovies and drinking bottle after bottle of wine; this must have improved their humour, for as a last gesture they lined up sausages on a cashier's desk like soldiers on parade.

A man who had taken £50,000 from a bank in the 1960s was moved to a certain professional pride, and wrote 'the boss was here' across his handiwork, but triumphant notes are very rare – it seems that happy thieves just melt into the night with their money. Signs of failure and frustration, on the other hand, have been scratched into paintwork, painted on walls, and written out neatly on headed company notepaper. I have been able to assemble a small collection of these touching plaints from newspaper cuttings spanning more than a century, and these anonymous lines are as vivid as any more considered memoirs:

A note left at Fulham football club in London: 'Sir, – Where the hell do you keep your money? We can't find any. Sorry for the mess.'

At a railway station in Scotland: 'THE INVENTOR OF THIS SAFE SHOULD BE HANGED WITH A SOAPY ROPE.'

A thief who had spent hours in ripping open a safe, but still could not reach the money: 'Time waits for no man – The Phantom'.

A rueful unsolicited testimonial: 'DEAR SIRS, – We have given your place a visit with the idea of getting about £100. But we were mistaken – bad luck. Better luck next time, – Yours truly, N. E. BODY. P.S. – Please exhibit this safe in the shop. We have had a lot of trouble with it.'

A literary touch: 'We are extremely disgusted. We sha'n't come back – Sikes and Co.'

A gruff complaint: 'NEXT TIME BUY A SAFE WITHOUT A CAST IRON BELLY. I'M STIFF, WHAT DO YOU THINK.'

And a selection of short laments: 'Sorry; your safe was too big for us.' 'TO [sic] TOUGH.' 'Very sorry we did not find the money, but will see you later.'

One of the longest and saddest notes was left in a Sailors' Home in Scotland, addressed to the manageress:

Dear Madame – Please accept my deepest apologies for putting your office in slight disorder and the Chubb lock hors de combat. But, candidly speaking, I think this is about the rottenest crib I've ever shot at cracking.

After four hours' elated hopes and exertions I find the truth of the proverb, 'We all come into this world with nothing, and we can't take anything out.' It's so with this place. After four hours' ineffectual exertion I haven't got the price of a stale doughnut.

I am, yours penitantly [sic]

MATHEW, the Midnight Marauder

PTO

And on the other side:

Dr to Mathew, the Midnight marauder	£	s	d
To a broken heart	2	0	0
To lost time	0	18	0
To lost trouble	0	0	5
	2	18	5

One very active safeman of the 1940s was either extremely cautious, obsessive, or perhaps superstitious about his rituals. With fireproof filling to be split, safe-cracking always left a mess, but this crook had the habit of meticulously cleaning up after he had blown the box, even dusting the furniture; one of his contemporaries said that this compulsive behaviour was controversial. 'Safe-crackers asserted that this style was a dead giveaway to the police. At the same time, he was known for his ability not to leave evidence that would be admissible in court.'

It is very easy to picture this houseproud thief, loot neatly packed, taking one last glance around the room before switching off the light to make his getaway into the night.

A Burglar's Tale

I interviewed Mike Jesswell for many hours, and the following is close to being a raw transcript of his detailed observations about the time when, in his early twenties, he was a successful safeblower. He went to prison in the early 1960s for a single offence, after nearly four years of persistent raiding; he and a friend began by making a large version of the old-style domestic canopener, but quickly moved to the use of explosives. When he left prison, he found a legitimate way to make a good living, and when I met him he was a contented man in robust early middle age; a cheerful, articulate, stocky man, he was nostalgically proud of having been a successful thief.

The first job was performed using a large home-made version of the old-fashioned domestic canopener.

We done our first one. In our manor where we worked . . . we had a guy who worked in a laundry, and he . . . we asked general questions like when do you get paid and . . . he actually came on the firm [joined the gang to do the job] and put us in the back of his van. He gave us the rough sketch of the layout of the building. We found one safe, the first one where we used the canopener and we found the keys to another safe and opened that up. We opened up five before we actually found the one that all the money was in, two we used the canopener and three we found the keys. There were seven altogether, there were a couple obviously just for files, insurance policies and bits and pieces.

[*Newspaper reports overstated the size of the haul, and*

Jesswell had to establish a way of dividing the loot.] We got out £2,000 in cash, now back in '66, '65, that was good money. We got very pissed off the next day to find out that there was a scream for £3,000, and that was our first thing that whatever you get you've got to now be careful. The ground rules were now drawn up: as and when you ever got anything out of a peter you put it in a bag and that bag was then . . . tied up and then it wasn't opened and it was always in the company of at least two of you, until it could be opened up in front of everybody, so there was never anything for anyone to quibble at.

Anyway, this was right opposite a police station, and we could see the police and it was quite simple. We just left the car then, went back to it and sort of wandered off. More than six months' wages each.

They moved on to use explosives.

So we then did a couple more – when we came across our first one we couldn't use our canopener. We'd seen a lot in the papers about gelly being used. One of our guys on our firm, his father was a well-known conman and he used to work the trains, with the cards – double aces and that – and he had a contact. I actually done the phone calls and met this guy. I got there – and again this is another important lesson I learned – I got there about fifteen minutes late. No sign of him. Went back, still hadn't turned up – made a couple of calls and I went and saw him this time. He actually turned up with the gelly, and he said to me, 'If you are ever more than one minute late, I don't hold the stuff – I throw it over the river, get rid of it. Never, ever, turn up late when I'm holding. I don't want to be sitting roasting.' So anyway we then made another visit and he got us this stuff – he got us this Polar Ammon [a brand of gelignite] and the first dets we got were the cord dets [the type which is lit rather than set off electrically]. The gelly – about this long, very

pliable. As long as the warning is, keep turning it, keep
it cool, don't put the dets next to it, keep it in its
wrapping. Later on we got hold of a big fat stick that was
the quarry stuff – a lump like that. *He described with his
hands a block the size of a half-brick*.

We then had a talk with another oldtimer . . . told us
how to hold it in your mouth to use and told us how to
place it, things like that, what packing to use. So we went
and tried our first one – it was out in the country on an
estate where there was absolutely no one within a mile
. . . more a practice run than anything else. He'd also
advised us how we had to time them: take the cord, take
a little bit off, like that, see how long it burns. You could
get two types of cord – you could get the very quick one,
and you got your slow burner – and you got obvious
problems with both of them. [The quick one] you can't
really stop safely, the other one if you leave too long a
fuse . . . takes up a two minute fuse, so you can't get far
enough away, you got the problem that you set it and all
of a sudden [with the fuse still burning] a security van
could come round and be checking . . . so obviously you
want to keep it as short as possible. So we did a practice
and it was successful, mind you we did have a little bit of
a mess . . . put too much in.

It was an experimental period. We wanted to know
just how loud the sound was, we wanted to know how
our reactions to it were.

But really as you go on in life you realize that with the
modern forensic methods now you really don't want to
be in there [*because dust from the scene could be identified*] – if you've got the time to leave it to settle. If you're
in there you're impregnated or you've got to go in the
skullcap [balaclava, or other hat to avoid trapping incriminating dust in the hair], you've got to go in buttoned up
– discard it all afterwards cause if the forensic get you

they comb all your hair out, scrape under your nails – they have everything off you for the tests.

The first one, there's no question about it, it was loud. You thought the whole world heard, there's no question about that. It mesmerized us for a second, there was the smell, and then you see your work, you know. It was the complete safe . . . once we opened it the back of the door was just pulverized inside. A lot of stuff was damaged. It was an exercise more than anything, we didn't expect there was any fortunes in there.

They learned to specialize in safes of a certain kind, concentrating on business premises and post offices for which they developed a systematic method.

I never saw a combination lock. If you set your sights high, and got into the league there was a degree of sophistication in the building, I think you have to work up to that. We did drill a couple, but we didn't really know what we were doing. We did not know enough. One of us was always going to do a course in it, go and work in a factory for six months in the hope we'd pick up . . . These safe manufacturers, you couldn't get round them all. Wasn't like now where you could go to a seminar and they have them all lined up . . . in those days everyone was very jealously guarding their safes.

Our business used to go out weekends hitting butchers, bakers, warehouses and laundries . . . The roundsmen would [bring in] all the cash, and it would be kept until the Monday . . . It didn't take long to sit outside on a Friday after the banks closed so you know they've got nowhere to put the money, and then hit there Saturday . . . You know that if there's twenty or thirty vehicles, they're going to bank a couple of hundred quid each . . . not a lot of money. It was just a simple rule of thumb really – we'd just study the thing, see how many vans they'd got in there. Go any day, sit there and watch it a

Above: The earliest vaults in Britain were like this – an underground cell built by the Romans to hold valuables

Below: To protect wealth in transit, portable safes such as this were used by nineteenth-century railways

Above: When banks might fail, and a little ostentation went a long way, the domestic safe could be sold as a fashion accessory

Left: This safecracker looks like a model of calm, but in fact he would have to leap from his stool, and peer carefully at the progress of the trickling nitro, then light his fuse very quickly to be sure of a perfectly timed detonation. There might still be much work to do with the hammer and levers at the foot of the safe

CRACKSMAN USING NITRO-GLYCERINE ON A SAFE.

Below: This was a child reputedly preserved by a Milner safe through a devastating fire. The resourceful waif apparently not only had the presence of mind to take in a luxurious cushion, but also presumably to hide a large oxygen tank beneath it

Above: Langdon W. Moore commissioned this fanciful picture of his first safeblowing to illustrate his auto-biography

Above: This Sargent and Greenleaf time-lock shows the elaboration of design which comforted the Victorian customer

Right: Portrait of a 'yegg': Maximilian ('Mark') Shinburn was both ruthless and skilful – legend has it that he picked the lock of a handcuff while his escort was asleep, using a piece of metal that he had hidden in his mouth

Fig. 1.

These 7 burglars failed to open The Chatwood Safe in 17 days!

To The Chatwood Safe Co., Ltd.
Bankers' Engineers,
BOLTON, England.

BUCHAREST,
March 19th, 1921.

Gentlemen,

Enclosed herewith I am forwarding you a photograph representing a band of 7 burglars and the gendarme in charge. These 7 men tried on January 2nd, 1921, to steal the contents of THE CHATWOOD SAFE No. 32404 belonging to the Petroleum Refinery "Helios," Société Anonyme, in Tirgoviste, Roumania.

THEY BROKE THROUGH THE WALL OF THE HOUSE, TOOK THE SAFE OUT AND TRANSPORTED IT, PER CART, A DISTANCE OF 9 MILES, where they left it for some time buried in the sand and gravel of a river bed.

THEY AFTERWARDS WORKED 17 (SEVENTEEN) DAYS ON THE SAFE, exhausting all ordinary devices of safe opening known in this country trying to open it, but beyond succeeding in breaking off the hinges and the handle and severely battering the outside of the safe and the lock, they FAILED UTTERLY in getting at the contents of the safe.

The safe was eventually found, and it took skilled mechanics a whole day to straighten out the key-hole, after which, by turning the bolts with the aid of a strong pair of pliers (the handle having been knocked off), the contents of the safe were found in perfect order.

Yours faithfully,

. . . .

The Chatwood Safe Book containing full details of the various Models, together with many excellent illustrations, will be sent gratis and post free to any address on application.

THE CHATWOOD SAFE

THE CHATWOOD SAFE CO. Ltd.
Bankers' Engineers.
Head Offices and Works : BOLTON, England.

LONDON   MANCHESTER   GLASGOW
59 Leadenhall St.   Royal Exchange   12 Gracealarge Tce. Crosshead

Above left: A. C. Hobbs, the man who picked the Bramah Lock, demonstrating how he did it

Above right: The Corliss safe, its shell cast in a single piece of manganese steel, was for a generation the most effective of safes

Left: Glum and incompetent, these bungling burglars served the Chatwood publicity department well

Left: The effect of a well-placed charge: from this safe in Hatton Garden thieves took jewels worth £7,000 in 1926, probably equivalent to £150,000 today
(Courtesy The Hulton-Deutsch Collection)

Right: The extraordinary depth and complexity of a vault door made plain: the elaborate system operated from what looks like a ship's wheel is no part of the lockwork, but serves to fit the door snugly into its aperture

Below: This device from 1936, when triggered by an alarm system, would laboriously dial the number of the local police station, then play a 78-rpm record announcing the break-in

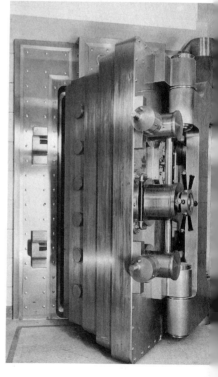

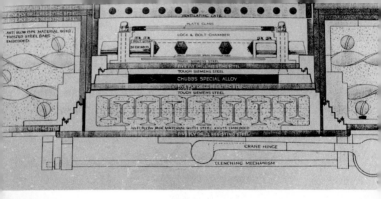

Above: Within the fourteen-inch thickness of a vault door are hidden layers`, each designed to defeat a specific method of attack

Centre: With four key locks and two combinations, this Chubb safe was apparently commissioned for the valuables of a royal household. It was common to use a glass plate on the inner face of a door, to place all the intricacy of the lockwork on show to the owner

Foot: A factory technician demonstrates the use of tools recovered from thieves: at the bottom of the safe is a frame used to hold a ratcheted drill, while into the holes thus made a powerful lever such as the one a the top of the safe could be bolted. The man can easily exer enough pressure on the top left-hand corner of the safe door to deform it, and then perhaps employ the wedges which lie or the floor about him

Right: For the very largest vault doors, circular doors and doorways can be machined much more easily and accurately. In the very centre of the door can be seen three of the four dials of a time lock

Left: Here a policeman is showing how the use of a core drill, which removed a circular plate from the side of the safe, allowed the thieves simply to reach in and take their loot

Right: Here is the result of peeling a safe. Each thin layer was cut then tugged until the entire top of the safe lay open

QUARRYING EXPLOSIVES.

Right: The faithful friends of British safecrackers – the fuses, the detonators, and the rolls of explosive used in quarries

Left: This shot from *Time Lock*, made in 1957, is remarkable for showing one of the more accurate studio-built safe doors, and for disguising the very young Sean Connery so effectively behind goggles (*Courtesy British Film Institute*)

Below: In 1965 thieves fired twenty-two rounds from an anti-tank gun to breach a vault; for the 1974 film *Thunderbolt and Lightfoot*, Clint Eastwood borrowed the method, but the cinema's favourite gunslinger was through the wall with just three well-placed shots (*Courtesy British Film Institute*)

couple of hours, couple of days, take your time. It wasn't hard in those days to find the number of roundsmen, the places you could go and take good money. Obviously the bonus would be if you could find someone who did it on a monthly basis – if you could find that out, and work it nicely, then you was on to a good earner then. Some tallymen . . . post offices didn't seem to realize the value of postage stamps, insurance stamps, postal orders, and the amount of cash they used to carry.

On the subject of armed robbery: It's not a nice world out there at the moment, unfortunately. We never went in for confrontation – in the whole time in the whole three-and-a-half, four years that I did it – I think we only ever got hold of two people that stumbled in. It was a matter of just holding them down, and saying, 'Just be very quiet. We're leaving now,' and just tap them on the arm, and get out. My favourite tactic . . . was to smile at them, and I've seen people actually turn their backs: 'I can't see nothing, I'm not listening!'

On carrying weapons: Never, ever tooled up. It was not on, it added to what you was going to get. The most you could get done, if you could bury your gelly and dets, all you got done was office-breaking. If you got caught with the gelly and dets, you were on a different charge, if you got caught with a tool then it was even bigger, and the old coppers would give a splosh anyway [hit anyone caught with weapons], and I think they were justified.

On getting in: We used to plan our entries quite meticulously. I loved the rain – I was a great man for going in horrible, nasty horrible weather – I loved the noise of rain because that covered up nearly every sound you heard. Loved rainy nights, loved fairly dark places – not industrial estates: too open, too well lit, too many police snooping around. We got in this place – we blew it – and all we caught for [understood] was the little lock was still jammed. We come, we really got the hump. [In fact, the lock was not jammed – the safe had a relocking device, the first the team had encountered. They soon spotted the problem and came up with a solution.] Lo and behold, the next weekend there was another one. Blew it – the lock disappeared inside. So that made me take it out – we took it with us. This was a bakery, we brought our van in. It weighed about three-and-a-half, four hundredweight . . . We took it up to an engineering yard, and really had just all the time in the world to attack it. Took the back off, got inside to the box, got the box off, then sawed the lock. Cleaned all the inside out – I think there was about two-and-a-half grand in it – then looked inside the lock and could see where the little thing had dropped in. So once we lifted it up, put it back on its base, and it was just a matter of looking for something, and we got a [tool] and that was the perfect length. So the next one we blew, we cracked the back open, put it in, turned it and caught the lever up and opened the door. Very simple, very very simple.

We had a good run on that . . . we used to go, 'Oh great!' Post offices liked them, every Co-op had one. 'Oh great, we're away.'

He found that simple pressure on the handle would throw the lock before the relockers could operate: If you had a strong tension on the handle, when the thing went before the lever could drop in, it would pull past it . . .

On the problems of handling explosive: The other thing was when you got the Polar Ammon on your fingers it gave you the most incredible headaches – we didn't realize this. It's very hard to put it in wearing gloves and you know that if it goes off there's going to be nothing there they can actually get a good fingerprint off. The det's going to be fragmented, but you can actually wipe that and put that in after. But when you're putting it in, if you picked your nose or rubbed your nose . . . Me and the other guys, we used to handle it, we used to perhaps mould, we'd get these headaches, and it wasn't until we started really thinking about it . . . we washed our hands. At first we thought it was the adrenaline, the excitement – it was frightful.

On the threat from alarms: The other thing is, there's a psychological thing about peters – they see this safe, especially concrete all embedded in . . . you get in these other places where they're more security conscious, you look around and you know it's alarmed up, so you're very careful how you get through these doors and these walls and then when you find this safe, or a wooden cupboard – especially if it's got a key in the door – you open it up and the alarm goes off. It was a fatal error – if you saw a key in a door you never opened that door – that was your tempter.

Once we worked out what the system was in there, we would then study it, and we know that if we could get in there we've got all the time in the world – we know there's no night visits – there is no rush. Once we got in if we knew it was belled up we would take our time and find out all the exterior bells – that was the important thing, that was only going to alert local people.

Then, once we'd located where the bells were, what we used to do [was] find out where the switchboard was. If there was one alarm – it would say ALARM – we'd have that one out so you'd straighten that. [For a criminal, to 'straighten' is always to remove an obstacle – so that a bribed watchman, for instance, is straightened rather than bent, a neat reversal of meaning. The details Jesswell gave of just how he tackled that alarm are rather too precise for publication, but he went on to describe the automatic dialling alarm.] You'd hear the little record player go: 'This is such-and-such a company . . .' Once that had gone, we used to get near an exit, or probably we'd actually leave and just run outside for about half an hour, to see if there was another telephone line. I didn't like that – didn't like going out and coming back in – then if no bells had gone, we'd take our time and work through it, work on the safe in your own good time.

What was the mood during a raid? When the adrenalin's pumping . . . if I said to do something, I wanted it done, I didn't want an argument. I found that . . . you get very snappy, very terse . . . if they start wasting time looking at other things, and wandering off, I'd get the hump. I want to get it done, get it all completed. Then once you've got what you've gone in for, then you've still got a bit of time, then you can take your time and have a look around, start looking for your little prizes, little things you want to take with you. One of our guys was very impetuous – I remember we did a job up in the Midlands, and we was opening up the basement entry, it was fairly isolated – we were removing this grille; it takes a bit of time, because you've got to get in to get to the alarm. I said to him, 'Take your time.' 'Nah, nah, it's all right.' 'No, take your time,' and all of a sudden – WHAH – off this thing screamed. So I tell him, 'Better go.' You know you've got a few minutes, you don't panic. The first bell, when it first goes, it frightens the life out of you. It really sounds like the whole world is ringing. Don't let anyone tell you that, 'Oh, you know, it does sound,' but it is the dead of night, and that thing clanging away – Oh my God.

Notwithstanding you're on an estate and the nearest person is quite a while away, the idea is to frighten you, and it really does. But we don't know if there is an alarm off to the station. If you're inside, you know what they've got, but when you're outside when the alarm goes, don't ever assume that's the only thing, up there, that bell. If you do that, you'll get nicked. If the bell went off before we went in, or as we were getting in, we'd leave it. Cause it would just look like a normal breaking and entering, and we could then go back another time, a few months later, with a bit of care.

So, anyway, as we run, we stumbled into a herd of cows, which is the most frightening thing I could ever think of . . . Suddenly you fall flat on a cow, and it's a big lump, and you get this warm . . . and it moves! You can't see and you've slammed into something. You can't see them, they can't see you. Oh, I tell you something – I just, I don't know what happened, I mean it's just a complete blur from that point . . . these things moved . . . aargh!

On setting off the charge: The last one we did, I literally stood – if that's the safe there, I stood here [he showed how he stood just eight feet away] – it was the loudest one ever, my ears went for a long time – it was how confident you got in your packing – the less explosive you used and the better packing the more flash you could hide and the more deadening sound overall, you could get fairly close.

On another job, in Nottingham: We took it in a field, put it on its back, which was a good way of blowing them, putting them on their back, because that way when you put the stuff in the door, it didn't actually drop down. That was when we started using the condoms, [to retain the explosive where it had been inserted, close to the lock] but this way you could just pack it in, pack a nice bit around the outside, put your det in. We really moved quite a bit away . . . it was a moonlit night, and as it blew, everything blew up – 'The door's come off!' [throwing his hand up, to show how the door had disappeared high into the sky, had not yet landed, and how the thieves realized it might drop on them] – and we're all sitting there. 'Fucking hell, no!' But with four of you scattered around you've got to be a bit unlucky to catch one of them. That was quite a memorable time.

How was a raid organized? The first thing you always did was have several escape routes, not just leave the door open, but subtle ones so that you've got a chance so that if you can't get back you've got another route out.

There was only two of us that used to do the main work on the peter; the other two were like the backup . . . if you need a lot of help to get it up in the van; you always need lookouts – it may have been boring, but they weren't really on offer, they wasn't really getting involved in it . . . Over the three years we had a couple of changes – a couple of the original ones fell out because – didn't like their style, they'd be indulging in big flash American cars, spending all their money, and talking a little too much about it, and that was never my style.

On the problems of running a good team: Not one of us got nicked at any time, but after they left they got caught on silly things – the impetuous one, he left after the herd of cows; he wanted to be a leader, and I wouldn't let him because there could only be one real leader on the firm, and he went back to drumming [household burglary]. He was a drinker and a club man. Another thing that turned me off was we went to meet his father in a pub and he was there with a few of his cronies and he announces, 'Here's my son, he's a top safeblower.' I could not believe he said it, and that was the very last time . . . I haven't really seen any of them since we parted. I don't keep close to any of them, except one who came on the last two or three jobs, a very very close friend of mine.

I grew up with him. My brain told me stay away . . . because it's all very well the villains get together and all talk about the old times . . . I'm a bit of a loner. I did love it, I absolutely loved it . . . A couple of big ones got on television, but the best one was we actually broke into one of Her Majesty's establishments [he set up a raid in which the payroll of a prison was stolen] – that was absolutely . . . thoroughly enjoyed it, and to get away with all the screws' money . . . absolutely loved that.

The end of the game, when his wife asked him to give up the work: Then one day, I was going out with my current wife – I was married before – and word came round [an invitation to join in a job], when I used to go out every weekend, and she said, 'Do us a favour, knock it on the head.' And here was another challenge, [to get into a legitimate business] and I love a challenge. I never went back to grafting after that.

I think the writing was on the wall, because over the years we'd had such a terrific run, and we got complacent – sheer fluke, absolute fluke . . .

The gang was simply stopped at night in a van, after failing to recognize a police car coming up behind them. One of them had a dusty mark on his face from the packing they had placed around the safe, which aroused suspicion. A discarded detonator was found, they were all arrested, and one made a statement which incriminated them. Jesswell served three years.

13

Muscle Power, Motor Power

The simplest way to open an early safe was to hit it with a hammer. The sheets of iron which made up the top, back and sides were thin enough to deform after a few heavy blows, and pull away from the rivets which held them in place. Then a muscular pull on a lever long enough and strong enough would peel away one face of the box far enough for an outstretched hand to reach the contents. There were a very few improvements in technique – wedges were employed to help in peeling off the iron, and the thoughtful thief would use a hammer with a head of copper or lead to reduce the noise he made during the attack. If this all seemed too complicated, many a safebreaker used an axe: sections of soft metal could be chopped out, so long as the thief ignored or protected himself against the dangers of working past the sharp and protruding edges of the gashes.

For cheap safes, the same methods have worked well ever since, and quite recently I saw the result of an attack by young teenagers on an ancient youth club safe – they had successfully reinvented for themselves the style of an 1830s burglar. With customary criminal ingenuity, levers for breaking safes have been made from half-shafts of motor cars, extended with lengths of scaffolding poles; the sources have changed, but the tools would have been familiar a century ago.

It was one of the earliest moves in the security arms race for manufacturers to strengthen their boxes against primitive assault. The easiest way was to retain the same construction but to use thicker metal for the frame and for the covering. The iron was still soft and penetrable but it now took more force, more noise, and more time to break, and the extra weight made it much more difficult for thieves to remove the safe. These were useful achievements and if the safeowner took the precaution of leaving his safe where it might be seen by passing police patrols, he could be confident of finding his cash and stock intact in the morning. It was the Cornhill case which brought this comfortable age to a close.

The Cornhill burglars attacked the shell of the safe, but force was sometimes the simplest way to attack just the lock, which in many early safes was riveted to the inside of a simple sheet-metal door. A hole could be drilled over the lock, and a stout rod pushed in: then a couple of blows on the end of the rod with a heavy hammer would part the lock from the door, leaving the handle free to turn and withdraw the bolts. A version of this attack, used on combination safes, is 'punching the can', in which the aim is simply to smash the lock inward, to disconnect it from the locking bar. To accomplish this the safebreaker would first drop the safe onto its back and knock off the dial of the combination lock with a heavy hammer. Using a long, hard spike or punch the burglar would then hit the exposed spindle until he heard the lockwork drop. If he had been successful, a swift turn of the handle would open the door.

'Punching a can' was primitive but useful, requiring little equipment or expertise. This attack only works on the most elementary safes, but to this day is the first method that an American working criminal would try. It has served to provide many a freshly-discharged prisoner with his first small stake for a new start. A very common target has been a garage, where all the tools would be conveniently to hand.

Strengthened lock mountings resist most blows, but

were overcome by the ingenuity of criminal toolmakers in the 1850s who sold small devices which brought a screw to bear, turned by a long lever to give a steadily rising pressure. The mechanical advantage offered by this 'jack-in-the-box' and its copies made the job easier and quieter, but it was one of the specialized criminal tools known as 'unlawful', and a thief caught in possession of one could be arrested and convicted.

British burglars in Victorian times divided their tools and equipment into two categories, the 'lawful' and the 'unlawful'. The first type were portable tools, preferably conventional and easily explained away; not too obvious to carry about and comparatively noiseless on the job. The 'unlawfuls' included, apart from the specialist tools, bulky items such as elaborate drilling apparatus which often had to be dismantled and assembled on site, and the grossly heavy tools which were impossible to conceal, such as large sledgehammers, and long crowbars made in a single piece.

Even when criminal technology had advanced enormously to include intricate tools and powerful explosives, a safeman needed to take along his 'peter cane', the lever that would finish the job of wrenching open a jammed door or a distorted shell. It seems almost as if the work of a nineteenth-century policeman was made easier by the extraordinary bulk and weight of a working burglar's equipment. A thief should have been easily identifiable by his stooped shoulders and permanent expression of pain. Pity poor Cully Lockwood, who is remembered only because in 1873 he had a little difficulty explaining away the 108 pieces in his burglary outfit, or the American twenty years later whose equipment included:

> . . . the pusher, for opening combination locks, extremely rare and expensive. The jimmies included a sectional one,

five feet long, in three joints, and a smaller one sixteen inches long. There was a bellows worked by the feet, a lot of half-inch rubber hose and seven tin tubes for powder to be forced through in blowing open safes. This powder, contained in two flasks and a bottle, was very fine and well-adapted to the work. Besides this explosive were several pounds of nitroglycerine and atlas powder, in cartridges, so arranged as to be exploded by electricity if desired.

There were three coils of waterproof fuse, a fur muff, intended to deaden sound, and a gossamer to hide rays of light, two pocket dark lanterns, a thin spatula to work window fastenings, an adjustable wrench, a bit-stock, fifty-eight drills of silver steel, and thirty-four steel wedges, ranging from three-quarters of an inch to four inches in length. For coercion and defence there were four new-pattern revolvers and two pairs of Bean's improved handcuffs.

Maps, whisky and a machine for cutting out door locks completed this vast kit.

The toolmakers who provided thieves with their equipment didn't just adapt and strengthen conventional tools. For a good price they also sold very specialized items of equipment. The jack-in-the-box was one of the first, but when combination locks were first introduced, and none of the established methods would work, these underworld craftsmen provided the means for an indirect attack. In the 'drag' they invented a screw device which ignored the lock, but applied pressure to the walls of the safe and distorted them so that the ends of the lock bolts were drawn free of their sockets. Safemakers learned to increase the strength and rigidity of doors, but some also made greater use of a feature first intended to stop wedging and levering – they gave each bolt a hooked end to engage in the frame which was too strong for the drag to dislodge.

If the hammer and lever were the crudest tools, the

early drill was little better. Before safes, before safecracking, burglars had developed a variety of drilling methods for use in housebreaking. With a simple chest brace a burglar would cut a hole through which he could poke a cord or stick to snag a bolt and draw it, or he might take along a larger rig with a cutter that traced a circle around the central bit. A disc could thus be removed from a door panel and leave a hole big enough for an arm, even a person, to pass through. With these familiar pieces already in their toolkits, working burglars tried them on the new strongboxes, but they performed poorly.

It became clear very quickly that it was beyond the strength of a man to hold his drill bit against a thick metal door with enough pressure to penetrate, and a variety of devices were designed to brace the drill against the floor or the safe itself. To increase the pressure which could be applied, the bit was attached to the end of a rod carrying a fine thread, which gave greater leverage to the arm which turned the drill. Now the greatest limitation on drilling was the hardness of the bit. By the middle of the nineteenth century, steel was in common use, but was expensive, and lacked the later, more exotic ingredients which would help to overcome the essential problem of making a bit hard enough to cut effectively, yet not so brittle as to shatter under stress. Even today apprentices in many trades are taught how to re-harden and re-sharpen worn and broken bits, and many a burglar would take along with him the means of reconditioning his tools as the job progressed, making sure that he had with him as large a supply of bits as he could sensibly carry, for bits notoriously break at a point which leaves just too small a stump to be useful.

Early burglars used their drills in a variety of ways but usually to provide a first purchase for other tools. A line of holes could be used to allow the blade of a canopener to enter, or rob a panel of its strength and allow simple ripping to proceed. Holes could be clustered over a lock to weaken it; a stubborn rivet close to a corner could be drilled out to help in peeling off a side. This was as much as could be achieved, and measures which hardened the metal could repel all these attacks. George Price, an English safemaker, was one of the first to case-harden his safes, and he made great advertising capital out of the 'largest burglar's machine ever constructed for the purpose of opening iron safes' – a mighty drilling rig over four feet long, which had required seven men to carry it to the job on which it was found abandoned. Price organized a public test of the drill against his own safe, and although 'practical mechanics . . . applied drill after drill of the hardest metal . . . not one of them would bite, and to all appearance the onlookers seemed perfectly satisfied as to the impregnability of the safe.'

Other manufacturers promoted rival approaches which they claimed would resist drilling. Locks were defended by layers and plates intended to snap the drill bit, grind it down, or deflect it. One maker inserted an iron sheet dotted with harder studs which would turn aside, then snap off the drill; another tried inserting into the door a layer of hardened discs, which were left free to revolve so that a drill could gain no purchase. Much simpler, just as effective, and closer to modern practice was to attach a case-hardened plate behind the keyhole. It seems to have been one of those phases in technological history when it was as important to steer around a competitor's patents as to turn out a rational product.

Harder cases could be beaten by harder drills. Diamond was long known to be capable of cutting through anything a thief might encounter, and some successful safecrackers had the money needed to equip themselves with diamond-tipped bits. The efficiency of the cutting action depended not just on the hardness of the material but how rapidly the drill could be made to turn; at high speeds the tiny fragments of stone needed to be cemented firmly to the bit and the early drills were rarely reliable.

The demand from industry for a means to work the new harder alloy steels led to the invention at the end of the nineteenth century of a drill bit which could cut at five times the speed of the best tool-steel, using an alloy containing a moderate amount of carbon, some chromium and a substantial amount of tungsten. The tungsten carbide within this alloy allowed the bit to be used even when it was red hot. Later, as bonding techniques improved, it became more common to employ the carbide itself as minute chippings, along with a little cobalt, and such bits have found a place in the household toolbox as the common masonry drill. Do-it-yourselfers should not plan for a life of crime: safemakers have developed materials to resist even these bits.

Drilling was often used not as a means to open the safe directly, but to allow explosive to be introduced. Langdon Moore, a very successful American safecracker of Victorian times, designed a very powerful rig, a back brace with extension legs. The whole device was bolted to the floor, and adjusted to the height of the lock dial; into the head piece of the rig was mounted a quarter-inch diamond-pointed drill. In half an hour or so, this drill would make a hole right through two inches of solid chilled steel and the lock casing, so that with a small bellows Moore could blow through a charge of gunpowder. It was the diamond bit which made Moore's machine a winner.

Quiet precision drilling is the most impressive but the rarest form of safecracking. It is quick, unobtrusive and carries no risk of damaging the safe contents, but demands accurate technical knowledge and practical skill. The task is to place a drill bit where it will make a hole directly into the mechanism of the lock, so that the levers or dials of the lock can be directly manipulated. The room for error is very small indeed: in 1887 burglars foiled in a raid in north London had 'by the aid of a parallel rule . . . gauged the position of the lock and bored the hole but an eighth of an inch out of a direct line with the vital part of the lock.'

Expertise in the mechanical tasks was worthless without a precise guide to a safe's lockwork, and even a very busy thief could not hope to calculate for himself the vulnerable points of every safe that he might encounter. There was always a ready market for bulletins such as this sheet of notes taken from a burglar named Timothy Kelly who was sentenced to two years' hard labour at the Old Bailey in June 1931.

Through the mark on the dial ring drill a 5/16″ or 3/8″ hole at an angle of about 25 to 30 degrees towards the dial spindle. This should bring the hole just inside the lock casing and at the top of the tumbler wheels. Through this hole pick up the tumblers 'by sight if possible', beginning with the furtherest one in and working to the front, keeping track of the combination numbers. Now make a pencil mark on the ring exactly one quarter turn to the left and work out the combination to this line, if you were careful to keep the numbers correct through the hole you should have no trouble opening the safe, working the combination a degree or two on each side of the pencil mark often helps to do the trick. You can also drill a 1/2″ hole to the left centre of the dial and a 30 degree angle towards the spindle shaft and pick up the tumblers from this position or punch off the lock back and the bolt part far enough to miss the spindle wheel. The safe will now open.

Kelly was not the author of this list, but a customer who had bought from a knowledgeable colleague a burglar's guidebook to assist him in his work. A total of eighteen current makes of safe were listed, apparently all of American manufacture, so it may be that the original list had travelled across the Atlantic. The final note on the list was that 'other dimentions [sic] will be added to this list from time to time'. The publisher plainly had faithful subscribers to his correspondence course.

For respectable locksmiths, precision drilling is always the first choice as a method of opening the accidentally locked safe. It causes so little external damage that if the hole made can be concealed, the safe may be refurbished and reused. The locksmith has the benefit of regular study of the position and arrangement of locks within safe doors, is trained and experienced in the manual techniques, and even for unfamiliar safes can call upon published details circulated only with great care among recognized and trustworthy craftsmen. Kelly had bought a substantial list, but it is tiny when compared with the material available to master-locksmiths – charts, lists, and paper templates which can be applied to the face of the door to establish very precisely the point at which the drill should be applied.

Even having made a well-placed hole, and with a clear line of sight into the lock, the burglar may be defeated simply because he cannot make sense of what he sees, and has not learned the art of manipulation. I sat with a skilled locksmith as he opened safes for which no key was available – he was able to open several in the course of a morning without difficulty, but when he invited me to peer into the small holes he created, I could make out nothing but a succession of metal edges, steel and brass, some scarred by the drill – I could see what he could see, but even with a running commentary it was very tricky to interpret what I saw. To be able to look within the lock is only a part of the task: once a tool is placed in the hole, that line of sight is blocked, and the opener has to be able to make sense of the messages transmitted through the fingertips.

My guide was able to work through a succession of levers, shining a pen torch into the holes, then retaining an image of what he had seen in his mind, he moved each lever with a thin flat-bladed screwdriver, until he had set all to his satisfaction, and then with the fine flourish of a conjuror he could turn the handle and throw wide the door. As these safes were ultimately to be resold, and because it was a measure of his professional skill to operate within the smallest of holes, he had been at pains to use the slimmest possible drill, but even a hole twice the size would have been of little use without his knowledge and practised expertise.

All this was a demonstration of the conventional approach through the front face of the door, but in the right circumstances it is even possible to manipulate a combination lock by drilling through the back of the safe. One modern keysmith – he was proud of the extra professional status given to the men who make keys rather than locks – told me how he had drilled from the rear of a safe, and poked a long thin rod past the money on the shelf inside, to allow him to reach the lock on the inner face of the door. It had been a demanding job, and I was intrigued later to find that a very similar approach had been used criminally sixty years before. Long before the days of convenient battery-powered torches one old-time safecracker used to take a length of wick stripped from a candle and bind it to a thin wire which was poked through a hole drilled in the back of the safe. By the light of the wick the safeman could see and find the hole in the back of the door which was used in resetting the combination – he pushed a long wire into this hole to manipulate the lock while a confederate at the front of the safe turned the dial, following instructions until the lock was unfastened.

Such a level of skill was always rare, and where the method had more than occasional success, it was often because the safe design was flawed. A fully-armoured vault door should resist drilling well enough to prevent manipulation of the works of a lock, but in some smaller American bank branches a less secure door, made of thinner steel filled with concrete, was once tried. The error of saving money in this way was revealed when one burglar opened a door within thirty-three minutes by first drilling a half-inch hole, and then, 'With mirrors, probes and a tiny side light (called a nasopharyngeoscope) [he] expertly felt the intricate way through the next few steps of the operation.'

The ordinary defence against a drill attack is invisible and passive, and requires no priming or other action on the part of the safeowner. Like most efficient and reliable machinery it is simple: covering the area in front of the lock, and impossible to avoid if the drill is intended to reach the lockwork, is a pane of glass. Attached to the glass is a wire cable which holds back extra bolts against spring pressure. A drill must break the glass, releasing the bolts, and the burglar then has the much more demanding task of working out how to defeat a system which he cannot see or reach.

The use of internal defences such as extra toughened layers and relocking devices does not make the use of precision drilling impossible, but now several holes will have to be made to break into a good safe, each hole giving access to a particular part of the locking system. Legitimate locksmiths know how to do this, with the aid of manuals and special tools, but it is beyond any ordinary burglar's capabilities; in fact, the use of such methods nowadays would immediately throw suspicion on qualified craftsmen in the neighbourhood.

Safecracking with small drills was never truly popular or successful, but there was a short triumphant season for a drill which required power but no finesse – the core drill. Like the thermic lance and the disc cutter, the core drill is a recruit from the building industry, designed to make large bore holes through rock or concrete. The drill bit is a tube an inch to nine inches across, with diamond or carbon chips embedded around the rim like salt around the edge of a glass of tequila. This tube is attached to an electric drill and spun at high speed, generating so much heat that a water cooling system has to be used.

The core drill has been described as the ultimate burglar tool: safe, quick and sure. Most drills have been used only in the first stages of a safe attack, to make way for tools or explosives, but used on its own the core drill removes enough of the vault wall or safe casing to leave a hole large enough for a hand and arm, or even a person, to pass through. The principle is simple, and the cutting speed of the core drill is extraordinary when compared with the rate at which other methods progress, but every minute saved in the course of the raid itself requires hours spent in surveillance and preparation before ever the team sets out.

This has made the core drill the tool of experienced and skilled safemen with an important haul in mind. The equipment is heavy and bulky to store and carry; it draws a great deal of electric current and it must be connected to a water supply. Each of these factors must be provided for before the raid, and once on the premises the thieves need time to install the drill rig. That cutting tube has to be applied with much greater pressure and for longer than the strength of a man could normally provide, so the thieves must devise a means of bolting down the rig and pushing it tightly against the surface to be penetrated.

One of the best-documented raids to use the device was carried out in 1974 at the Woodland, Washington State branch of the Bank of the West, and gives us examples of how the safecrackers overcame each of these obstacles. During months of preparation the team had travelled to the small town several times, even visiting the bank itself to survey the layout and surroundings. Behind the bank was a yard where trucks belonging to a logging company were taken for repair, and this offered a simple way to take the gear to the raid without being spotted – a company pickup was stolen, loaded with the equipment, and then simply returned to the yard.

The 110-volt American domestic electricity supply could not power the drill, but the thieves had spotted on the roof a source of 220-volt power. While the cables were being rigged, another member of the team was cutting into the pipe which brought cold water to the ladies' toilet in the bank, and running from it an ordinary green garden hose which would supply the coolant to the drill. The vault was to be attacked from above, so the rig was bolted to drill downwards, and several thick lengths of wood set up as wedges and levers to press home the drill.

The concrete was thirteen inches thick, but the nine-inch bit was capable of cutting through an inch each minute; three holes were drilled, overlapping in a clover-leaf pattern to yield a hole twenty-two inches wide and about a foot high, big enough for one of the team to squirm through head-first while his colleagues clung to his feet.

Almost directly beneath him was the safe which was opened with a gas-oxygen outfit, and around him were shelves on which securities and travellers' cheques were stacked. Burning into the safe was a foul task – the only ventilation to the vault was the hole which the thieves had cut – but the haul came to more than $360,000 in cash. The loot was so bulky and heavy (including cash weighing more than 700 lbs) that the torch man decided to leave through the vault door, and since he could not deactivate the timelock he simply cut through the main locking bolt. Neither he, nor any of his accomplices, has ever been caught.

The tools of mechanical safecracking are rarely different in kind from those used in basic carpentry – hammers, chisels, drills and screw-driven contraptions like the drag which use the same principles as a vice. Cutting and sawing have also been tried, most recently with attempts using disc cutters of the kind that will slice through masonry. Just as there have been fashions in safecracking method which have changed over time, so there have been national and continental favourites. In the United States explosives lost popularity before the British gave them up; on the continent of Europe preference was given to techniques for cutting into a safe, and much ingenuity was applied to making better, faster, more effective apparatus. At about the time that the very first petrol-driven car took to the road, French crooks used the internal combustion engine to power a safe-cutting saw.

This continental preference for cutting helped the Australian police in the 1920s when they had to deal with a series of safe burglaries which were plainly the work of a new gang. Most local cracksmen of the time were using fuses and gelignite, and just a few the oxyacetylene torch, but during the latest thefts no explosives had been used, and the safes carried no sign of having been heated. Something had cut through the chilled steel doors of the safes leaving marks which looked just as if they had been made with a giant tinopener, but neither the police nor any of the experts summoned from safemaking companies could suggest where and how such a blade might have been made, or how the means of applying such enormous pressure to it had been created.

The broad guess was made that a new team had arrived from Europe but the investigation made no progress until, near one of the safes, a scrap of fabric was found which was identified as having come from Italy, but not through any known importer. A watch was kept on criminals in the Italian community, and eventually an informant who was too scared to name them, or even to point them out, tipped off the police that there were three new men in town worth watching, and named a restaurant in which they regularly ate. Once the three men had been spotted a routine of very close surveillance began. Just once did they show any signs of shiftiness, meandering across town before going into a factory which one of them had been seen to visit occasionally, and this time the detective who was following crept close enough to be able to see through a small crack into a basement room.

What he saw was at first baffling. Two men he had not seen before were fixing a pair of blades to the spokes of a large wheel, then the man who had seemed to be the leader of the group took the wheel, fixed it to the face of a thick sheet of steel, and attached a smaller control wheel bearing a lever. Then the purpose of the rig became clear – as the leader turned the wheel, the blades cut a sharp groove in the steel. But he seemed to be dissatisfied, and the blades were removed for further work.

For the next two weeks the police were able to watch test and re-test as the blades were improved, until at last a satisfactory hole in the plate had been made. By day, detectives learned that the leader had rented a small office on Castlereagh Street. He made little use of it, receiving neither mail nor messages there, but police interest quickened when they saw that the office was directly above the banking hall of the Union Bank.

When the gang broke through into the bank a few nights later the police were able to seize them and their cutting machine: fully assembled, it included bolt cutters with handles nearly four feet long to provide the necessary leverage, and a drill to bore into the safe so that the clamps could be fitted. Police testers were astonished when the cutters proved capable of slicing through two inches of chilled steel in less than thirty minutes.

Similar cutters have been invented again and again by men who studied the problems of safe-cutting, and each fresh machine has had to be tested and refined. A Scot living in London had gained a reputation as a fine keyman, with many satisfied clients, when he had a brainwave, and began work on his own version of a gadget which would act like a powerful set of compasses to cut a disc from the back of a safe. So that he could carry out experiments at home he bought a second-hand safe, and invited interested thieves to a display of the clean hole which he had made after just an hour's labour.

Visitors were horrified that he had such incriminating evidence in his own home, and persuaded him to get rid of the box, but they were impressed by the machine. All of them wanted to buy or hire it, but for the first time the inventor insisted that he would entrust his handiwork to nobody – he must come on jobs himself. Time after time the gadget succeeded, and his clients were very pleased, but the keymaker was a man of strong views and short temper; one Sunday he began a political punchup at Speakers' Corner and was arrested. When two young police officers visited his home they were puzzled to find under the bed a circular, cleanly-cut piece of steel, so they took it back to the police station. That was enough to start an investigation which led in the end to a seven-year stretch for the Scot.

There was a less punitive end to the story of two amateurs of the 1950s who took the development of cutting gear still further by adding a little automation. Two young men from Hertfordshire went together to watch the French thriller film *Rififi*, and as precision engineers were intrigued to see the device used by the thieves to open a safe. Talking it over, they came to the conclusion that with their skills they could do better: they could design and construct a much more efficient safe-cutting machine. Christmas was close, and they were broke. The late-night idea, the technical challenge, the what-if, turned into a methodical plan.

A first prototype didn't cut as quickly as they wanted, and was discarded into a canal, but the performance of the second version powered by a small motor was extra-ordinary. It was capable of cutting a five-inch circular hole through most safe doors in just half an hour; just as impressively it needed only the right lubricant to carry out the task in silence. The amateur thieves carried out just two raids, on Inland Revenue and electricity board offices. The cutter went to work with great efficiency: it had a self-tapping action, and once switched on could continue to cut without adjustment. Tension can bring on sudden lethargy, and once the machine was installed and quietly running the burglars had so little to do that they dozed off. During the second burglary they were inter-rupted and fled, leaving the machine behind.

On it was a single fingerprint, enough for the thieves to be traced and convicted, but the story of their trial and sentence tells us how seriously the threat of their inven-tion was taken. The first version was recovered and examined, but neither model was ever exhibited in a courtroom where the design might be revealed. The authorities had become very nervous indeed about the capabilities of the device and saw great danger even in imprisoning the thieves, in case they let slip the secret of their invention. The burglars might normally have expected to serve years inside, but when they gave lifetime undertakings never to disclose their method, the police spoke up for them at the trial, with the remarkable result that both men were conditionally discharged, left the court and returned quietly to their respectable lives.

Physical attack was the commonest method for beginners and the lowest grade of safecracker, but there were times when hammering and cutting had advantages and would be used by safemen who were perfectly skilled in other methods. On the right safe, cutting could be just as quick as explosives, given the time needed to prepare a charge and check for patrols and passers-by who might overhear. Slow hammering and drilling were always more controllable than any method which might burn the goods, and it was often worthwhile to take a safe away for a prolonged attack rather than risk destroying the loot on site. The main disadvantage was the size of the equipment, which could not be carried with ease like 'gelly and dets', and was hard to discard in an emergency. If they were not thrown away, specialized tools could be the only evidence needed to send thieves away for a long time – there are no obvious legitimate explanations for a mammoth canopener.

The best safecrackers were versatile enough to keep these basic muscular methods in their repertoire. The proof comes from Herbert Emerson Wilson, the man who claimed to have stolen $16,000,000. He was sure that his greatest single triumph was to defeat the cannonball safe, and to pull off this feat he commissioned a special tool – an axe.

First I applied the tongued flame of my torch to the chalk mark I had made directly around the safe – the big end of my 'egg' as I was mentally calling it. Great care had to be taken, however, for if I were to let the flame get out of hand, the paper money and securities within the safe could be destroyed, burned to a crisp. So I cut only a one-inch groove all the way around the safe. When I had finished, Tony Masino poured cold water on the heated metal. This case-hardened my egg and I was ready for my next movement. Into the burned groove went the edge of the new tool, the hatchet the blacksmith had made for me. Then as Lou swung an eight-pound copper hammer against the hatchet, I methodically followed the groove till we had circled the safe. There was not much sound, since copper against steel makes little noise. With that work completed . . . I took aim with the blacksmith's tool, prayed my hunch was right, hit the groove at the top of the safe only one sharp blow, just one . . . The haul came to a hundred and seventy thousand dollars!

Never a modest man, Wilson claimed that this was the only time that a cannonball was cracked. In fact he had a rival, who adopted the cruder approach of making a hole, pouring in water to protect the money inside from heat, then torching the top off. The money was soggy but the safeman was successful.

14

Explosives

Any explosive is portable force. In the palm of one hand a child can carry, and conceal, a charge which can perform in a fraction of a second the long destructive work of a dozen strong men. For the safecracker who learned to use explosives in safety, they were for a long time the quickest, most effective tool.

The earliest explosive was gunpowder. This mixture of charcoal, saltpetre and sulphur was discovered in thirteenth-century China, and remained the principal propellant and explosive for the next six hundred years. The very first gunpowder was very crudely made, and so impure that it would have produced little more than impressive flames, sparks and fumes – decorative and entertaining but little more. By 1325 lessons had been learned; the saltpetre was now purified, the need for thorough mixing was understood, and from that year we have the first picture of a gun. Surrounded by superstition and awe, the manufacture of gunpowder was commonly seen as the work of the devil, for who else could take three ingredients each harmless in itself, and create a devastatingly powerful agent of destruction? Unintended explosions were common during manufacture and from time to time engineers contrived big bangs in the course of sieges, but it was usually regarded as folly to amass a large quantity of powder in one spot. In mines, excavation was still by hand; the highest technology used in quarrying was to drive in wooden wedges, then soak them in water until they expanded enough to split a rock face, and not until seventeenth-century Hungary, we are told, did civilian blasting begin.

As propellant or explosive gunpowder still had short-comings. Apart from the constant danger of unwanted detonation, it was always difficult to achieve consistency when using it. The first enemy was moisture, which reduced the explosive power of the powder and was very readily absorbed, unless the powder was carefully wrapped and stored from powdermill to the moment of use. Various methods of impregnating skins, then paper, with wax and grease were used – some say that one of the causes of the Indian Mutiny was the coating on cartridges issued to Indian troops: these were coated with beef fat, and to load his musket the soldier had to tear open the cartridge with his teeth, an offensive breach of religious dietary laws.

It was important, but difficult, to use a reliably consistent size of powder grain: the size of each particle, and the air retained among the grains, affected the rate at which combustion progressed through the charge. Powdermills would grade the powder as best they could, but the early product was soft, and crumbled easily as it shifted in transit. This damage could be limited by packing the powder firmly, but gunpowder too tightly pressed will blow up. In five centuries of development, the process of manufacture was improved, and by the nineteenth century the means had been found to 'corn' the powder into polished grains which would not absorb moisture nor crumble to dust, and to sell it in many forms, from the finest granules to cubes fully two inches square, each weighing half a pound. The qualities required by the soldier and the miner would now aid the safeblower.

Crude early gunpowder attacks used a charge to blow up the casing – a bag of powder was held against the door, a fuse lit, and with luck the door would be distorted enough to open with a lever. Next the safemen blew powder into the keyhole, but key locks were redesigned, and in the United States the success of the combination lock eliminated this approach. The last method to be of any use was 'puff and rod' – the burglar drilled into the casing of a cast iron or mild steel safe, and used bellows to blow in a charge of gunpowder; the introduction of hardened safes which would resist the drill put an end to this technique in about 1885.

Other forms of explosive had by this time been invented and understood, though not yet commercially developed. They had different characteristics from the familiar gunpowder, and for the first time scientists distinguished between low and high explosive. This is not a measure of power, but of violence of explosion. A more powerful explosive would be one which produced a larger volume of gas for the same amount of solid explosive, but a higher explosive would be one which reacted to produce the gas more quickly. Higher explosives were not always more useful – they might well shatter the barrel of a gun if used as a propellant, and were too easily detonated to be used as filling for shells, since the shock of firing would again place the gunner in more danger than his target.

The new high explosives were said to be the result of a legendary accidental discovery. The story goes that a German chemist called Schonbein – he also discovered ozone – was experimenting in his kitchen with nitric and sulphuric acids. He spilled some of his mixture, and to avoid his wife's wrath he rapidly mopped up with a cotton apron that was to hand, leaving it to dry over a stove. A few minutes later the apron blew up. Guncotton – cellulose nitrate – had been discovered. This turned out to be useful for simple blasting, but in the same year of

1846 an Italian called Sobrero first made a liquid called glyceryl trinitrate – more familiarly if inaccurately known as nitroglycerine.

At first this too seemed like an experimental success but a practical failure. It was the first strictly high explosive, whose effect was caused by a shock wave rather than merely the rapid expansion of gas; however, it was lethally sensitive to shock. Drops falling on the floor went off like pistol shots, and when Sobrero gingerly tapped a minute quantity with a hammer the explosion came close to blowing out his windows. Each experiment seemed to be dangerously unpredictable: heat a sample, and it might burn steadily or blow up without warning; freeze it, and in thawing it could detonate. These random hazards turned out much later to be the effects of tiny impurities, but at the time they ruled the substance out for serious and regular use.

The work of the Nobel family of Sweden turned simple, powerful but dangerous nitroglycerine into dynamite, and eventually established the basis for the range of commercial explosives which predominated until halfway through the next century. Continuing his father's experiments with explosives (despite the fact that his brother, and indirectly his father, had both been killed by them) Alfred Nobel began by solving the problems of reliable detonation using gunpowder, and then mercury fulminate, to apply shock instead of flame to the charges.

He still needed a stable form of explosive, and his breakthrough was to concoct guhr dynamite, in which kieselguhr (diatomaceous earth) was mixed with nitroglycerine to make a solid which was safe to handle. First introduced in 1867, dynamite was immediately useful and popular – Nobel's annual sales were to rise in the next seven years from 10 tons to 3000 tons. Once Nobel had shown that adding inert filler to nitroglycerine worked, other manufacturers made up their own versions which evaded Nobel's patents, and their production would have to be added to these figures to grasp just how much of this first high explosive was now in circulation.

Such commercial competition was a major reason for the invention of gelignite: Nobel needed a new product, and in making Schonbein's guncotton with nitroglycerine he found it. This 'blasting gelatine' gained its name because it looked like a dessert jelly, though chemically it was quite unrelated. Also called gelignite, its formula was modified to give the modern smokeless powders which have almost totally replaced gunpowder as a propellant in cartridges.

To the lay filmgoer, dynamite is dynamite, the stuff that a James Coburn or Lee Van Cleef lights with his cigar and flings casually into the battle with the bad guys. As a safecracking explosive it seems to have been slow to challenge gunpowder, and to have been used only in the crudest ways to demolish safes. A stick or two would be placed on top of, or next to the box, perhaps underneath a layer of whatever blanket or sacking was available to deaden the sound of the explosion. This could be enough to blow apart a simple riveted safe, a quicker alternative to smashing it with a sledgehammer. Once in a while dynamite may have served to replace a jemmy, for the same labour-saving reasons – a gap would be opened at the edge of the door or between the bricks of a vault wall, and a stick of explosive rammed in.

For all that it was inefficient, dynamite had the great advantage of being widely available, and a travelling safecracker could rely on finding a local source when needed. On any major ground clearance site, at a mine or quarry, he could spot a small, badly-secured shack in which the stock was held, or trace a man who knew how to get into one.

As a stick, dynamite was not worth using, but it was eventually a powerful tool for the safecracker. As we have seen, the achievement of the Nobels was to stabilize an effective but dangerously unstable explosive – nitroglycerine – by mixing it with inert compounds which left it safer to handle. American legend has it that a man called Michigan Red was the first safecracker to reverse this process, by separating out the active explosive once more into a form which could be used in his specialized trade. Red probably did no more than place dynamite into a sack and squeeze it. The binding earth stayed in the bag, but through the fabric came the oily nitro, a yellow liquid which would always be known as 'grease' in the trade.

Nitroglycerine was useful to the safecracker because it was so concentrated. There was great explosive power in amounts small enough to be carried and hidden easily, and as a liquid it could penetrate round the door of a safe. But as Sobrero had discovered, nitro needs only a sudden shock to blow up, and the closer the liquid came to purity, the greater the danger in making or carrying it. Squeezing dynamite was an enterprise which became monstrously more dangerous as the process went on – a teaspoonful was enough to wreck a safe, or kill a clumsy refiner. Thieves soon learned to treat nitro with respect, and would carry it in small rubber bags tied at their waists as some protection against impact. Every time this failed to work another safeman would be killed when he slipped, or was jarred riding a train or just walking down the street. In the early days, using inconsistent supplies, safeblowers made many mistakes. Among the unlucky pioneers in the years when yeggs – travelling safecrackers – all seemed to have names from the pages of Damon Runyon were Denver Dude and Seldom Seen. They wanted to open a box in a Tennessee coalyard office, and since it looked tough they prescribed a two-ounce dose. Seldom Seen kept watch outside while Denver Dude lit the fuse, and was killed in a terrific explosion, just one of the twenty or more safecrackers to die before detonation techniques improved.

To find a safer way of extracting nitro, thieves took dynamite back to the kitchen: 'You – and you would just take it in a container of boiling water – you'd take the casings off the dynamite and you'd put it right in, and the heat separated the sawdust, the body – it wasn't a gelatine, but whatever it was . . . that held it together. The heat would just dissolve that and grease – nitro is heavier than water – and it would sink right to the bottom. And you'd pour off the water, and there it is.' This veteran safecracker commented with some regret that his simple process no longer worked – a new law in the 1940s required that a compound be added to dynamite which remained bonded to the nitro even after boiling and other simple attempts at separation.

When it became difficult to extract nitro from dynamite some thieves stole supplies of the raw liquid; one man made off with thirty quarts, enough to tackle about a thousand safes, but the dangers of the getaway and trying to store a stock which would become less stable each day made this a reckless undertaking. The most thoughtful crooks went back to basics and taught themselves how to manufacture nitro from raw materials. They went to libraries and, with an ease that is startling, found details of the processes they needed, and handy sources for their supplies. It turned out that the ingredients and techniques needed to make grease were described in encyclopaedias and schoolbooks, and once the news had spread that a few men had been successful, many others knew that they had only to expend a little effort to be back in business. Information about the ingredients and methods was passed by word of mouth among safecrackers, and the bolder criminals took a chance with no more than the most rudimentary recipe.

All the raw materials are common, and it took some time for the authorities to alert chemical suppliers that they should be cautious when selling the particular combination of chemicals that would be needed. Even then, it was simple enough for the crook to buy from separate sources, or spread his shopping over several days to avoid suspicion. If it seemed that an excuse would be needed, company letterheads could be printed up, or some other subterfuge used. A Canadian who put his story on paper in the 1950s had a cover story that worked: 'I used to pose as a schoolteacher. I would even get them to give me a receipt bill – so I could collect from petty cash, see.'

The process of manufacture was of course very dangerous and required patience and precision: 'Now this glycerine's got to be added. Say you got a five-gallon crock and you have that – you keep going around very slow – if you ever dropped it in there, well, it'd be disastrous – Oh God, I'm telling you! But you have to pour very thin, just the size of a needle . . .'

Only the most painstaking greasemakers produced an explosive which was both potent and consistent, and risks ranged from sudden death to frustrated failure. In the end, although many safemen knew the essentials of manufacture and had taken part in experiments, only a few persisted, and they were able to make money by selling grease to their colleagues.

Premature explosion was not the only hazard of separating or manufacturing nitro: 'During these experiments I began to get very severe headaches, and nothing seemed to do much good,' wrote one British safecracker of the 1950s. Nitro does not have to explode to harm bodies, though controlled doses of nitroglycerine, or glyceryl trinitrate, are used therapeutically to treat angina because they expand blood vessels and so reduce the workload of the heart and relieve chest pain. (Nobel himself was dosed with it, before he died of heart disease in 1896.) It is so easily absorbed into the body that it can be taken as a tablet, an ointment, an aerosol inhaler and even a poultice. Over time, the body learns to tolerate the ill effects, and patients, workers in the explosives industry, and the illicit makers of nitro have all found that after a time the flushes, headaches and slackness of the muscles would pass.

Once made or bought, nitro still leaves the thief with problems. There are no convincing, legitimate excuses for having bottles of nitroglycerine around the house, and a few very pressing reasons for keeping it at a distance. The custom was to 'plant' the store in open country, where it was unlikely to be discovered, and where any explosion would do least harm and draw least attention. It would be recovered just before setting off on a job, and transported with elaborate care. Even the weather could be a hazard: 'If you let it get too cold it gets touchy, and the older it gets the more touchy it gets. Usually we keep it in our pants right inside of our belt against our bodies to let the body temperature take care of it.'

Another safeman described the usual method of buffering the nitro to improve the chances of arriving alive. 'It's like if I had half a bottle, a medicine bottle, and if it was half full of grease I'd fill the other half full of water; now, grease won't mix with water. Now the water goes to the bottom and it cushions it – it keeps it from sloshing around. That's when it is dangerous – when it sloshes around. So, if you had a bottle, say with three ounces, and you use one ounce, you put another ounce of water in it.' This improvised solution of working safecrackers is very similar to the safety precaution taken during manufacture of explosives, in which the unstable nitroglycerine is moved by pumping it as an emulsion in water.

With all its dangers, nitro was the favourite of professional North American safecrackers for two generations; its liquid form made it very versatile, and several standard techniques were devised. The first target for the new explosive was usually the lock – gunpowder had generally been used on locks, and nitro could be used as a straight substitute. To blow out the mechanism of the new and popular combination locks, safemen invented the 'gutshot'; the other name for this technique, the 'spindle shot', tells us where the explosive was introduced:

> Now – this here's your dial. Now you just knock this off. That's just one blow with the hammer, and you tip the whole safe over on its back. Then you take an eyedropper, and the nitro will follow the path down. See – it's lying on its back, actually . . . And the gravity will pull the nitro and this is called the gut box, for very obvious reasons. Cause the – it contains the actual mechanism – the tumblers.
>
> Well, anyway – the gravity takes the grease down the spindle and it can't go any further, and you just pour it in with the dropper. Well, the most that you would use is a dropper and a half. That's all. And then you just lay your detonator right across it – oh, probably you build a little bridge, you know. Just sort of to form a cup, and you just put the cap in there, and boom! You let it go – with an electric detonator, you see.

This safeblower's estimate was that for a common safe it would take just four or five minutes to complete the work, leaving the innards of the lock destroyed, and a hole through which the burglar could reach and manipulate the locking bars to pull back the bolts.

There were some disadvantages, from the burglar's point of view, to the gutshot – for the safe to be tipped over, it had to be free to move, and small enough for the available muscle to shift it, and there had to be space in which to tip it over. Removing the dial might prove tricky or noisy, and the nitro might drain away within the door to explode uselessly or feebly at the wrong point. As a partial solution, it was sometimes possible to push in a rag soaked with grease, to retain enough nitroglycerine close to the mechanism.

This variety of attack, the rag shot, is described by Herbert Wilson:

> I gave the first door of the safe a light 'rag shot'. That is to say, with my money drill I bored a 5/8-inch hole directly above the combination dial. Then I saturated a piece of rag with my Thermol Solution, and with a lead pencil inserted the rag into the hole. Two lengths of wire followed the rag. The hole was then covered with kneaded laundry soap, and I reeled off about twenty feet of wire and touched off the charge with my hand battery. The 'shot' disarranged the tumblers within the 'gut box' (compartment behind the first door of a safe) and by turning the vault handle the bolts were thrown back.

Sometimes the lock would be clear and openable only for a brief moment, before the tumblers settled and jammed once more. Brave safemen, like Harry King's tutor Denver Dick, might stretch a hand across the door to apply pressure on the handle even as the charge went off, not to miss the vital instant, but a more prudent approach was to make a device which would allow the blower to stay out of range of debris. King himself preferred to 'take a stick and then a rubber band on the other end of the stick (a large rubber band from an inner tube) and run it over to the hinge. That puts pressure on the mit [handle]. When the shot goes off it will automatically turn the handle.' Most of these difficulties arose from the fact that nitroglycerine is a liquid. We shall see in later accounts how much simpler to use were the plastic, pliable explosives that were to come.

The safemakers found simple ways to prevent the lock spindle from being hammered in, and to divert poured nitro from the lock. Looking for a more reliable, and less exhausting way to blow safes, an unnamed thief invented the 'jam shot', which used the fluid properties of nitro to produce that most gratifying of results, an explosion which simply opened the door: 'The hinges remain intact. A good safeblowing is with the safe doors swinging properly.'

This simple result demanded considerable care in preparation and execution, and although the method was to become the most popular of all, it was very much a measure of the skill of the safeblower, and the source of his reputation, to be able to carry off the whole exploit with professional adroitness.

The essence of the technique is to pour the thick liquid nitroglycerine into the crack around the edge of the door, allowing it to trickle right around and down until, when it has filled all around the doorway and reaches the bottom of the door, it can be detonated, blowing the door open. To achieve this, the safeblower would prepare a kit containing, in addition to the explosive, a detonator or two, a length of fuse, and a few basic tools. For this new method he also required two vital items – a bar of soap which had been kneaded for about fifteen minutes, then wrapped in wax paper, and a prefolded strip of cellophane.

The safeman would set out his kit on top of the safe, and from it take the strip of cellophane, folded several times until it was no more than half an inch wide. This was pressed into the crack along the top of the door, and then around it the soap was formed into a cup or funnel, fitted snugly so that it would leak no grease onto the face of the door. (Some designs of safe attempted to prevent this entry of nitro by fitting a sealing strip of felt around the door edge; this could be dealt with by pouring in a concentrated acid which would eat away a space to introduce the explosive. Any remaining felt could only help the safeblower, by holding his nitro in just the right place.) Now the cellophane could be carefully withdrawn, and the knocker (detonator) placed into the cup, its fuse dangling three inches or so over the edge of the cup, enough to allow a delay of five seconds. Then the end of the fuse would be split with a razor blade – this cannot be done earlier, as the powder at the core of the fuse might spill, and prevent the fuse from lighting correctly.

Now the safeblower would with great care unscrew the cap of his little bottle of grease . . . 'And this is where the actual art of safeblowing comes in – right now – is when you load this can, you know – this cup,' one anonymous Canadian safeman told researchers. 'You watch to see, like – just how fast this grease is – what you call drinking.'

In the next seconds the nitroglycerine is slowly trickling invisibly around the door, and the blower must concentrate hard on the rate at which it is flowing out of sight, ready to light his fuse five seconds before the moment at which he believes the grease will have completed its run.

This can never have been easy. Those five seconds were needed to allow the blower to retreat twenty feet to safety, or to take shelter behind a substantial barrier. The thief had to keep in balance the immediate physical danger, the risk of discovery, and the need to do the job right.

If he became too nervous, too hasty, the charge would go off before the run was complete, and some of the charge would be left in the cup, to explode wastefully, perhaps even blowing the door inwards rather than out. If he were distracted, waited too long and allowed the moment for a good shot to pass, there would be too little grease left in the channel around the door to blow it off. Either way, the chance had been missed, the door remained closed, and the risks of a second shot had to be weighed. If that second shot was needed, the blower could not know how much of the original charge remained, unexploded, and possibly drained within the safe, where a second attempt would cause it to 'burn the money'.

It was vitally important to use the right amount of the right quality of nitroglycerine. Failure to blow the safe hard enough produced no more than a bulged door which might require a fresh attempt to blow it, or strenuous physical effort to try to jemmy the door open; after all the blast might have raised the alarm and many a safe was found jammed shut by a bungled attempt at blowing. However frustrating, this was at least the safer outcome. To use too much explosive was to 'make a bomb out of a safe', to blow off the door, damage the contents, blow out the windows and draw attention. At worst, lives were lost.

The skilled, the experienced and the lucky, however, would now be faced with a door still riding on its hinges, but swinging open.

Ears ringing, and covered with the fine dust of the safe's fireproofing scattered over him and everything else in the room, he would dive forward. The money might be burned and worthless to him; there might be another smaller safe-within-a-safe, called a 'Keister', undamaged within; perhaps the original observation or information had been totally misleading, and the cupboard would turn out to be bare.

Electric detonation made the jam shot technique much less chancy. It was instant and consistent, and removed all the problems of unpredictable variations in fuse speed. Instead of having to guess at the invisible flow of liquid, the blower could now wait until the moment when the grease reached the end of its path to set off his charge. Many blowers added a second cup at the lower edge of the door to catch the grease, and as it began to fill the blower would know that his charge was well placed and he had only to touch two wires, completing the circuit through a torch battery and the detonator.

This new and better way was not popular with everyone. Older safemen whose reputations had been earned over years of practice grumbled about a decline in craftsmanship, and resented losing all the prestige which their years of apprenticeship and experience had given them. In fact, the jam shot method could only be effective against earlier, less carefully-designed safes, and was often just a speedier substitute for direct physical attack. Safe manufacturers had developed a number of changes which made the jam shot ineffective: they manufactured to tighter tolerances to leave less space around the door, provided a small lip around the outer edge of doors to catch the nitroglycerine and prevent it from penetrating to a useful depth, and added various devices to the outside of the door to apply pressure inwards, sealing the aperture more tightly. For each of these, of course, fresh methods of attack were devised.

An alternative protection for a safe, suggested in 1914 by the Johnson-Bradford Company of Oregon, lay in a novel form of construction. They proposed a shell made of three spaced layers of manganese steel; unlike all other safe walls these would have holes ready-made at the factory in the two outer layers. The idea was that if explosive were introduced into the casing, it would rapidly flow down through the perforations, draining away where it could do no harm. An experimental charge blew out flames fully ten feet long, but left all the vital works still operable, and the contents protected by a fireproof partition inside the innermost shell. Technically a success, the design failed to find a market – safes have always to inspire confidence and a sense of security in the buyer, and the sales force may not have risen to the challenge of selling safes covered in a rash of holes.

It was more practical to close that gap around the safe door into which nitro could be poured, and safe manufacturers developed systems of external bars which would jam the door more tightly shut. Spanning the width, and sometimes the height of the door, these shiny chromium-plated rods were not only functional, but very probably a salesman's dream. The cunning of lock design is normally hidden from view, and the many metallurgical improvements were quite impossible to demonstrate, but the glittering shafts and cams and brackets of the new models reassured the customer that his money was truly going to buy him extra security.

Safecrackers called the new models 'harnessed' safes – experience was to prove that they could be tackled with explosives by setting the first charge at the most vulnerable point in the pressure-bar mechanism, and then following it with a conventional jam shot. By obliging the burglars to spend extra time at the scene, and to run the extra risk of detection that went both with delay and with the extra explosion, safemakers had achieved a partial success.

Even when the safe was not harnessed, the jam shot did not work every time. Poor quality grease, faulty technique, or an unsuitable safe could make life difficult for the safeman. 'They're starting to use these tubes, in the floor, you know, in the concrete . . . These can be blown, but . . . we blew up, I don't know how many – how much money. Just shredded bills, you know . . .' This destruction arose because with such a safe the use of several shots was not just a nuisance but a necessity, in the technique known as the space shot.

Shooting for space required a safe to be dropped on its back, if the door was not already set horizontally into the top, to build up the soap cup on the centre of the door, then detonate as in a jam shot: 'You're going to dish that door, no matter how well it is constructed, and it's going to get a severe enough jar from this shot to give you enough space to shoot.' The aim was to dish the door, pulling in the edge just enough to allow the next charge of explosive to find its way into the crack around the edges, but not so much that the second shot would find its way inside the safe and destroy the contents.

And this is where the steady development of American nitro techniques came to an end. Yeggs and their successors had dealt with each new design and refinement by careful study and resourceful change, but in the years after the Second World War nitro became obsolete. The tougher laws had caused a shortage of supplies, and there were new alternatives like core drills which were much safer to use and just as effective, especially against the newer safes fitted with relocking bolts ready to be triggered by an explosion. Even veteran safemen changed their ways.

In Britain there had long been a different tradition. Nitro was sometimes used before the First World War, but became a rarity which found favour only with visiting Americans and the occasional home experimenter, while most British users of explosives, including the crooks, had turned from dynamite to Nobel's other invention – gelignite.

Thieves obtained their gelignite in two traditional ways.

Some career criminals stole supplies for themselves, but the largest amounts seem to have come from men who had access to stores at work, such as miners, soldiers or demolition workers. They would pilfer what they could, and then sell it locally or even take a trip to London or another major city. Once they reached the criminal market, explosives were usually distributed quickly, rather as drugs are sold on today: apart from the physical hazards, possession of a large quantity would draw a very heavy sentence, and to make a quick profit the wholesaler would sell in small and relatively expensive packets.

Safeblowers developed ways of handling and using gelignite which took advantage of its physical characteristics. Dynamite was solid, fairly safe to handle but crude in its use, nitro a lethally touchy liquid but versatile. Gelignite comes as a putty-like block which can be cut into pieces and squeezed into new shapes; even a naked flame will not detonate it, and as long as it has been kept at a sensible temperature it is stable enough to carry in comfortable safety.

British safemen soon found that the simplest approach worked well: if just a very small amount of gelignite were pressed into the lock of a safe, it would stay in place while the detonator and fuse were attached, and very efficiently blow apart the mechanism to allow the handle to turn. The biggest drawback to gelignite was its power, and the biggest secret in using it lay in cutting off a block of explosive just enough to do the work, but not so much as to wreck the safe and the building in which it stood.

The standard techniques required very little equipment: the explosive itself, a couple of detonators and either a length of fuse or, later, long wires and a battery. Soap or modelling clay was used to seal the keyhole and hold the detonator. Everything could be hidden with ease, and carried to the job in two pockets – one raincoat pocket would hold the lot, but it was common sense to keep the gelly and the dets apart. The one major important refinement which was widely adopted added little to the load; to keep the charge exactly where it was wanted, the explosive was often packed into a balloon (or even better a condom) to make a strong flexible packet which could be pushed into place.

Most safeblowers would carry enough gelignite for two shots, in case the mechanism seized up on the first shot, but a thief who had done some homework could often diagnose just which part of the lockwork was unhelpfully out of shape and push in a bar or wire to dislodge it. When relocking devices became common, many of them could be defeated by keeping a steady pressure on the handle by hand, spring or weight, to pull back the bolts before the relocker could jump into place.

Users of gelignite had a much smaller target than the nitro men, and rarely needed to use the amounts of explosive required to blow off a door. This reduced the noise, and with a cover of office carpets, tarpaulins or any merchandise to hand a gelly explosion could be quite easily suppressed. A cautious single explosion might in any case be quite safe, since most of us, including any nightwatchmen, tend to wait for a second disturbance before we feel justified in raising the alarm.

In Britain, where the vast majority of crooks were wary of violence, and certainly shunned gunplay, explosives were too exotic for many safecrackers who preferred to work with hammer and crowbar, even where this often meant accepting the lower rewards of opening weaker safes. This hesitance increased the mystique attached to explosives, and the prestige of the safeblower: within a team, and among thieves in general, the man who held the gelly had the status. Official controls on the storage and transport of gelignite were tightened, but explosives went out of use because safecracking itself ceased to be a practical and profitable crime. By the middle of the 1960s safeblowing was a rarity, and by the end of that decade there was a new and powerful deterrent to any use of explosives: from being a tool for thieves, they had become a weapon for terrorists. The nervous increases in security, the vigour with which the police would pursue any theft of supplies, and the punishments for possession all increased so vastly that working criminals finally abandoned explosives.

15
New Flames

Just as soon as controllable heat became useful to the engineer it became a tool for the safecracker; less precise than a drill but less brutal than explosives, heat had tactical advantages of quietness and portability which no career safeman could ignore. The first important criminal use of a flame was not to cut but to reverse a manufacturing process. When safemakers began to use heat to harden their boxes, tempering the sheets of iron which covered the box, some safebreaking methods were defeated. Good safe casings were now tougher than any available drill, and stiff enough to prevent easy use of a lever.

Thieves realized that they could still use their drill and jemmies if the heating processes which produced the hardness could be reversed, if the temper could be taken out of the metal once more by annealing. This meant raising the temperature of the iron quickly and lowering it slowly.

Some safemen tried carrying off the whole safe, to build a bonfire around it which could be left to die down. This was an excellent test of the fireproofing, but could not normally heat the metal enough to have the required effect. Burglars were fortunate that a much more convenient means of applying heat – a public supply of gas for lighting – was now being installed in every large town. Into the burglar's bulging bag of equipment went a length of rubber tubing and the criminal equivalent of a Bunsen burner. On the job, he would choose the spot through which he hoped to drill, apply the flame until he saw it reach the right colour, then allow the box to cool steadily. The temperature of the flame could be increased further by supplying air under pressure, but the source of the air was not a convenient cylinder: the burglar himself had to blow long and hard through another pipe.

This exhausting work was enough to weaken an iron plate, but some thieves had higher hopes: that they could find a way to fuse or melt a hole right through the shell. They found that the iron used in basic safes was such a good conductor of heat that they could not keep the high spot temperatures needed, and the view of experts in 1871 was that 'the blowpipe . . . is a powerful auxiliary to the drill, but it cannot be used alone with success.' Even with its limitations the use of gas blowpipes was enough of a threat to the industry that the Herring safe factory, in the USA, conducted experiments which showed that the temper could be drawn from a steel plate up to an inch thick; with a vigorous use of a large bellows steel could also be melted enough to leave a hole, but iron tended to conduct the heat away from the point of application too quickly, while Spiegeleisen was as hard after treatment as before.

A drill manufacturer was called on to comment, and he believed that if the safe were made of spiegeleisen, even his best and hardest carbon-tipped drill would need to be used at a speed which burglars would not be able to achieve. His estimate was that with ordinary steel or iron, the combination of heat and drill would penetrate at a rate of an inch an hour – fifteen to twenty minutes of heating, the rest for drilling. All this research was intended to reassure the customers, but apart from the fairly exotic Spiegeleisen models the newer, harder steel safes were just as vulnerable as the old iron ones once the blowpipe had been applied.

For lack of a more thorough safeguard, one safe

manufacturer was reduced to recommending that the gas meter of a bank should be placed within the strongroom, and that all the pipes carrying gas to provide strongroom lighting should be case-hardened to resist any attempt by a burglar to tap into the supply. Otherwise, the best defence seemed only to be to increase the bulk of metal in the construction of strongroom walls, using steel reinforcement up to the thickness of a railway line. In fact, the coal gas and lung power torch was never put to general and systematic use because older methods still served most thieves well, with much less discomfort and risk to health.

Since gas could not yet provide a portable device which would burn through strong metal, some thieves turned to a rival approach which used a solid fuel called Thermit. This had been developed by a German technologist called Hans Goldschmidt as a means of heating large pieces of metal in the course of welding or repair. He had experimented until he found the right mixture of aluminium with iron oxide (or other oxide or peroxide according to need), and was now selling it as cartridges, tablets or a paste, all of which were easily ignited with a burning strip of magnesium. His mixture worked because as it burned it fed itself, producing the oxygen to keep the flame temperature high.

Thermit offered portability, ferocious speed, and silence in use, but required the greatest care, because once the reaction had started it would continue until every speck of fuel had been consumed. There was no convenient tap to cut off the supply when the job was done, or an accident threatened. One device tried was a small crucible or bowl with a fine hole drilled in the base: the mixture was placed in the bowl and ignited with an iron rod which had been raised to white heat. The intent was that by adding the mixture to the cup, the reaction could be fed slowly and steadily. In practice a jet of burning metal was sent through the hole in the base which would certainly penetrate iron and steel, but from the top came spitting, uncontrolled flames which could not be damped or extinguished.

For the thief this method had the same problems as all the other attempts to use Thermit – while threatening to set alight everything else in the room, it could cut only in one direction, vertically downwards. He couldn't turn off the fire if he heard a patrol coming, and more times than not the burning mixture would fall right into the safe and set all its contents on fire long before the burglar could reach them. Goldschmidt had been right to recognize the potential power of burning metal, but Thermit went too far.

Later metal-burning methods would always keep the metal and the oxygen apart, so that by turning the gas supply on and off the reaction could be controlled and halted. Another German attempt to use solid fuel enjoyed a brief vogue at the end of the nineteenth century. This was a strange coke-fired device called an 'automatic furnace', made from a semi-cylindrical piece of metal lined with asbestos and provided with a variety of blast or bellows. Charged with coke and charcoal, and supplied with air under pressure, the furnace produced a 'keen, biting flame which eats its way through the metal'. This would have been about as effective as the coal-gas blowpipe, and useful where no gas supply was available, but I could find no mention of just what quantity of coke was needed to penetrate the average safe. The burden of a heavy apparatus and sacks of the raw materials cannot have recommended the furnace to many safemen.

As we now know, gas was to provide an answer in the end, but only when a number of practical obstacles had been overcome. In 1886 the Brins Oxygen Co (later the

British Oxygen Co) began to produce oxygen on a scale and at a price which would permit commercial use, and just two years later Thomas Fletcher of Warrington staged a demonstration which caused great alarm among safemakers. Iron and steel will burn in an atmosphere of pure oxygen, and Fletcher's approach was to heat the surface of the safe, using a gas flame, then place a steel tube over the hot surface through which he could blow oxygen onto the spot.

Fletcher's guests saw how a single workman needed only seconds to cut a large hole in a slab of puddled iron. The startling, spark-spraying effectiveness of Fletcher's demonstration depended not so much on the gas flame but the combustion of the target in the burst of pure oxygen which followed, very much the principle of the thermic lance rather than an oxygen/gas cutter. Safemakers contested Fletcher's claims, and declared stoutly that the torch was no threat to their fine robust products, but within two years a burglar called Brown used a Fletcher apparatus in a raid on the Bank of Lower Saxony in Hanover.

The industrial production of cheap and plentiful oxygen was a stride forward, but there was no reliable means of storing and carrying it in useful quantities, until the latest military research programme yielded a spinoff: 'It came about in this wise. With a view to compress hydrogen gas, so that it could be carried about in tubes for the purpose of filling balloons, all sorts of experiments were made, till a description of steel was discovered which would hold the gas in a thin envelope.' This report from the late 1880s didn't miss the criminal possibilities in the new invention: it included a comment from an anxious policeman that, 'There are some people who think that the burglar cannot carry enough gas . . . and that, therefore, big safes are not to be attacked. But I have the authority of one of the greatest balloon engineers of the day . . . for saying that two tubes which would look like two umbrellas if properly fitted with silk and a nice handle would contain enough gas for the cutting of at least fifteen feet of such steel.'

No burglar seems ever to have adopted an umbrella disguise for his equipment, and fears of the misuse of hydrogen were also misplaced. It was too dangerous to handle, and another gas was needed which would be more easily made, stored and used; within seven years it had been found. In 1895 the French Academy of Sciences was told of an experiment in which acetylene had been burned to produce a flame temperature of 6000–7000 degrees Fahrenheit, and the scientist who performed this test encouraged a colleague to develop a torch suitable for welding. Changes in the adjustment of the flame and a new arrangement of the nozzles had produced by 1901 a torch which would cut metal. There was still a further obstacle to overcome, because acetylene was dangerously unstable under pressure, liable to explode if struck or jarred. In 1901 the law still required that it be kept only under low pressure but three years later this problem had been solved – the gas was dissolved in acetone, and the mixture absorbed into kapok or charcoal within a cylinder. The oxyacetylene cutter was ready to come out of the laboratory onto the market, and in 1907 it was first used in a safe attack during the burglary of a diamond merchant's premises in Antwerp.

Like so many technical advances, the criminal use of the oxyacetylene cutter was discovered independently in different parts of the world – the introduction of the skill to the USA has been attributed to a chance discovery by a nitroglycerine man called Oakland Tommy. The tale has it that one night when on his way to a job Tommy was thrown off a train in East Liberty, Pennsylvania, close by a steel mill. The night was cold, and Tommy was drawn by the glow from the mill, where he bluffed his way in with a fake union card. He was intrigued to see a workman using a torch to cut hardened slag out of a ladle, and by taking a job in the mill he learned enough to master the technique. Subsequently he led successful attacks on thirty-four bank vaults.

We have a full account of the first recorded use of oxyacetylene burning in Britain, in September 1910, and it was a fiasco which may have allowed the safemakers to feel secure just a little longer. The attempt began with a fine tale of a workshop for making silver-backed hair-brushes which the villains told to obtain the lease on empty premises next door to a firm of manufacturing jewellers in Birmingham.

Taxis arrived over the next few weeks carrying several large packing cases, some of them very heavy – taxi-drivers, unlike other carriers, made no enquiries about the address of the sender. In the cases were stowed two cylinders, containing one hundred cubic feet of oxygen and sixty cubic feet of acetylene, armoured piping for the oxygen, rubber piping for the acetylene, the blowpipe itself with a pair of nozzles, and a variety of conventional burglary tools. The thieves waited until the close of business on a Saturday and broke through the dividing wall to reach the strongroom, which held jewellery worth £40,000.

The new technology had held so much promise, but the burglars had very little idea of how to use it. Their first mistake was to burn out a nozzle by taking it too close to the door of the safe, and the second nozzle was soon damaged in the same way. Worse, they began to cut below the lock and then work steadily upwards, so that the metal they were melting could only run down the door to cool and harden in the first cuts – in effect, they were welding the door shut again as they went along. After some hours of this folly they switched to a drilling attack on the wall of the strongroom, but this was too strong for them: it was made of concrete into which had been embedded steel chain. Though they persisted well into the Sunday evening the burglars were able to carry away only a single ring worth about seven pounds, which had been left in an unlocked book safe.

A patrolling constable blew his whistle outside, trying to stop some youths from playing in the street, and the thieves took fright. They escaped in a taxi-cab which had been parked outside all through the burglary, the number of which had already been noted by a police patrol – first of the many clues which led the investigators to the thieves. They had intended to leave the taps of the oxygen and acetylene cylinders turned on when they left, to cause an explosion and wipe out evidence, but they bungled this too.

Such early criminal incompetence, and an understandable wish to make light of the threat of the new gas cutters, drew from safemakers some remarkable denials. In 1897 a firm in Brooklyn which made chrome steel was happy to say that, 'From what we have so far heard we attach no importance whatever to this blowpipe process,' and even as late as 1910 a British safemaker claimed, 'We are satisfied that we have discovered a means of absolutely preventing the practical use of the oxyacetylene flame by Burglars.' Their experiments with the technique had required cylinders weighing 210 pounds, which they had decided was too much for burglars to carry to a job.

What the safe manufacturer failed to take into account was that gas welding and cutting were so very useful that every kind of business which included the working of metal, from the largest factory to the small one-man workshop, would before long have all the equipment a burglar could need, ready to use and ready to steal. Thieves had good reason not to own gas equipment: for safety and security reasons, every cylinder carries a unique serial number, which is recorded every time it is sold or exchanged for recharge. No safeman dared abandon in his flight an incriminating item which could be traced back to him, so thieves looked hard at any company which had both a safe and a supply of cutting gear. Gas cutting sometimes helped to recruit safecrackers: the skill of using torches and cylinders would not be secret or obscure like the setting of explosive charges – tens of thousands of workers were trained to use the equipment safely and efficiently.

Oxyacetylene cutting was never a comfortable way to break a safe, since the burglar's trade could never meet ordinary industrial standards of space and ventilation. The heat was foul and the spitting of metal a torment; even wearing a welder's goggles and gloves, long work on a larger job would require special precautions. The American safeman Wilson 'stepped up to the safe and sank to one knee, looking like the Grand Wizard of the Ku Klux Klan, for I was dressed in a white apron of asbestos that covered most of me, and wore a hat and long gloves of the same material'. When they needed to hide the vivid glare given off by the torch, safemen used screens and tents of dense black fabric, which only made the heat and confinement more appalling.

The essential torch-cutting methods changed very little and, as ever, safe manufacturers found ways to combat such attack. They improved the shells of safes by changing to steels which resisted heat better, by using layers of copper to dissipate heat from the spot at which the torch is applied, and by replacing the old loose fireproof filling with a hard-set concrete lining which would not yield to burning alone. The torch remained a dangerous tool, but the construction of the newer safes forced the burglar to switch between methods as he worked his way through the wall of a safe, slowing him down drastically. These countermeasures could not defeat the last, and much the most powerful, of the burning tools available to the safecracker: the thermic lance, or burning bar as it is known in North America.

In the mid-1960s the British press reported the first raid to use a new technique, a safecracking method of quite stunning speed and effectiveness. One safemaker described the thermic lance as 'the most dangerous piece of equipment ever to fall into the hands of criminals'. The door of the vault in the Knightsbridge branch of Lloyds Bank in London was eighteen inches thick, of a steel made to resist drilling, oxyacetylene cutting and explosives, but in April 1965 raiders using a thermic lance were able to cut through it within less than two minutes, and escape with more than one million pounds.

This was an astonishing crime, but was in fact far from being the world's first criminal use of the device. Lances were a known threat in the United States in the 1930s, and the principle had been demonstrated as long ago as the 1880s: a metal brought to burning temperature in an atmosphere of pure oxygen under pressure will not only generate extraordinary temperatures, but as it melts, the metal itself will act as a flux to speed up still further the burning of the target, whether it be iron, steel, or even granite and reinforced concrete.

For all its devastating effect, the apparatus needed is very simple. A tank of oxygen is connected by tubing to a pipe, which may be made of wrought iron, or mild steel, can even be a plastic pipe stuffed full of metal filings. In use, the end of the tube is heated vigorously with a blowlamp or hand torch, to the point at which the metal can begin to burn, and then the oxygen is released to blow through the tube. The result is spectacular, as violent flames jet out from the tip, releasing clouds of thick and noxious smoke as they strike the target.

Long before its use in crime the lance was the standard method for unplugging the tap holes in the furnaces of metalworks, where the output had cooled to block the flow and needed a very hot, locally-applied jet of flame to remove it. Its power was well known, but it had seemed a very specialized tool until it was rediscovered and developed after the Second World War to help demolish obsolete fortifications and strongpoints. Massively reinforced submarine pens, gun emplacements, pillboxes and forts had all to be removed, and the lance methods used by the French Air Liquide company on the Atlantic Wall left by the Germans were soon adapted for civil use.

There was no delicacy in the task and the lance used was crude, much like a length of scaffolding pipe ten feet long and generating vast amounts of heat and smoke when lit, but it was serving contractors well. Crude also meant cheap (the lance used in the Lloyds job had a retail price of just over one pound), and lances were legally and quite freely available. Little wonder that the new tool caused such alarm – none of the materials that safemakers had been using, none of their traditional design expertise, seemed able to offer a defence.

Resourceful thieves were delighted to learn about the potential in the tool, and once raids such as the Lloyds success had pointed the way, others were quick to copy – in that same year the use of the thermic lance had reached as far as Australia, and by early July there had already been three raids in Sydney in which £31,000 was stolen, just a month after the police had been warned to look out for the latest threat. Although widespread, lance attacks formed just a small proportion of the world's safecrackings and produced no general response from the safemakers until a wave of strongroom attacks in Italy – sixty raids between January 1975 and December 1978 – raised customers' anxiety so much that some more substantial defence had to be provided.

For all their fear, safemakers were learning about the lance's limitations as well as its power. It was becoming clear that thermic lances were useful only against strong vaults – for minor jobs they were much too powerful. The gear was hard to carry and to conceal, the long lance could not be applied unless there was room to manoeuvre it, and was powerful enough to transform an ordinary safe into an eruption of vicious molten metal which no contents could survive. Even where the target was large, the ferocity of the heat and the volume of smoke produced made it dangerous and difficult to use. The thief could rarely work without breathing apparatus, and could not enter a breached vault with safety until the heat remaining in the metal had dissipated, which caused delays.

Vault constructors, while racing to find materials which could resist the lance, took care to reduce the available space around vault doors so that thieves could not bring the long lance pipes to bear on the doors, and at best would have to carry out their draining work in a tight, hellish space.

Almost before the lance was taken up as a criminal tool, it was discarded. To understand why such a powerful weapon can still fail, we have to remember the time factor: until the lance came into use, vault designers and owners thought themselves safe if the strongroom could resist attack by conventional methods for a given time – perhaps a couple of days, enough to cover a weekend. When the first panic had died down, they realized that

the importance of the lance was not that it could penetrate a vault, but that it could do so within hours.
Strengthening vaults was one very costly way of fighting
back to increase the time needed, but owners could
improve their ordinary security, with better alarm systems
and more efficient patrols. These measures were enough
to remove the thieves' temporary technical advantage,
and the lance threat could now be seen for what it was: a
brief period of opportunism, never to be repeated.

A last method of burning through steel which enjoyed
an even shorter vogue was to apply electrical current to
strike an arc which would melt through the metal casing
of a safe. In 1901 news reached the West of two daring
raids in Russia: the thefts in St Petersburg were both the
work of the same gang, but the methods could hardly
have been more different. In one case a safe had been
stolen from the very Criminal Court building itself, by
the simple expedient of getting the guards drunk. The
other raid was much more technically remarkable: thieves
had broken through a thick stone wall into the strongroom of a wholesale tobacco company, and had penetrated the safe itself by fusing the metal using electricity
drawn from the lighting system.

The London *Daily Express* was dismissive in its report:
'Those St Petersburglars who made a hole in a safe by
fusing it with electric wires must have had a soft thing to
tackle,' and went on to quote an expert who said that the
safe must have been a thin sheet-iron German one. He
was quite sure, of course, that his own company's safes
were of a steel which would resist such attack. The
method might just work, he said, but only after a week's
hard labour and only in laboratory conditions.

Companies always want to reassure their customers,
and perhaps this man really did not know that in New
York, just three months before, an electrician from the

Post Office had tackled a safe door two and a half inches thick, made of six layers of different alloys, when the combination had been mislaid and other methods had failed. The circuit he had created ran from one of the city's street lights to a carbon rod, which was applied to the door and formed an arc which reached temperatures of 2000 degrees Fahrenheit, the voltage controlled by a crude rheostat made of a bucket of water – not quite laboratory conditions, but effective overnight.

The safe company man did acknowledge that some had worried about electrical safecracking: 'Very careful folk, it seems, anticipating the electric dodge, have the means of switching on the electric current placed within the switch within the safe, so that to obtain the current a burglar would have to open the safe first.' He seemed to think that this was clever: 'This is as though one were to say to the burglar, "You may have the key, it's inside the safe".' Equally, the message might be that if the burglar thought he might need a convenient supply of electricity, one was laid on right to the safe itself.

The method of attack was powerful, but didn't find favour with thieves. Safemakers and safeowners were fortunate that examples of successful electrical burning raids were so very few; the last one that I could find was in Australia, no later than 1908. Electricity has certainly been used, but in more conventional ways, powering quite ordinary tools. In a time when suppliers of gas and electric power were still in fierce competition – gas refrigerators are still in use, and there were once serious attempts to sell gas-powered radios – electricity could still be newsworthy. None of us likes to be confronted with a high fuel bill, but one newspaper clipping from 1927 has made me chuckle:

£11,000 LONDON DIAMOND ROBBERY
THE SCIENTIFIC THIEVES OF THE EAST END
Jeweller's Own Electricity Used In Cutting Open His Safe.

The victim of this raid lost seventeen bags of loose diamonds, up to three hundred gold rings, some stone rings, gold watches and gold cigarette cases – it is hard to imagine that he was greatly troubled by the few extra pence that the burglars had added to his quarterly bill.

Whether by burning or blowing, hundreds of safecrackers have used heat to reach their loot. Just one man, a burglar called Bronco Bill Frane, is said to have frozen his way into a vault, during a bank burglary in Kingston, near London. Bank staff and police were baffled to find that the vault had been burst from within, apparently by a charge inside the strong room. £30,000 had been taken, but every part of the vault had in some mysterious way been washed down and all traces of the charge removed. Frane and three confederates had made their way from an empty adjoining building into the upper floors of the bank and cut their way, through floors and ceilings, to a point directly above the vault. They drilled just one hole, and pushed in a hose to fill the entire vault with water. In that viciously cold winter the water froze, expanded to tear the vault apart, and was then melted by a fire so that the money could be spirited away.

This is a great story, told in apparent good faith by an author who claimed intimate knowledge of the underworld, but he was either gullible or having a little fun at the expense of his readership. There seems to be no other record of this inventive success, and I calculate that when the temperature in Surrey last reached such a prolonged low there were mammoths in the High Street.

Nice, 1976

A man conceives a daring underground raid. He gathers an expert team about him, and after much careful planning they make their way, carrying all their equipment with them, through the sewers of a city, to break through the walls of a bank vault. Once inside, they break into safe deposit boxes and find enough money and valuables to make this the biggest bank theft anyone can remember. This is the plot of a book called *Loophole*, published in 1972 (from which a film was made in 1980), and a description of the real life raid in July 1976 on the Société Générale in Nice. Robert Pollock wrote the book, but the author of the raid was a man called Albert Spaggiari, an unsavoury right-wing political adventurer, soldier of fortune and thief. As so often, the reality was more inventive and extraordinary than even the best fiction.

Though very much a criminal, Spaggiari was not a safecracker by trade. In his own account of the raid, he claims that having been adventurous for many years, he had settled into a respectable tax-paying way of life, until seized by a fleeting mid-life crisis in which he quite suddenly chose to break into the bank.

To carry out his plan, he knew he had a lot to learn. His first step was to rent a safe deposit box, so that he could visit the bank to memorize the layout and study the alarm system. He was already sure that he would need to finance the big job with the proceeds of an easier, smaller one, so he spent a great deal of time learning about other banks in the area too, from staff movements to the smallest available technical detail. 'I devoured all the brochures, copies of *Science et Vie*, banking magazines, technical literature. It was becoming more exciting all the time.'

From the beginning he knew he would need accomplices, and the first of these was no waterfront heavy, but a respectable lady close to eighty years old with whom he had often daydreamed about the perfect robbery. This criminal counterpart to Miss Marple was taught to use a miniature spy-camera, and took photographs within the safe deposit; later, she even smuggled a radio transmitter into the vault which allowed Spaggiari to listen in to all that happened there for a day. Even better, she played to perfection the part of an inquisitive little old dear whose concern for the safety of her life's savings made her ask so very many complicated questions about the vault, the alarms and the patrols. Bank staff were at pains to reassure her with the fullest details of the bank's defences.

Although the raid may always have been an attempt to raise funds for the neo-fascists with whom he was connected, Spaggiari's own account is of a fantasy which became a personal obsession and made ordinary respectable life unbearable. When he was ready to move from preparation to action, he tried to buy a thermic lance, and attracted the attention of an experienced gang from Marseilles. Once they had heard just how grandly ambitious a scheme Spaggiari had in mind they offered their skills, and made an approach to the local crime boss in Nice to get his approval for such a major raid within his territory. He turned them down, fearful of the police heat that must surely follow, yet the Marseillais were determined to go ahead. Their offer to Spaggiari was simple – if he had misled them, he would die, but if there was truth in what he had to say, they wanted to press on. They were seven men – Spaggiari would have to muster an equal number himself to make up the workforce needed for the job, and he recruited the rest of his team from among the ex-military lowlife who had worked with him before: one was believed to have defrauded the aircraft company Dassault of one million pounds, another had tried to assassinate De Gaulle in 1962.

The sewers seemed to offer a way in, and they must first be reconnoitred. Here Spaggiari showed the thoroughness that was to mark all of his preparations. The team drove a van of the make and model used by the public works department, wore the right uniforms and equipped themselves with official-seeming tools and road signs. Down in the four-foot by three-foot tunnels they made a full underground map of the area by pacing out the distances between manholes and junctions, and leaving markers to guide the team through the days and weeks of working. They were looking in particular for an entrance to the sewer system large enough to allow the heavy gear to be moved in, and found one close to a helpful source of electric power.

In the next weeks Spaggiari's men went shopping, and occasionally stealing: from Milan some toolbags, from Belgium scissors; three hundred metres of cable, bought in small lengths in different French towns; thirty chisels, thirty handlamps, more than thirty hammers; dynamite; oxyacetylene torches and dozens of gas cylinders; a wheelbarrow; buckets; wooden beams and cement to help in shoring up the walls of the hole they were to make. The list ran on through overalls and boots, scores of pairs of gauntlets and surgical gloves, a portable stove, and an industrial smoke extractor. Two electric drills and a heavy-duty hydraulic lever were fairly conventional tools, but Spaggiari also spent thousands of dollars on a small laser and a set of walkie-talkie radios.

From the beginning the Marseilles men had been wary

of alarms, and no matter how many times they were reassured by Spaggiari that no alarms were set which could interfere with the job, they became obsessive, and Spaggiari went to bizarre lengths to provide proof. They felt certain that there must be microphones, so he lodged an alarm clock in his safe deposit box – it went off, but triggered nothing; he put in a radio and timer – nothing; he put in a raucous siren – nothing.

He won them over, and in May the major work of setting up an underground base began, with the men making three or four trips through the tunnels, stooped over, carrying sixty, even one hundred pounds at a time. The twisting one-hundred-yard route led to a depot, a concealed dump cut into the tunnel wall.

Drilling the final tunnel, the one which would lead from the sewer to the wall of the vault, had to be slow work. The vault engineers had fitted no alarm because the rock beneath the bank had seemed so solid an obstacle, and for each hour's drilling and hammering the gang made only four inches of progress. Drill bits broke, one after another, and when they tried to divert around the toughest rock the diggers met with sand which could not be shored up safely. There was physical strain and emotional stress – the men, especially Spaggiari's adventurers, were used to rapid action and quick results and they became touchy, ready to brawl with each other. Just in time the team hit a layer of clay which would yield, but then more rock, and tension rose once more. At last, after two weeks' work and having excavated a shaft of twenty feet, they found the concrete of the bank's foundations.

For the plan to run to time, and take advantage of a holiday weekend, the team now had just one week to break through into the vault. The safecracking gear – blowtorches with forty gas cylinders – was taken down ready for the final attack, but at the end of that week they were no further than halfway through the foundations, having ruined three pneumatic jacks and more than one hundred drill bits. Not only was the foundation tough, but the bank walls were carrying the sound of their work and they had to stop whenever a lookout signalled the approach of a passer-by.

Not until 24 June, after a total of seven weeks underground, could the men break through the five feet of foundation to see the vault wall. The wall itself proved easy to breach, but then they found their way blocked by a fifty-ton safe. It took nearly three weeks to clear a path: even with a jack they could shift the safe just a fraction of an inch, so they tried to cut through with the torches. This worked for the outer layer of steel, but made no impression on the concrete lining, and only when a much more powerful jack was found and brought could the safe be moved and wedged out of the way. On Friday 16 July the team was at last able to get into the vault and face the next task of opening the safes, and the deposit boxes inside them.

The thieves mistakenly assumed that the greatest spoils would lie behind the strongest defences and spent hours cutting into a very few of the 1500 boxes. By four o'clock on Saturday afternoon only twenty-eight, by ten o'clock just thirty more; a rhythm and a routine carried them on, but by the Sunday morning as they reached the two hundred mark they were having to take short breaks to sleep. Not all the boxes were yielding cash – everything from mouldy biscuits to blackmail letters, pornography to a drawer full of sugar and lentils.

In one corner of the vault they set up a place to sleep and eat, sustained by soup cooked on a set of butane stoves they had carried in. With comparable forethought someone had brought cans of pine scent for the patch that would be used as a latrine, but the general stench was so foul that they were useless.

By midnight on the Sunday they were packing up the haul, and when the final, 107th box had been emptied they used a blowtorch to weld shut the main entrance from the bank to delay discovery of the theft for a few hours. They discussed what message might be left, rejecting 'we wish to extend our sincerest thanks to the management' and 'interesting work in pleasant surroundings' to settle on 'no hate, no violence and no guns'. Fire extinguishers were sprayed over spots where fingerprints might have been left, and the team moved out, struggling under the great weight of their haul through sewers that were rising.

Three months later Spaggiari was arrested: someone had told the police of a store of arms and explosives at his house. While in custody he talked, though he was later to claim that he had been doped with amphetamines in a cup of coffee. It seemed certain that he had talked himself into a long sentence, but in the middle of his trial he broke free from his escort, leaped from a courtroom window, and was carried away by an accomplice on a motorcycle. He has never been recaptured, and the stolen money seems to have reached the hands of right-wing terrorists in Lebanon and Italy.

PART FOUR

The Payoff

16

Government Burglars

> The plans, which are exceedingly intricate, comprising some thirty separate patents, each essential to the working of the whole, are kept in an elaborate safe in a confidential office adjoining the arsenal, with burglar-proof doors and windows.
>
> *The Adventure of the Bruce-Partington Plans*
> Sir Arthur Conan Doyle

To governments, their secrets are more precious than gold, and more difficult to protect: they are worthless when revealed, but worth twice as much to the thief if their loss is undiscovered. So nations lock their plans and papers away, and try very hard to steal those of other nations, and not only their enemies.

The arts of burglary may be useful to government agencies, yet only in wartime, when so many other social taboos are lifted, are they a fit study for gentlemen. Elementary lockpicking and the rudiments of house-breaking were parts of the core curriculum for the respectable young people recruited and trained in haste for clandestine service in both world wars. The safemaking companies provided their expert tutors, but it does appear that until quite recently the difficult field work was carried out by hired hands drawn from among honest working locksmiths and, where they might have to be disowned, experienced criminals. These are not men who have been quick to write memoirs, but their stories sometimes emerge.

I can find no trace of their names, but among the most extraordinary of official safecrackers were two Italians called to the colours during the First World War. Italy was allied with Britain and France, and vulnerable to German spying; among the foremost operatives for the Kaiser was a Cardinal Gerlach, who hatched all manner of dastardly plots from his post at the Vatican. On the night of 6 April 1917 Gerlach's house was raided by Italian secret service agents, but too late – His Eminence had fled to Switzerland. Nonetheless the next day, more than three hundred arrests were made across Italy of those believed to have been involved in the Cardinal's machinations.

The raid and the arrests were not the result of chance or guesswork. The tale had begun in January of that year with the escape of our two safecrackers from the prison in Rome where they were serving life sentences. Readers of thrillers will have guessed that in fact their release was ordered by the prefect of the Italian police himself, and a reward of £2000 was promised to each man for undertaking a most daring raid, over the Austrian border into Vienna. There, in a house next to the German embassy, was the nerve centre of the German spying operation, and in April the Italian plan was put into action.

The London *Daily Express* told the story:

Had they burgled hastily, the spies might have burgled the house, robbed the safe, and even laid hands on a certain set of precious papers . . . That, however, is as far as they would have got, for attached to the bundle of documents so highly desired by three Governments was an intricate series of wires.

With almost devilish ingenuity the Germans had provided that if the safe was opened and the papers moved, a cloud of poison gas, deadly in effect, would envelop the disturber, and render the entire room . . . uninhabitable. At the same time, a cleverly devised burglar alarm would call military police to the scene to deal with any number of intruders . . .

How [the burglars] were smuggled into Vienna no one will ever know, but when they did undertake the robbery of the safe they were provided with gas-masks and every tool for safe-opening known to the police or criminal world . . .

While announcing the robbery of a 'large sum of money', the Austrians succeeded, by means of a secret wireless, in communicating with Cardinal Gerlach, who departed unceremoniously from the Papal Court . . . However, the Italian police were able to round up several hundred of the most dangerous German plotters and to strike into the heart of the Teutonic element in the highest Church circles of Rome.

There was a further exploit that seems likely to have been the work of these same two safecrackers. The Italians learned of a plot to blow up their warships in the Mediterranean; documents which would reveal the details were believed to be held in a foreign consulate in Zurich. Enter the dashing Baron Aloisi, then Italian Minister at Tirana in Albania, who made the journey to Switzerland with two expert safebreakers – surely those heroes of the Vienna Raid – and a full kit of oxy-hydrogen cutting gear. Working all night they succeeded in breaking into the safe just before dawn, then made their escape back over the border in a powerful car – the stuff of Biggles and Richard Hannay.

After the Great War most countries dismantled their spying operations. Although counter-espionage remained a task for agencies such as the British Special Branch and the American FBI, which worked with a policeman's respect for the value of information, intelligence had usually been a matter for military authorities. Peacetime career officers took no more pleasure in shady snooping activities than they did in filthy modern inventions like the tank and the aeroplane, and were relieved not to have to soil themselves further. Although there was no longer a threat of national defeat, politicians in many Western countries were very fearful of revolution. They knew that war had come just in time to interrupt the growth of class anger at home, and dreaded that Bolshevik success in Russia would infect their own workers and cause insurrections across Europe.

This nervousness was to lead to the most spectacular government safecracking ever seen. When governments want to break safes, they are usually as secretive as any burglar, and as ready as any fence to deny all knowledge of a theft, but in 1927 the British broke into Soviet vaults in front of an audience of thousands, with every step recorded in full by the press.

During the Cold War we became used to the idea that Russian spies were dedicated to penetrating the defences of the West, but in the years between the world wars there was just one substantial attempt to establish a Soviet intelligence base in the United Kingdom. When diplomatic relations were reopened between Britain and the Soviet Union in 1924, the Russians sent to London not only an ambassador and his staff, but a trade delegation. Trading as Arcos Limited, the delegation took over two large office blocks in Moorgate. Then as now it was important to obtain hard Western currencies, then as now the commercial operation provided cover for numbers of spies.

The Russian spying effort in Britain was not intense, and the British Communist Party has always been small and insignificant; nonetheless, the British police and intelligence services were astoundingly complacent about the Moorgate operation. No one seems to have wondered why the low levels of trade between the two countries needed a staff of three hundred, nor to have realized that one of the Arcos bosses, and the Commercial Counsellor at the embassy, were both identifiably members of Russian Intelligence.

A crude blunder by the Russian Communist Party became the downfall of Arcos. During the 1926 General Strike the Party sent more than a quarter of a million pounds to the English miners, an interference with domestic politics which outraged the British government, and the Trades Union Congress, which promptly returned the money. The Chancellor of the Exchequer threatened to break off all trade with the Soviet Union, and attention was at last paid to Arcos; MI5 discovered the intelligence connection, and when a new Commercial Counsellor was appointed, diplomatic immunity was withheld.

An immediate result was a Russian dispatch from London to Moscow calling for a suspension of the traffic in espionage documents. A copy of the dispatch fell into the hands of MI5; an RAF technician who had stolen drawings and calculations was found to be sending material to Arcos; another English spy was discovered trading with the Soviet organization in Germany – in the face of all this evidence the British began to move against Arcos. The final straw was the disappearance in early 1927 of a document containing strategic bombing plans: the Special Branch and MI5 believed that the document had been given to Arcos.

Pressure was applied to the government for a full raid on the Moorgate offices, and after worried consideration of the political and diplomatic implications of such a move, the Prime Minister ordered the police in. At dawn on 12 May the buildings were surrounded, and having forced an entry police found the chief cipher clerk from the Russian embassy burning papers. A list of agents' cover addresses was found. The decision was made to seize every file, and seven tons of documents were carried away, but as they searched, the police found three well-concealed safes – the Russians refused to open either these safes or two others within a strong vault.

Expert help was sought, and draughtsmen from a City architect's office prepared drawings of the strongroom and safes which were delivered to a safe manufacturer, with a request that they provide men and equipment to force an entry. Access to the safe doors was very constricted, and the most promising approach seemed to be to cut through the walls of the vault, so the thousands in the crowd which had gathered outside were treated to the sight of tons of equipment arriving, and then the sound of pneumatic drills as the break-in progressed.

The original document whose loss had prompted the raid was never found. It may have left with one of the female employees – with a concern for delicacy, the police searched none of the women in the building – or been spirited away through a secret passageway which the Russians had constructed but which remained undiscovered until much later. It hardly mattered now, since the search had shown that Soviet agents had penetrated every important military and naval centre, in particular Aldershot and Plymouth. Diplomatic relations with Russia were broken off, the trade delegation deported, and a total ban placed on the entry of Russians into Britain.

Until the states of Europe began to prepare for war yet again, there was little demand for state burglars, but there was a remarkable example of safecracking by royal appointment. In 1927 King Victor of Italy lost the key to the safe in which he kept one of his most prized possessions, his collection of rare coins. Rather like the kings in the fairy stories, he called a courtier, who called a higher courtier, who called the Prime Minister, asking that someone in the realm be found who could open the king's safe. In particular, could the prisons of the kingdom be searched for a man who would come to the palace and help the king?

From the main prison in Rome a notorious thief was brought in handcuffs, with a collection of suitable and useful tools, to an impatient Victor. The king watched as the burglar, whose knowledge of bank safes was said to be peculiar and extensive, set to work; the safecracker was nervous, but the king got into the spirit of the occasion, and asked the prisoner to work slowly so that he could see how it was done.

The safe was opened. The king was delighted, shook the man's hand: 'I think the banks ought to pension you off,' he said. 'In a little villa on, say, Capri, you would be – er – harmless.' But at that moment the prison official returned, the cuffs wère locked back on, and the prisoner taken back to his cell in a royal car. Nothing ever came, apparently, of the king's retirement suggestion, and the prison sentence was not reduced. The safecracker was perhaps unfortunate that the Minister of the Interior, who was also the Prime Minister, and for that matter the Chief of the Black Shirt Militia, was a man never famous for his generous spirit – Benito Mussolini.

Through the years when Germany was rearming under Hitler, democratic governments allowed their hopes for peace to lead them into the diplomacy of appeasement. German rearmament was tolerated. And there was a wilful refusal either to recognize the risks of German spying or to expand Britain's own intelligence services. Only after the debacle of Munich did serious military and intelligence preparations begin.

I was told by a craftsman called Brewer, who then worked for a safe company, how, in the last months of peace, his employers had summoned him to meet a very distinguished-looking man who gave no name. He was questioned about his attitude to breaking the law, and his answer – that he might have been guilty of speeding, but had never contemplated theft – seemed to satisfy. Then he was asked if, having been instructed to do so, he could enter premises, pick the lock on a safe, then relock everything so that there was no evidence of any intrusion. Cautiously he agreed that this was quite possible, if the circumstances permitted, and so long as whoever was giving the instructions would guarantee his immunity from any prosecution.

This seemed to be good enough, and Brewer was soon sent on the first job of many, keeping a rendezvous with watchful men for whom he opened doors, drawers and a safe which he relocked after the men had finished their inspection. Back at work, his boss told him that the job had been regarded as satisfactory, but he was curious about the speed with which the safe lock had been picked. When shown the special tool used, he asked to borrow it, then never brought it back; the tool emerged many years later among the safebreaking exhibits in the Metropolitan Police Black Museum, and my conclusion is that it passed into the hands of the Special Branch.

Again and again Brewer was given instructions at short notice to make his way to a house, an office or a hotel room, and each time the rule was the same: if he judged that any attempt to enter would leave tell-tale signs, the job was off for the night. Every mission was sensitive: these raids were not only aimed at obvious German targets, but at Britons whose loyalties were suspect, or residents whose files might give useful information. Had they ever been caught or discovered, the legal and diplomatic consequences would have been very damaging.

It is a shame that Brewer's most ingenious manoeuvre was never to pay off as it might have done. Hitler had ordered the refurbishment of the German Embassy in London, and all the craftsmen to carry out the work had been sent from Germany, until it came to the tricky installation of some very large safes. This was a fairly short job, but it would require skilled labourers to avoid danger to the men and damage to the safes. An exception was made to the rule about German workers and a large British company was asked to send along an experienced team.

This was too good an opportunity to miss, and Brewer was instructed to join the gang to learn what he could about security within the embassy. He did even better; while moving one of the safes he managed to land a blow on one of the combination locks which displaced the dial, and when embassy officials tried to open it the numbers supplied by the factory would not work. Prompted by the locksmith, another member of the gang suggested that Brewer might be able to put matters right, and by allowing for the dial shift which he himself had caused, he had no difficulty in opening the door. Further, Brewer suggested that he could prepare the safe so that the staff could set their own codes, and in the process was able to examine and memorize the internal structure of the lockwork in detail.

The Germans were impressed and the Ambassador, von Ribbentrop himself, came to express his gratitude. For his part, Brewer couldn't wait to get out of the building to record what he had seen, and as soon as he reached the pavement he set every detail down on paper. In his retirement in a South Coast resort he still has the notebook, with all its sketches and dimensions, and wishes that he had had just one shot at using it.

When war came, the undercover work continued, and the burglary teams found that air raids were splendid cover for their activities: when the warning sirens sounded, everyone took to the shelters, including their targets and potential inconvenient witnesses. Unnoticed among all the explosions and fires, the teams went about their business confident that they could work uninterrupted until the All Clear.

There were other tasks for a man who could open safes. After Dunkirk, when Britain was desperate to buy arms to replace the equipment abandoned in France, the Treasury drew up lists of all the safe deposit boxes in Britain rented by people known to have remained in territory occupied by the Germans. In a discreet but complicated operation, legitimate locksmiths were sent to open every box, partly to look for any evidence of Nazi sympathies or conspiracy – there was great dread of a Fifth Column – but also to help the Government to get its hands on gold which could be traded for food and armaments. They took all the gold they found, and left an official deposit note as a receipt so that the value of the gold could be reclaimed after the war. As a further step, all records of use were checked, and any box which had remained unopened for twenty-five years was similarly searched and stripped of gold.

Just as in Britain, the development in America of effective intelligence agencies came late; after all, had not President Woodrow Wilson said that 'a gentleman does not read another gentleman's letters'? For most of the years between the World Wars the government of the United States had little need or appetite for espionage, but once the war in Europe broke out in 1939, hurried attempts were made to build a modern intelligence service. Like the British in their last months of peace, the Americans needed to check the loyalties and the intentions of individuals and nations, and chose discreet burglary when it seemed the most promising approach.

Consulates were obvious targets, not only those of

potential enemies but of nations which were officially neutral, but burglary always carried the risk of causing an embarrassing diplomatic row. Businesses handling strategic goods for the combatants or believed to provide a front for subversive operations were worth a visit, and of course the homes of individuals suspected of spying. Just as in Britain, the only rule was to leave no trace, and the British were happy to lend the services of a woman who had perfected undetectable techniques of opening and resealing envelopes and parcels. 'It took two men to carry her assortment of pots, pans, steam-kettles and packages,' a memoir recorded.

When safecracking went to war, it was used by soldiers as well as spies. The same British locksmith who was a government burglar by night trained squads of commandos by day. There were official fears that men who had learned the secrets of stealthy housebreaking might be tempted into crime when they went back to civilian life, but the authorities decided to take the risk. There is no evidence that a lockpicking course led to lives of crime, and the knowledge of explosives needed to demolish enemy installations was not always useful in a criminal career. One safeblower brought to court in 1956 had learned the elements of his trade in sabotage operations behind enemy lines in Italy. He and his accomplices were caught before they could detonate the charge they had placed against the lock of a restaurant safe, but they should have been grateful: a safe is not a bridge nor a railway, and the amount of explosive they had applied was quite enough to have killed all of them.

There were immediate postwar tasks which needed the skills of official safecrackers: in Europe the chilling, meticulous records of the Nazi bureaucracy had to be exposed, and throughout the territories which had been occupied by the Axis powers banks and treasuries had to be opened so that economic life could return to normal. Brewer, the locksmith who had found the blitz such excellent cover for burglary, was sent to the Far East to open safes and vaults abandoned by the Japanese, and when I interviewed him he told of the need for care when so many of the doors had been boobytrapped. Our conversation had until then included a great deal of technical detail, and I could clearly picture this heartstopping task, like that of defusing an unexploded bomb – wires of different colours, hairtrigger second detonators, dummy devices and hidden springs.

When I asked just how he had tackled the problem he looked surprised that I should ask: 'You sort out the lock,' he said, 'then take a very long piece of rope, tie it to the handle, take cover as far away as you can, and pull that rope. If it goes BANG! it was booby-trapped.'

Before the war was over, suspicion of Soviet intentions and the possibility of Communist subversion at home ensured that the intelligence agencies would survive the peace. The spy scandals of the Cold War usually arose from treachery rather than theft, but among them is a case which involved both, remarkable for the scale of the spymasters' effort – all of it needed to make up for the incompetence of the spy.

An agent who is recruited when he already occupies a position of trust will always be difficult to train, since he cannot be removed without explanation for months of tuition and grooming. Sergeant Robert Lee Johnson in the US Army was on a posting in Berlin in 1952 when he offered his services to the USSR in the bizarre belief that if he defected he would be able to become a radio star in Russia. He was given elementary instruction and a little money for the few items he could provide, but he was of very little use to either of his employers. Before long he was posted back to the USA and left the army, but made little progress as a civilian and obeyed a KGB instruction to re-enlist and secure a posting to Paris. The Russians had hoped that he would be attached to SHAPE head-quarters, but they were lucky. He went instead to the Armed Forces Courier Station at Orly airport, through which the most secret written communications were transmitted between the Pentagon and the forces in Europe.

Johnson was one of the guards, and often on duty alone, but he was dimwitted and a drunk. He could not be expected to penetrate the system of steel doors and multiple locks which protected the secrets, so the KGB brought in teams of experts and elaborate equipment to exploit Johnson's position, and it was they who enabled him to get into the vaults. In traditional style they taught him how to take wax impressions of keys which passed through his hands, and made the necessary duplicates, but they also used technology which would have been the envy of civilian safecrackers. They were able to provide Johnson with a small portable X-ray device specially shipped from Moscow, and interpreted the plates he brought back, identifying the locking devices within the doors and calculating the combinations to which they were set.

Given the keys and combinations, even the inept Johnson was able to enter the vaults and make off with packets of documents on seven occasions when he was alone in the centre. He had then only to pass the material to agents who were ready to whisk it away to the Russian embassy to be photographed and returned, but he put the operation in danger by falling asleep and missing a vital rendezvous. The KGB had received information about US planning, dispositions and codes of the very highest quality: it was now more important to keep the thefts secret than to risk discovery with a further raid, so they suspended operations. Johnson was posted back to the USA, and was revealed as a spy only after he had disappeared from work and home to take a drunken trip to Las Vegas following a row with his wife. FBI agents looking into his disappearance interviewed Mrs Johnson, who told the tale of her husband's spying. The remote-controlled safecracker was sentenced to twenty-five years in prison. He died in jail, stabbed by his son during a visit.

The huge operation to support Johnson was perhaps in keeping with a Soviet military doctrine that large numbers would always carry the day. When they launched their own burglary and safecracking operations, the KGB seem to have used enormous teams, sacrificing stealth for thoroughness: mounting a tricky nocturnal burglary of the Swedish embassy in Moscow they sent in a team of no less than twelve burglars and safemen.

Billy Hill, the British safecracker, claimed that he had been approached by an East European agent with an offer of £100,000 if he would take documents from a safe in a London embassy, with a promise that he could keep a further £100,000 which lay ready for the taking in the safe. He was told that the safe was protected by an armed guard, and Hill himself carried a pistol to shoot if necessary, but his team was safely smuggled in by the agent, and was helped during the raid by a guard who was either a spy or a bribed hand. Rather than try to break into the safe at the embassy, they dragged it out, opened it at leisure out of town, and found £72,000 and the documents. Hill says that he was curious, and secured a translation which showed that he had stolen a list of anti-communists in an Iron Curtain country, with plans for the sabotage of various installations there. His conclusion was that a thousand people might die, so he burned the papers, lamenting only that he was £28,000 short.

Hill probably overstated many of the details, but it is certain that agencies of both East and West have used criminal subcontractors in what has become the Golden Age of government burglary. It is ironic that during the years which have known the virtual disappearance of private enterprise safecracking the state has employed, on salary and occasional contract, men whom it has trained in the very best techniques. The most famous government burglary of all time was the break-in at a Democratic Party office which caused the Watergate scandal and eventually forced the resignation of President Nixon, and it was a classic of ineptitude. Any burglar fails if he is caught; any official burglar fails if there is a trail of evidence leading back to his masters, and he cannot be disowned.

A government burglar must be technically competent to a degree no mere criminal can expect to achieve – he must be able not only to penetrate all the defences of locks and alarms to reach the material he wants to see, take or copy, but to do so without rousing any suspicion that he has been successful. From time to time an attempt may be made to disguise the entry as a common theft, but this is never satisfactory: the victim is unlikely to be deceived, and will take steps to make sure that target material is in future kept elsewhere, or will so improve his security that future attempts will be much more difficult. At worst, the entire point of the burglary may be lost if it is discovered – plans changed, suspects warned, broken codes replaced.

Official burglaries are the work of several types of expert – safe companies still offer the services of their craftsmen, and those in the know say that experienced criminals are hired from time to time. Thieves rarely have the skill to make a clean entry and exit, and are probably used when subtlety is not required, and when it is particularly important to be able to abandon anyone who has been caught or identified – what could be more convincing than a record of convictions and imprisonment?

More useful than either of these are members of the teams which agencies themselves have created and equipped. I have been told of a particularly efficient official operation in London whose van carries a full workshop of all the apparatus necessary to bypass alarms, make keys, X-ray and manipulate combination locks, even to neutralize electronic locks. This technical efficiency is not the only reason why loyal regular employees are the best choice: a criminal may work alone or with a couple of accomplices, but an unseen and unsuspected official burglary may require elaborate teamwork between lookouts at the job, observers to keep an eye on the targets to make sure they do not return to interrupt the job, and the technicians who can take care of photography or other specialized tasks.

Victims of official burglars include traditional targets such as the diplomats of enemies, potential enemies and their suspected sympathizers, but also commercial and technological rivals. Eastern bloc countries have been very keen in recent years to gain by espionage the commercial information denied them by bans on the export of any equipment and techniques regarded as strategically important.

The quotation which opened this chapter describes a kind of secret, and a kind of security, long gone. The plans for the Bruce-Partington submarine, recovered of course by Sherlock and Mycroft Holmes, represent the most obvious form of secret – the pieces of paper which, by themselves, gave the holder technology which would grant enormous power. In real life, such secrets are rare. The French government in the 1860s became obsessed with protecting the technical details of a quite unremarkable rifle, while the postwar defence of atomic secrets against the Soviet Union became absurd. Absurd because the greatest secret of all, the reason why none of the other nations who had nuclear bomb research programmes – including both Germany and Japan – had invested enough time and money to succeed, was that no one knew whether they could succeed. With the first explosion, the secret was out.

In fact, on both sides of the Iron Curtain the favourite target of government burglary, the one which used most manpower and absorbed most funds was the surveillance of dissidents, whether underground publishers in the East, or anti-nuclear campaigners in the West. Burglary is now as ordinary as telephone tapping and mail interception and is used less than either only because it is more expensive and less easily concealed. Safecrackers used to be underworld characters, living risky lives in which they gambled their liberty against an uncertain profit; their heirs are likely to be smart men with shortish hair and a military bearing, civil servants with index-linked pensions.

17

Catching the Safecracker

Every crime has features which help or hinder the working detective, and safecracking had special characteristics which shaped any investigation. Working both for and against the police was the fact that few safecrackers had led previously blameless lives. Their names and faces were usually known, their fingerprints already on file, and news about them was carried through the system of informers and police station gossip on which all thief-takers depend. Against this, safemen were often the smart ones, and had usually risen to the class of crook who had the best connections for the disposal of valuables and the best intelligence networks. The technical demands of the crime took it beyond simple thieving, and successful practitioners went about their work with a planned methodical maturity.

Those same technicalities could be the detective's greatest ally: every attack on a safe must leave evidence of the way in which the safecracker went about his work, and clear marks of the tools and devices used. The method could point to the identity of a safeman, and the physical evidence seal his conviction.

It has been such a long time since safecracking was common that today even senior, very experienced police officers have never tackled such a case. What they do recall is the advice they were given as young officers about what to do at the scene of a safeblowing.

Every police officer knows the importance of caution at the scene of a crime, where vital evidence can much too easily be destroyed or compromised by clumsiness or misplaced curiosity. When the use of explosives was common, the danger was not only to evidence but to the police themselves. An interrupted burglar could leave a charge primed, needing only an electric current to detonate it, and when the burglars had chosen to use the mains supply it was dangerous to operate any switches. In one case a patrolman who flicked a light switch was greeted with a sudden sharp explosion; believing he had been shot at, he threw off the light, dived for cover, and yelled for assistance. Only later was it discovered that he had set off a detonator, wired ready but not yet inserted into the waiting explosive. Incidents like this are much funnier later, and I suspect that the panicky policeman was much teased by his colleagues, but he had been a lucky man. Other officers found that even where there had already been an explosion they could be in great danger if a second charge lay prepared. Less risky, but alarming, was the excess explosive which could be left in a fine film over walls and floors, ready to explode with a very disconcerting BANG under a policeman's boot.

A fresh danger to the police came from an invention of the resourceful safecracker Harold Lough White, who also contrived to recruit a passing policeman as an unwitting accomplice. White raided a jeweller's shop, blew the safe and made off with gold leaf and jewellery to the value of £37,000. The theft was successful but White had indulged himself with a piece of bravado which would cost him his freedom: having set his charge, he left the shop, walked up to a constable on patrol and asked for change to make a telephone call. This officer was later able to recall White, his voice and his clothing accurately enough to identify him, and White was convicted and sentenced to seven years' imprisonment.

What was not revealed in court was the reason why White needed the coins, and the call. He had wanted to avoid the risks of injury and capture which he would risk if he stayed on the premises to use a conventional firing circuit, so he made up a remote triggering device and attached it to the telephone – if the phone rang, the charge went off. Getting change from the police was not merely bold, it was bare-faced cheek, but in keeping this out of the trial record, the prosecution was not just trying to avoid embarrassment.

Telephone triggering, and later radio control, were ingenious but potentially very dangerous indeed, and the authorities dreaded that a copycat safeblower would set a charge which could be detonated by chance. Worst of all, they knew how often thieves abandoned a job when interrupted – what might happen if police went into premises to investigate a burglary, and the fleeing thieves chose to pick up a phone during the getaway?

An unfired charge of an explosive such as gelignite, used as a solid, could usually be taken away with common sense and care; safeblowers rarely used any but the most straightforward fuses and circuits which could be traced and neutralized. Liquid nitroglycerine was much more hazardous. It was prone to detonation with any rough handling, and could seep invisibly into the cavities of a safe's wall and casing. The police could not know how much explosive might be hidden, nor its position; there was no safe way to remove it, and the process of trying to neutralize it was long and tedious.

When police arrived to find that the safe had been blown, the scene would be very messy indeed. Anything packed around an explosive charge on the door would have been hurled across the room, windows and internal glass shattered, and often as not a thick layer of dust would lie over everything in the room where the fireproof filling had been blown out or scattered by the thieves as they fought through the casing. Attack a safe, with explosive, drill or cutter, and some of the stuffing will be knocked out of it, and once out it will attach itself to the burglar, his tools and his clothing. It was an important first step to take and keep a sample of the filling; a laboratory match with a trace from a thief could be all the proof needed to secure a conviction.

Examining a sample of dust from a car, tools or clothing, it was often enough to arouse an investigator's suspicion merely to discover some substances in combination. A mixture of diatomaceous earth, Portland cement, and vermiculite mica has been used to insulate many twentieth-century safes, but for no other purpose – a sample from a suspect would be very difficult to explain away for a person who could claim no legitimate access to safes. Establishing that a specific sample came originally from a known crime scene has been made easier by manufacturers' concern to offer a distinctive product on the market. The choice of fillings, and the proportions in which they are used were often enough for a laboratory to be sure of the brand of safe which had been attacked.

Even where the filling was a common mixture, such as gypsum with woodchips, which was used in many safes, there could still be identifiable qualities to the sample, such as particle size, or the effects of the safebreaking method used, which might enable a good match to be made. Expert botanical opinion could be sought to establish the links – in one Scottish case it was a Lecturer in Indian and Colonial Forest Trees who was able not only to identify four distinct woods in combination, but to spot that all four were infected with a fungus. That was the mixture in the safe and in the samples taken from the turn-ups of the accused man's trousers: not an easy coincidence to explain to a jury.

Just as important to the investigation was a record of any marks of force on the safe itself and on any door or window which had been broken through. It could be good news for the police to find that no tools had been abandoned on the job: good safebreaking tools were specialized, often made by the safeman to his own requirements for strength and leverage. Tools which required exact dimensions or treatment such as hardening were often costly and difficult to obtain, and even when the very possession of specialized equipment was enough to draw a substantial prison sentence, many burglars would take considerable risks to hang on to tools which they had found effective. This was to prove ever more hazardous as forensic laboratories developed ways of proving the connection between marks at the scene of a crime and the tools which had made them.

The essential apparatus was the comparison microscope, which was invented in the early 1920s to enable bullets to be examined side by side. The lines engraved on a bullet by the barrel of the gun from which it had been fired were found to be quite unique, distinguishable even from other guns of the same model from the same manufacturer. When a bullet recovered during an investigation was placed under one side of the microscope, and a test-fired sample from a known weapon under the other, it was swiftly possible to declare with certainty whether this was the weapon used in the crime.

It was an easy step to use the same method in matching tools with the marks they had made. Even an edge which is utterly smooth to the naked eye will prove under the microscope to have irregularities, nicks, an individual pattern acquired during manufacture and use, which will be engraved into any material on which it is used. Scratches around a safe door, even a cut across a wire in an alarm system can be proved to be the work of a specific tool. Sometimes tools had been abandoned at the scene, but it is easy to see how an unbroken chain of evidence might lead from the attacked safe to the tool to a partial handprint to the man in the dock.

Even paintwork can betray. The composition of the painted finish on some safes has been formulated in such a way that it can be identified, and any fleck or trace is evidence that its carrier has been in contact with a safe of given manufacture.

Although safecrackers were rarely amateurish enough to leave fingerprints all over the scene, a check had to be made, and would occasionally pay off. The time spent at the scene of the crime, as all the preparations are made and the work of opening the safe goes on, might cause a lapse of concentration and an incautious ungloved fingerprint, but few safemen can have been so unlucky as one man who left a piece of skin from one of his fingers on broken glass during a bank burglary in Kingston. The investigators stretched the fragment back into shape, protected it with layers of plastic, and had a perfect specimen from which a match could be made with fingerprints on file.

Some crimes could be solved in the laboratory, but most safecrackers were caught because they made the same mistakes as any other failed crook. They trusted the wrong people, allowed greed to overcome common sense, and kept distinctive habits long enough for the police to recognize their style. If anything, safecrackers tended to put a great deal of thought and effort into the exciting preparation and execution of a raid but too little into planning how to hang on to the money in security and comfort.

Safecrackers may have been among the most ingenious of thieves, but they could fall victim to their own excessive cleverness: the case of Mike Tokar's socks is a fair example.

On the night of 26 August 1954 the McCaskey safe of

the Co-Operative store in Percival, a tiny outpost in
Saskatchewan, was blown, and $421 stolen. On his way
out, the thief had also taken clothing and a wrist watch.
The RCMP officers called to the scene found that the
safe had been opened by the rimshot or outside shot
method, using a trickle of nitroglycerine around the door.
The door had swung open in the blast, but not hard
enough to swing right around and damage the wall against
which the safe stood, and this seemed to indicate that the
thief was experienced enough to be a good judge of the
charge required. He was also wily enough to have left no
fingerprints.

Inspecting the muddy ground outside the store the
Mounties found strange footprints which seemed at first
to have been made by very finely patterned rubber soles.
Someone suggested that it looked as if the culprit had
worn leather-soled shoes, but covered them with socks in
an attempt to disguise them; tests proved this to be true,
and the investigators recalled reports of other crimes in
which socks had been used in this way, crimes in which a
Winnipeg safeblower called Mike Tokar was strongly
suspected.

Now they had not only a name but a trail of footprints
unlike any other in the whole of Percival, easy to follow
all over the village, and it showed the police how the
thief had failed in a series of attempts to steal a car for
his getaway, then led them to the spot where the thief
had abandoned the socks and a ball of soap which had
been used to seal the door of the safe.

A photograph of Mike Tokar was shown to citizens of
Percival and to the drivers of buses on local routes, and
he was recognized as a man who had been hanging around
the Co-Operative, then boarded a bus just outside Percival at four o'clock in the morning. Best of all, the $5 bill
offered for the bus fare was firmly identified as having

been stolen from the safe. Now there was more than enough evidence to obtain a warrant. Tokar was captured, convicted and sentenced to six years in the dauntingly-named Stony Mountain Penitentiary, for the crime of safecracking and the indiscretion of wearing his socks outside his boots.

An American textbook on the investigation of safecracking contains an absorbing guide to incompetent crime, intended to help police officers by pointing out the difference between amateur and professional attacks. To set against the accounts elsewhere in this book of thieves who used craftsmanship, lengthy training, research and expertise, it may be as well to remember how thoroughly ineffective many failed safecrackers could be. There were thieves who couldn't even get into the building with ease, leaving evidence of several attempts to get in at a number of different windows and doors; having struggled to get in, the incompetent safecracker simply attacked the wrong parts of a safe – the hinges, for instance, which are tough but play no part in locking a door. While on the premises, they would pointlessly steal property which had little value but was much more easily traced than anything in the safe.

Far from having respect for their equipment the inexperienced thieves not only broke tools, but left them as evidence. Where real expertise was needed it was totally lacking: the cutting tip of an oxyacetylene rig, for instance, has to be selected to suit the thickness of steel to be cut, and an incorrect mixture of gases will produce the wrong flame. Instead of opening boxes, incompetents left many a safe welded tightly shut.

There were safecracking schools, but the evidence of many investigations showed the need for more vocational guidance for criminals. If one characteristic of the professional is his manual skill, another is his ability to concentrate and remain cool for long enough to complete his work. Many of the failed thieves, even when they had made a good start, simply lacked the resolve under pressure to carry on with the work, and abandoned it after just a few minutes.

Inspiration, scientific method and plain dumb luck helped police to catch safecrackers, but none of them was ever as important as steady pursuit of sensible lines of enquiry. Gelignite can have a distinctive smell, and a sergeant of the Flying Squad claimed in 1958 that it was the characteristic whiff of pear drops which led him to discover hidden explosive while talking to a woman in a West End office. The newspaper report of her conviction made this sound like the workings of a helpful Providence, but it was no chance call – whether 'acting on information received', or 'pursuing routine enquiries', the sergeant was paying a visit to a woman whose ex-husband was in prison, and whose boyfriend had just been sentenced to ten years for his part in a bank robbery.

18
The End of the Game

The push-over thieve became harder to find and tougher to carry out.

L. J. Cunliffe, close to his retirement
from safecracking in 1965

The story of safecracking has an end. After more than a hundred years, and with amazing speed, it ceased to be a career for working criminals. When the sixties began, it was still a fairly common and profitable crime which could offer money and status to a young ambitious criminal, but by the end of the decade it was work for older men who could not change their ways, a dead-end trade for little reward.

The safecrackers were defeated, but it was not a victory for safemakers, for all the ingenuity and research of lockmakers and engineers. Alarms became more sensitive, more reliable, and much more widely used, but electronics alone could never stop professional thieves from going about their business. The end of safecracking came, with a logic which will appeal to anyone who thinks that history acts like a wheel, for many of the same reasons that it began. When we put our wealth into strong boxes, thieves learned how to take it out – when we removed the wealth, the crime stopped. Almost all of the many changes in the way that we handle our money have helped to remove cash further and further from the grasp of the safecracker.

Companies no longer hang on to their cash. Nothing provided the safemen with a steadier living than the habit of letting all the week's takings from a business pile up in the safe, ready for a weekly trip to the bank. This was always risky, always foolish, but nothing that the police and the banks could say or do was persuasive. Managers and owners seemed only to reason that if they had yet to be burgled their security was adequate or, if they had already been burgled, that lightning would not strike them twice. Such an attitude is the stuff of dreams for crooks.

Other reasons were practical: some managers preferred to cut the risk of a snatch attack in the street by carrying cash as rarely as possible, and others found it too much trouble to work on their books daily rather than weekly. Of course there were always those benefactors of the working burglar, owners who were much keener to hide cash from the taxman than protect it from the thief.

Businesses are now more cautious, and there have been big changes in the way that we pay our debts, settling with cheques and credit cards where once we used banknotes. Now that interest rates are higher, wise companies keep smaller cash floats, and deposit every unneeded penny where it can earn interest by the day.

Storing wages in the company safe was as common as storing takings. Bulk cash was often delivered the day before it was needed, to give time for wages staff to count it out; lodged in the safe it gave a full night of opportunity to thieves, who often marvelled at this idiocy. Now, even where staff are paid in cash, larger businesses contract out the work of sorting the cash to security companies who deliver as late as possible.

This extra cost of wages preparation is one of the reasons why businesses are eager to pay their employees by cheque or direct transfer, but to persuade workers to accept this sort of payment, banks had to change their ways. They competed to shed their austere images, to offer easier ways to save, spend and borrow. Once the move from cash had begun, it gathered enormous speed. Our real incomes have grown, but we don't spend our extra wealth in banknotes. Cash has been displaced, and cash has been concentrated from the many insecure safes into banks and security company depots.

When the money went out of safes, there were three career choices open to the safemen, all of them with equivalents in respectable society among workers whose craft skills were no longer wanted. They could stay in the specialism, remaining a burglar, but accept that jobs would be rarer and less rewarding – this would mean having to look much harder for work, then take home less. Younger, fitter, more adaptable men might do what Willie Sutton and Buster Edwards did, and turn to robbery in a sort of underworld industrial retraining. The last option was to get out of direct theft: either to retire into a civilian trade or drift into the way of life usually described as 'a bit of this and a bit of that'. There was no official pension or redundancy payment to underwrite a new life, but a resourceful working criminal would certainly have the contacts and the market knowledge to come up with an alternative.

Veterans who stayed in the trade made a poor choice. On both sides of the Atlantic there was much less money to be had, but in Britain sentences for serious crimes were rising steeply and fear of terrorism led to much stricter supervision of the stocks of explosive which had been so easily and cheaply available. Many of the old-timers took one more trip to prison, for longer than they had expected, and faded from view.

American safemen who took to armed robbery picked up guns, but in 1960s Britain intimidation was often achieved with pickaxe handles and iron bars: there was a general reluctance to use firearms, and changes in security measures had reduced the need. It had been quite common for private companies which protected cash and valuables in transit to issue firearms to nervous, untrained, unskilled guards – this had encouraged ambitious criminals who wanted to survive to go into safecracking. In the early 1960s, just when safemen were casting about for new opportunities, police pressure took the guns out of security vans.

Men who were active criminals in those days say that only a very few of the most reckless younger safemen were ever tempted into robbery. It called for a different kind of boldness, the psychological makeup of the sprinter not the middle-distance runner, and if they tried it at all, they didn't much like it.

It is my guess, from conversations with those whose careers spanned the end of safecracking, that very few redundant safemen were of an age and temperament to stay in high-value theft when this meant switching to robbery, but equally few retired immediately from crime. For many men it took no more than a single arrest after a successful run, or the arrest of a colleague, to help them take the decision to give up safe burglary: they had been aware just how scarce the decent jobs were becoming, and the intelligence which had made them effective planners and leaders prevented them from chasing smaller returns for ever greater risks.

There is another parallel with legitimate trades. Membership of the criminal world carried many of the same privileges as being a member in good standing of a specialist trade union; a legitimate worker who has been made redundant, but with a reputation as a good worker and reliable colleague, will be approached with tips and rumours of any employment which he can follow up, as well as direct offers. Just as a man who has been a supervisor in his last firm may be unwilling to take the first manual job, it was probably not easy to tempt a safeman to make up someone else's burglary team unless the job demanded some expertise, such as being a good bellman, which would maintain his status and his share in the proceeds.

Many used their contacts and cash in hand to establish themselves as self-employed, usually in one of the many trades in which flexible book-keeping is traditional; others had the acumen and man management skills to be hired, especially if they had been smart enough not to have a serious criminal record, by legitimate and semi-legitimate businesses. The safecracking days now seem very distant to these men: when I made an appeal on a television programme for retired safecrackers to get in touch, it was the daughter of one man, who had been told the old stories of jobs carried out before she was born, who coaxed her father into giving me a call.

These are settled years for the retired safemen, but dismal for the traditional locksmith or safe engineer: safes are made, safes are sold and used, but very rarely broken or blown, and the industry is suffering from success. Every reputable company now makes safes more than good enough to give solid protection to the smaller amounts of cash and valuables entrusted to them, and for more than a generation the older vulnerable designs have been steadily replaced. Now the market has become too small to support all the companies which competed so vigorously, and commercial pressure has produced all the changes so familiar in other traditional engineering industries. The better-run or luckier firms took over their old rivals, in a steady sequence of national and international amalgamations. Even these concentrated companies were relatively small, and vulnerable to takeover. Large conglomerates found them attractive because they had a very useful broad knowledge of security, and as trusted contractors to governments, banks and large corporations they have high-level access to the valuable customers on their lists.

Physical protection is now seen as just a part of overall security against theft and industrial spying. There have been useful improvements in the design and construction of safes, but the major innovations have been electronic: alarms and closed-circuit surveillance add to the protection given by mechanical locks and boxes, and their development has been little more than a sideline for the rich electronic corporations; yet one more application for their expertise and products.

Now electronics has begun to usurp traditional locksmithing, replacing the keys cut by the most respected craftsmen with cards which are magnetically coded on the production line. At first sight, the coded lock has many advantages: the card is hard to duplicate without expensive equipment, a lost master calls for quick recoding not expensive and obstructive reworking of every lock, and every lock can be centrally controlled and monitored.

There are ways of defeating electronic locks, which depend more on the cunning of the designer than the skill of the thief; once a working tool has been made, it can be put into series production for use by anyone. Every security system has flaws, but with mechanical systems the knowledge of a weakness was only a part of the solution – to know that the Bramah lock could be picked, even to have a full set of tools identical to the ones which Hobbs used, would not help the average citizen to open a Bramah.

Electronic systems, by contrast, are acutely vulnerable at the instant that the secret of their coding is known to a single untrustworthy person. This need not mean betrayal of a code number or word, but the use made of the code, the logic applied to the system is enough. With mechanical systems thieves could accumulate knowledge by taking the risk of burgling, or going to the expense of obtaining a lock or safe on which to practise, but the electronic thief can remain many miles distant from his target, testing his ideas and hypotheses about the system at almost no risk to himself until he is quite ready to make a move. The gap in skill and understanding between makers and breakers of codes is much smaller than the old gap between locksmith and thief. The experienced rogue locksmith was very rare, but now it is as if a traditional safemaker were trying to protect his clients from a large population of other very skilled locksmiths, all cooperating rather than competing, and having collectively an almost infinite amount of time to give to the task. The safemaker's old friend, time, is no longer a reliable ally.

All this applies not just to computer fraud, the most obvious breach of electronic security, but to every feature of an electronically monitored system. Even the supplementary cross-check on which banks once relied is accomplished with the greatest ease now that information can be surreptitiously retrieved. My own bank used to ask an account-holder for their mother's maiden name if a confirmation of identity was required. It might then have taken a check of parish records to come up with the answer, now it could come from any of a number of databases.

It is interesting that hackers have cracked personal codes just as burglars deduced combinations – a little knowledge of the interests of the target goes a long way. A friend with very limited computer knowledge used a few idle minutes to set himself the task of learning the passwords of a couple of colleagues: one man was known to be enthusiastic about old steam trains, and the number

of the Royal Scot proved to be his code, while another
was a Tolkien addict, and his word was found very quickly
among the names of characters from *The Hobbit*. Rum-
maging electronically through these possibilities took less
time than shuffling through numbers on a combination
dial.

Of course electronic security will improve, but it is
intrinsically much less secure than physical defences, if
only because the kind of courage required to tap out a
sequence of numbers is a great deal more common than
the boldness the safemen needed to carry gelignite over a
fence at dead of night, listening for dogs and police cars.

Appendix:

Raffles and Rififi – Safecracking in Films

Film-makers love crime. Their obvious favourite is murder, but if we disregard the total of all those routine bank hold-ups in Westerns, they have made greater use of safecracking than any other form of theft to make heavily dramatic thrillers and the occasional comedy.

There have been two traditions of film safecracking, which can comfortably be called the Raffles and the Rififi. Raffles stories not only concentrate on the gentlemanly art of jewel theft, but make light of the technicalities: the thief has merely to furrow his brow in concentrated effort, cock an ear to the mechanism, apply a cultured fingertip to the dial, and the booty is his. (A novel variation was provided in a spy film, *The Kremlin Letter*, when Barbara Parkins contrived to open safes with her toes.) Practitioners have included David Niven and Ronald Colman, each of whom played Raffles himself, Cary Grant and Michael Caine. You will find no nasty noisy drills and explosives in these stories, no sweating toil with a jemmy. As befits their amateur status, these safecrackers may lose their loot in a final twist of the plot, but they are rarely caught, and certainly never killed off. The essence of the Rififi approach, on the other hand, is to set out for the audience every stage in the preparation and execution of the crime, explaining and displaying as much technical detail and expertise as possible. Rififi crooks are occasionally gentlemen, but if they are, they have already fallen from grace; more usually they are professional thieves who labour hard and then fall out, coming to a sticky end at the hands of their colleagues or the law.

Although not the first caper movie, Jules Dassin's *Rififi* was much the most successful in grasping the popular imagination. It tells a story of professional criminals who conduct an elaborate raid on a jeweller's shop, only later to fall out violently. It is the raid – the caper – which so impressed cinemagoers and prompted many similar scenes in later films such as *Topkapi* and *Gambit*. Central to a film is a twenty-five-minute sequence in which the thieves penetrate the shop through the ceiling, first making a small hole through which they ease an umbrella. When opened the umbrella is able to catch debris as they enlarge the hole enough to make a man-sized aperture. The viewer knows that if a part of the ceiling hits the floor an alarm will be triggered, and this device keeps the tension high. Not a word is spoken throughout the raid, which not only applies an extra twist to the viewer's nerves but may have helped *Rififi* to join the small number of French films to enjoy major success in the English-speaking market. This was a film which seemed authentic, and the umbrella trick had occasionally been used by thieves in real life – one report tells of a German team which used the same trick in a hotel raid in 1907. In turn the caper inspired not only other film directors, but a few criminals who borrowed from the techniques, and a London restaurateur who took the name and installed a sign showing an inverted umbrella.

Rififi, though famous, was by no means the first caper movie. Five years before Dassin, John Huston had called on expert advice from safecrackers to make *The Asphalt Jungle* as realistic as possible, and told his tale from the perspective of the crooks themselves, to show the audience that 'crime is a left-handed form of human endeavour'. Anthony Caruso played the safecracker, a family man lured into one last job after an interview in which he must establish his professional credentials :

'What boxes have you opened?'
'Cannonball, double-door, even a few fire chest, all of them.'

He shows up for work with his kit of drill, bits and crowbar neatly racked in the lining of his coat, and the little bottle of nitro slung on a cord around his neck – a place for everything and everything in its place. The opening of the target vault, a classic use of a high drilled hole and a seeping of nitro, goes well but the boxman is shot in error by another gang member and the whole job goes sour. The plot was good enough to be used for at least three remakes in the following twenty years, one set in the Middle East – *Cairo*, one in the Wild West – *The Badlanders* and a Los Angeles version with an all-black cast called *A Cool Breeze*.

There's a book still to be written about underground films: not Andy Warhol art flicks but the many subterranean scenarios from prisoner-of-war getaways (*The Wooden Horse*, *The Great Escape*) to dead-end sewer finales (*The Third Man*, *Kanal*) taking in vault attacks on the way. A fairly recent example which intrigues is *Loophole*, in which Albert Finney and Martin Sheen penetrated from sewer to safe deposit in a raid which resembles very closely indeed the Nice raid of 1976. The film was made in 1980, but was based on a novel by Robert Pollock published eight years before, and both book and film concentrate on the technical details of the crime. The odd relationship between art and life went even further: poor Mr Pollock was apparently reported to the police by a vigilant citizen who thought that he had betrayed too accurate a knowledge of technique.

There have been comic safecrackers: in *Two Way Stretch*, made in 1960, David Lodge played a prisoner who gave hands-on tuition to his fellow cons to while away those tedious times behind bars, while comedian Charlie Drake, in one splendid scene in *The Cracksman*, (1963, GB) made fun of the ear-to-the-dial method. Crouched over a safe, surrounded by menacing heavies, the cracksman attaches wires to the combination lock which lead to a black box. The box produces a sound whose pitch rises and falls as the dial is turned, but Drake gets carried away, finding notes up and down the scale until he is playing a tune so catchy that all the crooks begin to sway in time to the music. In *No Deposit, No Return* (1976, US), two lovable safecrackers make a career switch into kidnapping, but the smart kids they snatch (this is a Disney film) make their lives a misery by playing catch with their dynamite and tinkering with the tools of their trade. The crooks redeem themselves by using their professional skills (headphones and manipulation) to rescue the brats when they are trapped in a safe. In this they are aided by a skunk, which seems appropriate to the film as a whole.

Not every film has adhered to standard criminal operating procedure: confronted by the 27-inch-thick walls of a safe deposit, the hero of *The Hot Rock* (1972, US), the unflappably incompetent Dortmunder, played by Robert Redford, opted to have a bank official accosted in a lift by a transvestite hypnotist, and instructed to obey the commands of anyone who said the code words 'Afghanistan Bananastan'. None of my researches have been able to yield a true-life example of this approach.

While safes were still being robbed, every aspect of safes and their cracking appears to have found favour with a film-maker: *Time Lock*, (1957, GB), was about a boy trapped within a bank vault for the weekend; hostages were locked away in *Strongroom* (1961, GB); wartime exploits of safecrackers who rallied to the colours were covered in the fictional *The Safecracker* (1958, GB) and the story of Eddie Chapman, a small-time safeman who claimed to have been a useful spy for the British after he was trapped in the Channel Islands during the German occupation; since he also signed on for the Germans, it was filmed as *Triple Cross* (1967, GB). Donald Sutherland played the most sophisticated of safemen, planning an attack in *A Man, A Woman and A Bank* (1979, Canada) before even the building is complete. By this stage a caper had come to need not only a knowledge of engineering but computer expertise. He has also played the most clumsy and incompetent safeman as a neighbourhood layabout who conspires with a crew of comparable losers in *Big Deal on Madonna Street* (unknown, US), a remake of an Italian film of the 1950s.

In one elaborately-plotted low-to-medium budget film called *The Act* (unknown, US) is a splendid technological update of the pressed-ear approach. In the *Raffles* tradition, the safecracker is a good guy and the job goes off without a shot being fired: he isn't a real crook, but an amateur who has been given a quick lesson by a real safeman. The money is an underhand payoff belonging to bad guys (so that's all right), held overnight in a hotel vault with an imposing door which carries two combination locks. Our hero assembles a complicated rig of wires, little boxes, and stethoscopic earphones; licking the suction pads on three little microphones he carefully applies them around each lock in turn – at least six inches from the mechanisms they are supposed to monitor. Since we in the audience cannot hear the signal (nor, probably, can the hero over the rapid bongo drumming on the sound track), so one of the little boxes conveniently carries three red lights, and we know that the lock will open as soon as all three are glowing. Sure enough, they come on like the cockpit lights which tell a pilot that all three legs of an aircraft's undercarriage are down and locked; 1 . . . 2 . . . 3 . . . and the door can be flung wide.

Traditionalists who want to see the old manual method are recommended to look out for *Checkpoint* (1956, GB): I have seen only a still from this film, which seems to concern the activities of an industrial spy in the motor industry, but the photograph clearly shows Stanley Baker in the time-honoured stoop by the safe door, eyes conventionally focused far far away as he listens intently through a stethoscope applied to the safe door. Ten years later in *Gambit* (1966, US) Michael Caine merely cocked an ear to his safe, with no artificial aids at all, but was also reduced to the crude and back-straining expedient of carrying off an unopened box by brute force; he was lucky that he had a flight of stairs leading down rather than up.

The use of explosives is rarely shown in explicit detail, but the technique which Mike Jesswell describes, of applying steady pressure to a safe handle to defeat a relocking device, was shown in *The Informers*, an otherwise unremarkable British film from 1963. The whole sequence is very brief and takes place in a dimly-lit room, but during it the burglars run a rope or cable from the handle to a spring-loaded gadget which seems to be attached to the floor. Its use was in no way necessary to the plot, was neither explained nor commented upon, and would have made no sense to the lay viewer, but shows that the film-makers were unusually thorough in their research. I have found no references to this refinement in contemporary books or newspapers, and can only suppose that a working criminal, or a serving police officer, contributed his knowledge of current practice. Perhaps a single cinemagoer in each full house would have nodded in quiet recognition of this attention to detail.

Hitchcock provided us with a rare female safe thief in *Marnie* (1964, US). Tippi Hedren, pursued by ghastly memories, becomes a kleptomaniac who takes jobs only to steal from her employers. As the film opens she has stolen nearly $10,000, a large amount for the rather flimsy fire cabinet we are shown. In her one theft on screen she takes advantage of the boss's absentmindedness: although the combination of his strong double-door safe has just five numbers, he can never remember it, and keeps a note locked in a drawer. To take advantage of this classic folly, all Hedren has to do is steal a key to the drawer, hide in the toilets at the close of business and rifle the safe.

Dollars (1971, US, shown as *The Heist* in the UK) seems to have been made with the best of professional advice. All the major characters have their own safes, and the hero is Warren Beatty as a security expert, who displays a variety of safecracking tools as part of his reassurance to his German banker clients – drills, oxy-acetylene cutters and even a thermic lance are left casually by the vault entrance for most of the action. Beatty himself has designs upon some of the safe deposit contents, and files keys to fit at speeds which would do credit to the deftest locksmith or thief. He even contrives to open the odd combination by ear, but the high point for a student of technique is the demonstration of how to use a thermic lance: to allow air into the vault where Beatty has deliberately trapped himself, a lance – a $7 burning bar, as it is described – is rigged with oxygen cylinders, lit with a gas torch and makes quick work of penetrating the vault wall. The intensity of the flame and the profusion of smoke produced by a bar no more than an inch thick are startling.

Safes in Westerns usually yield to a single pistol shot or a crude charge of dynamite, but in *For a Few Dollars*

More (1965, Italy/Spain/West Germany) Lee Van Cleef gains the confidence of the bandit chief by showing that he need not destroy the contents of the safe he has stolen by blowing it up. With a fine dramatic flourish he pours into the lock a powerful acid: the heavy fumes tell us that the innards are being eaten away, and with just a practised twirl of a piece of steel Van Cleef is able to throw wide the door. All this in a small village chosen for its remoteness, and with no explanation of how Van Cleef obtained the acid, or happened to have it with him!

Movies are expensive to make, and their producers cannily commercial men who make their money by being alert to the feelings of audiences, so it seems likely that the safecracker shown on screen is close to the one of popular imagination. He is a calculating man with secret skills, who may still be charming; a thief who is bold, but not menacing. He is a determined criminal but uses no violence, so we accept him as a sympathetic hero, or even a comic character. He is an individualist, but pulls his weight; he may sometimes be betrayed, but doesn't let others down. He doesn't threaten us on the streets, and our own homes are not at risk: only rich households have safes, and we are happy to see a cheeky jewel thief plunder them. The image which emerges is that of a crook almost as endearing as an old-style poacher, warmer and more worldly than a computer hacker – a rogue rather than a villain.

It was a view shared by some safemen themselves, but rarely by judges.

A Note on Sources

In recent years locksmithing seems to have joined the topics which fascinate an oddball fringe of survivalists and weapons freaks. It is a technical subject whose principles can be fairly easily understood, but has the appeal of being surrounded by secrecy, and there is a market for lockpicking manuals among some who buy books about guns, knives, explosives and nuclear shelters. Armchair guerillas are ordinarily pathetic creatures, but among them have been men so disturbed that they have taken guns onto the street to kill. I have no fears that this book could reverse history and lead to a revival in safecracking – the reader will already have learned why it is no longer a profitable line of work for criminals – but there is still potential for abuse of sensitive information by fantasists.

Safecrackers' memoirs make it clear that a determined thief will easily find accurate and useful information. During the research for this book I have been allowed access to archives and libraries not normally open to the public, but I have to acknowledge that in matters of technique public sources were just as revealing.

Because I will not give encouragement to anyone foolish or deranged enough to attempt experiments with dangerous materials I have excluded about a dozen books from this bibliography which are openly available – some have been on library shelves for decades – but which seem to me to go into too much accurate detail about the extraction, manufacture or use of explosives, or which by their tone make safecracking appear temptingly easy. I apologize to anyone with a legitimate interest in the subject – even an ordinary curiosity – who would wish to consult other sources, and hope that they will accept my reasoning. I remain perfectly willing to help any other researcher who wishes to explore further, and would indeed welcome correspondence forwarded by the publisher which bears a full name and address.

Where a correspondent can reassure me – by membership of the Police Historical Society, for instance, or some other legitimate affiliation – of the reasonableness of their interest, then I will be happy to offer what I can.

For anyone wanting to read a little further, there is no better starting point than *Safe Bind, Safe Find: the story of locks, bolts and bars*, Garry Hogg (Phoenix House, London; 1961), an excellent shortish history for the lay reader covering locks from the earliest times. Although this has been out of print for some time, it has kept its place on library shelves because nothing written since has been quite so useful an introduction to the subject. *From Boniface to Bank Burglar*, George M. White (Seaboard Press, New York; 1907), and *Langdon W. Moore: His Own Story of His Eventful Life* (Langdon W. Moore, Boston; 1893), are both substantial autobiographies of safecrackers. Neither of them is cheaply or luridly produced, which seems to mean that there was respectable public interest in this sort of crime. The style had changed a little by the time Herbert Emerson Wilson wrote his *I Stole $16,000,000* (the copy I have is Digit, London; undated). This is a rather more breathless, egotistical book but interesting in its technical details. There are now plenty of books about murderers, but the age of big career-criminal lifestories probably ended with *Where The Money Was* by Willie Sutton, with Edward Linn (Viking Press, New York; 1976). This was the better of two autobiographies by America's most famous safeman/ bank robber.

Boss of Britain's Underworld, Billy Hill (Heinemann, London; 1955): Hill's claim to be more than a single fairly important crook among many is over the top, but he gives a fairly breezy account of his career, and is at his most interesting when he explains how he went into, and then out of safecracking.

Grafters All, Eric Parr (Max Reinhardt, London; 1964): A lively account of British crime and criminals which includes a chapter on safemen. *Having It Away*, L. J. Cunliffe (Gerald Duckworth, London; 1965) is a racy first-person account by one of the later British safecrackers. *Inside the Underworld*, Peta Fordham (George Allen and Unwin, London; 1972) contains interesting observations on London criminal life just as safecracking was going out of fashion.

The Sewers of Gold, Albert Spaggiari, translated by Martin Sokolinsky (Granada, London; 1979): this is apparently Spaggiari's own version of the big Nice bank job of 1976, and the technical details of the raid itself seem sound. For the rest, it seems to me to be as imaginative as the novel *Loophole* by Robert Pollock (Hodder and Stoughton, London; 1972) which had already described a burglary via the sewers remarkably similar to the real-life theft.

Third Time Unlucky, Larry Pryce (Star, London; 1979) is a detailed account of the Bank of America raid, telling most of the story that was known at the time.

Criminals were not the only ones to write their memoirs: *Banker Tells All*, Thurston Hopkins (Frederick Muller, London; 1956) includes stories of safecracking alongside frauds and forgeries.

Science Catches the Criminal (published earlier as *Science Versus Crime*), Henry Morton Robinson (Blue

Ribbon Books, New York; 1935) is an account of forensic investigation from the golden age of safecracking, with chapters on safes and alarms.

Game of Thieves, Robert Rosberg (Everest House, New York; 1981) includes a selection of very detailed case histories, written by a high-powered American safes and security expert.

INDEX

Index

Accidents with locks and keys, 71–6, 90, 192
Acetylene, 228
Air raids as cover for burglaries, 255–6
Alarm systems, 62–70, 166–7, 179–81, 273, 278
Aloisi, Baron, 249
Animals as alarms, 62, 166
Antique value of safes, 37
Apprenticeship in safecracking, 154–5
Armed robbery, 149, 177, 275–6
Atomic demolition munitions (ADMs), 127

Banking, 25
  loss of confidence in, 26
Bank of America raid, 122–6
Bank of France vault, 77–9
Bank of the West raid, 196–7
Bernasconi, John, 104–5
Bessemer, Henry, 51
Blowing open safes *see* Explosives
Booby traps, 47–8, 69, 258
  for the police, 265
Borgmann, Kirsten, 93–4
Boxes for valuables, 22–3
Bramah, Joseph, 109
Bramah locks, 102, 109–15
Brewer (locksmith), 253–5, 258
Bricks, 83

Brink's Mat raid, 11
Bronco Bill Frane, 237
Burglaries, 27
  skills needed for, 159–72
  see also under individual raids
Byrnes, Thomas, 118–19, 147

Cannonball design, 41
Carey, Francis, 73–4
Cars used in burglaries, 165–6
Caseley, Thomas, 14–16
Cash, 26, 161–2, 274
Casing premises, 162–4
Cast iron, 49–50, 51–2
Charles I, 24
Chatwood, 28, 30, 54, 152–3
Chests for valuables, 22–3
Chubb company, 8, 60–61
  Anti-Concussion Spring Diaphragm Plate, 55
  Extra Heavy Triple Treasury Doors, 55
  locks, 102–3, 112
  Special Alloy, 55
Chubb, George H., 28–31, 32
Chubb, Jeremiah, 110
Cold War espionage, 250–52, 258–60
Combination locks, 116–32, 185
  compared to key locks, 116
  difficulty of cracking, 127–8
  how they work, 116–17

manipulation of, 128–31, 192–4

Commercial information, theft of, 262

Company records, 81

Competition between burglars, 169

Concrete, 83–5

Copper, 54

Core drills, 195–6, 219

Corliss safe, 41, 43

Cornhill burglary, 11–17, 185

Courtney, Charles, 141–2

Crime as war, 12

Crocodile as guard, 62

Cunliffe, L. J., 70, 166, 273

Cutting tools, 197–202
  see also Drills, Oxyacetylene cutters

Daily Express, 235, 248

Daily Mail, 66

Daily Mirror, 64

Daily Telegraph, 16

Darby Abraham, 50

Deaths during burglaries, 169, 208–9

Defensive mechanisms, 45–8

Delano safes, 57

Denver Dick, 154–5, 213

Denver Dude, 208–9

Deposit boxes, 79–80

Derr, Geoff, 161

Dickens, Charles, 136

Dissidents, information about, 263

Dogs
  as guards, 62, 166
  simulations of, 64

Doors of vaults, 87–90

'Drag' tool, 187

Drills, 188–91, 192–6

defences against, 194
  see also Cutting tools

Dynamite *see* Explosives

Earthquakes, 81–2

Edwards, Buster, 275

Electricity used for safecracking, 235–6

Electronics, 277–80

Ellis, Peter, 150, 152

Entrapment inside safes, 71–6, 90

Escapology, 139–43

Estimating a safe's date, 37–8

Eugene, 47

Explosives, 39–41, 181, 203–22, 289
  ADMs, 127
  dynamite, 40, 154, 207–9, 220
  gelignite, 43, 158, 165, 174–5, 207, 219–21, 266, 272
  guhr dynamite, 206
  guncotton, 205
  gunpowder, 107, 203–5
  manufacture of, 209–11
  nitroglycerine, 39–40, 42, 86, 165, 206, 208, 209–19, 266
  physical effects of handling, 178–9, 210–11

False alarms, 69

Feynman, Richard, 120

Filling from safes, 266–7

Films, 130–31, 200, 281–8

Fire, resistance to, 57–61
  see also Heat

Fletcher, Thomas, 227

Forensic tests, 175–6, 198, 268
  see also Police work

Frustrated burglars, 171–2

Fusible link, 134

Gas, 223–5, 226–8
Geese as guards, 62
Gelignite *see* Explosives
George, Willis, 131
Gerlach, Cardinal, 248, 249
Germany and espionage, 253–6
Goldschmidt, Hans, 225, 226
Government report (USA), 39–41
Government secrets, thefts of, 247–63
Great Train Robbery, 11, 150, 152
Guidebooks for burglars, 191–2
Guinness Book of Records, 125
Gunpowder *see* Explosives
Gutshot, 212–13

Hadfield, Sir Robert, 53
Hamilton, 'Shell', 119
Heat, 223–37
Heatproofing, 57–61
Herring safe factory, 224
Hill, Billy, 166, 260–61
Hinges, 42–3
Hitler, Adolf, 120, 254–5
Hobbs, A. C., 112–14
Holmes, Eldwin, 63
Hostage-taking, 135–6
Houdini, 139–42
Hough and Harper vault, 83
Hydrogen, 227–8

Ice used to crack a safe, 237
Information sources, 9, 159–61
Infra-red beams, 66, 69
Inside jobs, 90–91
Invisible locks, 133–8
Iron, 49–51

Jack, 7–8, 9
Jack-in-the-box tool, 106–7, 186

'Jamshot', 214–19
protection against, 217–18
Japan, 81–2
Jemmying, 15
Jesswell, Mike, 160, 173–83, 286
Johnson-Bradford Company, 217
Johnson, Sergeant Robert Lee, 258–60
Joliet Prison, 73
Judge and Jury Clubs, 16

Keister safes, 216
Kelly, Timothy, 191–2
Keys, 99–101
copying, 103–6
skeleton, 101
KGB, 259–60
King, Harry, 119, 149, 154–5, 163, 213
King Victor of Italy's safe, 252–3
Knightsbridge safe deposit theft, 90–91
Kreuger, Ivar, 72

Latif, Mr, 91
Lauson, Joseph, 157
Leslie, George Leonidas, 164
Lever locks, 102, 107–8
Lloyd's Bank, Knightsbridge, 232
Lock-outs, 89
Locks, 31–2, 44, 88–9, 99–108
combination locks, 116–32
interference with, 93, 191
lever locks, 102, 107–8
public demonstrations of, 110–13
relocking devices, 133–8, 219, 221
time-locks, 136–8

visible mechanisms, 218
Lockwood, Cully, 186
Loophole, 238, 283
Los Alamos, 120
Luxury goods, 26

Mandelbaum, Frederika, 156, 157
Manganese steel, 42, 53, 217
manipulation of combination locks, 128–31, 192–4
as myth, 130
Marquis of Worcester, 47
Masino, Tony, 202
Materials
external, 42–4, 49–56, 82–5
internal, 57–61
Michigan Red, 208
Milner's List 3 safe, 11, 14, 15
Mint, The, 24
Mistakes made by safecrackers, 269–72
Mitchell, Rhona, 8
Moore, Langdon, 190

National Archives Exhibition Hall, USA, 45
National Safe Deposit, 79–80
Nazi records, 257
Newell Parautoptic Lock, 111
New York Times, 147
Night watchmen, 63
Nitroglycerine *see* Explosives
Nixon, President, 261
Nobel, Alfred, 206–7, 211, 219
Nobel family, 206, 208
Nuclear attack, 81, 82
Nuclear devices, protection of, 127
Numbers for combination locks, 119–22

Oakland, Tommy, 228–9
Oxyacetylene cutters, 228–32, 271
Oxygen as source of heat, 226–9

Paris Exhibition 1867, 29
Police work, 264–72
see also Forensic tests
Politics, 77
Pollock, Robert, 238, 283
Premises, 162–4
Pressure differential system, 66–7
Prestige of safecracking, 147–53
Price, George, 52, 150–51, 189
Prison sentences, 177, 275
Publicity stunts, 28–9, 110–13
'Punching a can' method of safebreaking, 185

Raffles (film character), 130, 281
Rain, 177
Reinforcement of concrete, 84–6
Reliability of alarm systems, 69
Relocking devices, 133–8, 178, 219, 221
Rififi (film), 200, 281–2
Romans, 21–2
Russian spies, 250–52

Sabotaging alarm systems, 68–9
Safe deposit boxes, 79–80, 242
government raids on, 256
Safemakers, 27–8
company closures, 34
Safes
as bomb shelters, 143
design, 32, 41–3
early forms of, 23

estimating date of, 37–8
fake, 31–2, 38
harnessed, 218
manufacturing methods, 32, 36
materials, 42–4, 57–61, 82–5
moving for cracking, 168–9
public demonstrations of, 28–9
reduced demand for, 277
reinforcement of, 38
sinking, 45
sliding, 46–7
spherical, 41
spinning, 45
testing, 34–5
Victorian, 27, 37
weight, 44, 185
wooden, 57
Sandwiched metals, 54–5
Sargent, James, 117, 137
Schonbein (chemist), 205
Schools for safecrackers, 156–7
Science and technology, 151–2
Seized-up doors, 89
Seldom Seen, 208–9
Sewers as access to vaults, 240, 241
Shinburn, Mark, 105–6, 119
Siemens steel, 55
Sinking safes, 45
Skeleton keys, 101
Sliding safes, 46–7
Sobrero (chemist), 206, 208
Société Générale, Nice, 238–43
Soldiers as safecrackers, 257
Space shot, 219
Spaggiari, Albert, 238–43
Spaggiari burglars, 170
Spiegeleisen, 224
Spies as safecrackers, 247–63
Spinning safes, 45

Star, The, 152
Steel, 50–55
  alloy, 52–3, 55
  manganese, 42, 53
  stainless, 53
Strongrooms, 77–91
Sunday Times, 158
Surveillance of dissidents, 263
Sutton, Willie, 275
Swartz brothers, 93–5

Teamwork, 182
Technical challenge of safecracking, 155–7
Telephone triggers of explosives, 266
Terrorism, fear of, 222, 275
Testing, 85–6
Thermic lance, 232–4
Thermit, 225–6
Time-locks, 136–8
Tokar, Mike, 269–71
Tools, 186–202, 268–9
Trusty Alarm Box, 64
Tumbler gate, 117

Ultrasound, 66
Underground vaults, 81, 82–3
Underworld, the, 148

Valuables to be safeguarded, 81
Vaults, 77–91, 234–5
Ventilation shafts, 83–4

Wages thefts, 161, 274
Walker, John (Cornhill), 11, 14
Watergate break-in, 261
Wayne Strong School of Safework, 157
Wealth
  forms of, 21, 24, 35, 273, 275
Weather, 177

Westinghouse, 66
White, Harold Lough, 265–6
Wilson, Herbert, 156, 201, 213, 231
Wooden safes, 57

Worcester Sam, 72
Wrought iron, 50

X-ray equipment, 126–7